The Kingdom of

GOD

and Playboys

The Kingdom of
GOD
and Playboys

An Adventurous Journey to Faith and Wholeness

To Nelli,
With love
Tina.

2024

TINA ASSANTI

Printed in the United States of America

Published by Author Academy Elite
P.O. Box 43, Powell, OH 43035

www.AuthorAcademyElite.com

Paperback: 978-1-64085-256-3
Hardback: 978-1-64085-257-0
Ebook: 978-1-64085-258-7

Library of Congress Control Number (LCCN): 2018938016
Unless otherwise indicated,
Scripture quotations are from the New English Bible (NEB)
Copyright © Cambridge University Press and Oxford University Press,
1961, 1970.
All Rights Reserved.
Names and locations and identifying details have been changed for
confidentiality.
www.TinaAssantiBooks.Com

*This book is dedicated with boundless love
to my two amazing sons, and with gratitude and love
to my father, mother, Andy, Elyse, Reuven, and Lothar.
And, of course, Sam.
This is also dedicated to the members of my extended family who
were part of this adventurous journey. I refer to them in this book
without any names. Fellow travellers, I am so very proud
to be part of you. You are all heroes to me.*

Table of Contents

BOOK THREE: The Holy Years

BOOK FOUR: The Unsettled Years

BOOK FIVE: The Rocky Years

BOOK SIX: The Later Years

Preface

"The most common formulation of Buddhist Ethics is the five precepts.

1. Refraining from harming living beings/practicing loving-kindness.

2. Refraining from taking the non-given/practicing generosity.

3. Refraining from committing sexual misconduct/practicing contentment.

4. Refraining from false speech/practicing truthful communications.

5. Refraining from intoxicants/practicing mindfulness.

"If in our lives we act non-violently, do not take what is not freely given, do not deceive, and do not act out of delusive and irresponsible mind states, we cannot fall foul of the third precept anyway.

"*Sexual misconduct means any sexual conduct involving violence, manipulation or deceit—conduct that therefore leads to suffering and trouble.*"[1]

---

[1]   Buddha Net's Magazine Article, Buddhist Sexual Ethics by Winton Higgins

Introduction

My formative years were quite an adventure. My predominantly male-oriented, extended family, all worked in the family business. They grew up over the shop in Europe, then lived in one house in Toronto as they established themselves, and then eventually spread out into the suburbs to live side-by-side on the same street going to the same family business each and every morning. They worked long hours and they spent their spare time together evenings the odd time, and weekends they played cards. They had meetings or they simply 'hung' together, but it seemed every moment they shared was filled with anger, curses and shouting. It was to be an intense love and hate relationship affecting every member of the growing family.

Testosterone was like rocket fuel in this environment. As the eldest of the cousins, and one of the few females, it couldn't help but have a twisted and adverse effect on me and my views on this world. My uncles were very young when we first came to the New World, the youngest only four years older than me. They came with their own particular baggage that was as fresh as flowers plucked from the field seconds before wilting. Their own scars and deep emotional pain suffered during their own upbringing played out in subtle and not-so-subtle ways. The world I shared with them reflected their 'maleness' which almost eradicated everything gentle and nourishing, elements in life which they themselves craved.

But they were taught to see these virtues as weak.

And so was I.

To ensure our shared dysfunction continued in full force, the environment outside of our family cocoon spoon fed us more fuel for this particular fire through *Playboy*, *James Bond*, sexy and sensual music, fashion, sports and the media. But these views were just as fiercely fed to all males, young and old.

This upside-down world saw women as mere playthings for men's own entertainment, egos, and sexual fulfillment. What was worse, these effects were to feed on the original Victorian principles which already taught that men were the heads of their families, they were to be obeyed, and they were to be given the best of what women could offer. All while women were relegated to the back seat. They were only given the glory of their hair (preferably done in seemly and modest fashion) and the bearing of their children.

I was taught these principles through family, church and school. At the same time, because of when I was born, I almost grew into this new environment along with my young uncles and young father.

Generally, I received conflicting messages about my sexuality. At church, you did not talk about your body, or nudity, and, God forbid, sex. But major aspects of the world around us screamed it out loud—blatantly or subtly.

What was true? It was extremely bewildering.

As a little girl, I felt as low as a snake crawling out from underneath a rock while the sun continuously shone on the boys. Combine this male favoritism with the fact that in our family, domestic abuse (the term of which we never heard at the time) and violence were the norm—well, as far as a well-balanced adulthood was concerned, forget it. I didn't have much to go by. Just like my family before me.

For example, on Saturdays, as a young child, I accompanied my father to the family's auto body shop where my eyes were inundated with piles of well-fingered editions of *Playboy* magazines. They were scattered in the waiting room and office. The centerfolds were tacked up on the walls of the bathroom, above work stations, and even taped to tool boxes. Someone would pencil in moustaches, and goatees, and the odd bull's-eye on the private parts. At seventeen, it was my job to clean the offices and bathroom where reminders of how a woman's body was continually ogled at and played with, left me feeling depressed and anxious, though I didn't know the words to describe what I felt at the time.

Shopping with my mother brought me face to face with *Playboy* and *Esquire*. Every checkout sold them. First, they were on the lower shelves. Later, they were displayed out of reach but still evident. As a child and teenager, I panicked, thinking I would never be as beautiful or perfect as the women who were portrayed. More importantly however, my subconscious also picked up the vibe that *even in their perfection*, these beautiful women were worthless and dispensable creatures. The scribblings over their images continuously screamed this message to me and to the rest of the women of my generation.

So, I am here to use my snakes and ladders of a life within a *Playboy* society as an example of where a family, the church, and the media can directly and negatively affect the life of a young girl practically *guaranteeing* a life of molestation, rape, suicide attempts, depression, and domestic violence. Personally, I hid it behind a smile and a thick wall of great secrecy and shame. It was an extremely heavy burden to bear. But the main point of this book is: *I survived it all.*

Written in a matter of fact manner and with some humor, these stories study the *larger picture* of my life which *takes away the blame* from any one individual who may have had a negative impact on my life in any way. It's the only manner in which I can come to understand the important white elephant in the room: the massive *why*. Only through this broader perspective can I, or for that matter can *anyone*, move on. It's through this broader perspective that I learned how to forgive. And how to be able to 'refresh' the page in order to become the me I should have been right from the beginning.

This book is also a testament to the number of times *something* intervened in my life. It bungled my two suicide attempts as a young teenager in startling ways. It also intervened in such exotic and initially crazy ways that it took a while for me to get the message: *I wasn't alone.* But knowing this sill didn't prevent me from making further mistakes or falling into more traps. Nevertheless, each new mistake or negative episode was slightly less destructive until, finally, as I turned 60, the lessons seem to *take* and this particular drama in my life disappeared.

So now I am left with an amazing story of survival: of rape, depression, domestic violence, and resulting physical challenges.

But more importantly, this is also an amazing story of how I came face to face with God.

You can torture me, you can argue with me, but it will never change what I experienced. What I am experiencing to this day.

When you cut your finger, I am incorrect when I tell *you* that it's only your imagination. That the blood *you* see is a result of an active imagination. That the pain *you* feel is psychosomatic. But it's real. You have empirical experiential knowledge. It all happened. Nothing can change the facts you have. And though some facts are not tangible, they are still an immensely important part of the experience.

I believe we need more censorship of sexism. And that we should protect the young and the innocent from distorted versions of sexuality—quite the challenge in the face of our almost unlimited access to the internet on any subject.

I also believe that we would be much healthier as a society if we teach our children there is a higher purpose. And if you who reads this do not lean towards this way of thinking, then at least I ask you to believe that we should teach each of these precious ones the simple stand-by we used to have: the Golden Rule.

Tina Assanti, February 2, 2019
Kissimmee, Florida

BOOK ONE:

The Early Years

"Suffer the children
come to me; do not try to stop them: for
the Kingdom of Heaven belongs to such as these."

(Matthew 19:14, NEB)

ONE

The Imperfect Conditioning
of a Child and How She
Met an Angel

wo generations ago, my very innocent but plain great aunt on my father's side fell in love with a soldier who disappeared into the deep, muddy trenches of the First World War. He left behind the seed of a new life which was clandestinely born into our very strict Catholic family. And, according to the whisperings of my youth, the burden of shame was such that the child was placed by an open window to be left to the winter's elements. The hope was the baby would be carried back to Heaven by a stork with "Return to Sender" stamped on its head.

Years later, this great aunt insisted on being my godmother since I had been conceived out of wedlock. Therefore, I was a soul in need of saving. By the time I was born, my parents still had not had a church wedding. Civil marriages were not ordained by God according to the Catholic Church at the time. She insisted I at least be christened. On the day of my christening, she announced that I could now die in peace because I had been given my own wings to fly directly to God. Her way, I suppose, of easing her own pain and making up for not christening her little bundle before it was sent back so many years before.

My Nonno, my great aunt's brother, was taught by their father never to kiss a woman on the lips because they were dirty creatures. As a starving young man during the depression, he befriended my Nonna. She was a beautiful, young cook-in-training at a ritzy hotel who had pity on him, and secretly fed him in the basement of the said ritzy hotel. During an inebriated moment, he became bold, forced himself on her, and she conceived. He did not disappear into any trenches. He did the right thing and married her. She didn't like him and didn't want to get married but she had no choice. During their marriage, each of their seven children was conceived as a result of marital rape.

But he was careful not to kiss her.

These are the foundations upon which my own parents stood. Good looking kids with movie star looks. He was dark, sweet, and handsome. Posing on the day of their quick civil wedding in 1953, three months in my making, she could have been a double for Grace Kelly. She wearing a cigar paper ring and a borrowed aqua outfit; he in a borrowed suit.

• • •

Two months later in Chicago, Hugh Hefner gathered $8,000 and, on his kitchen table, created *Playboy* magazine. Marilyn Monroe glowed on the front cover, spread out on satin with her arms and legs discreetly positioned *just so*.[2]

The *Playboy* centerfold was born, and this baby was *not* stamped "Return to Sender."

Because this first unofficial edition was so well accepted, Mr. Hefner recouped the original investment within two weeks. He had enough to officially launch the January 1954 edition of his *Playboy Magazine: Entertainment for Men.*

Slowly, but steadily, as *Playboy* magazine changed the very fabric of society, it would intricately weave its tentacles into my own life. It became an unwanted, but steady, companion until well after my formative years were thoroughly programmed.

• • •

---

[2]   The famous calendar shot of Marilyn Munroe from the Baumgarth Calendar Co.

Back in the homeland, four months later, I was launched.

The stork did not take me back, either.

A little later, I quite abruptly became aware of life while clinging to an icy wrought iron grate at an open window. I was naked save for a frozen, sodden diaper scraping the tender skin on the inside of my plump thighs. It burned terribly and no matter what position my legs were in, I could not prevent the chafing and stinging. I screamed down into the street below, desperately bellowing for my mother who, to my understanding, seemed to have disappeared. It was dark and into the freezing months of winter. There wasn't a living soul on the black streets below.

My parents had gone to see a film, the first evening out since I had been born, leaving me in the care of my paternal Nonna. In the house also lived my spinster afore-mentioned Godmother a widowed second cousin, and three of my father's younger brothers. But no one came in response to my cries.

Nonno forbade my Nonna to leave their bed.

How I had gotten out of that tall crib without toppling it, and ended up half naked at that open window which was opened on a late wintry night, no one could say.

Upon my parents' return, they heard a baby cry before realizing it was me up at the open attic window. My mother had rushed in to save me, comforted me, and then changed my diaper. Freshly-clothed, she held me over her shoulder. I spied a rosary draped over a small pile of little toys stored in a white enamel wash basin. My first recollection of a crucifix.

Only days later, I was busy biting and rubbing my gums on the edge of one of the square rungs of the wooden playpen I shared with my cousin. She was greeted by admiring adults bowing down, craning their faces towards her with open smiles and cooing sounds. I, on the other hand, somehow brought out the sad sounds and whispers. I could tell the difference at less than a year old.

• • •

During that year, Playboy portrayed ten to twelve women in their birthday suits, their personal body measurements were listed as if they were cars on display or as sex slaves on the block:

Bust: 36 inches
Waist: 23 inches
Hips 36.5 inches
Height 5 ft. 5.5 inches
Weight 128 pounds

The front covers, in contrast, were still quite playful with a hint of the truly artistic. One month, the back of a woman in the newly-introduced two-piece—a conservative forerunner of the bikini— depicted her back free of the clasped top. The white profile image of the Playboy Bunny jumped out of the page in stark contrast to the sunburn on her naked back, surrounded by the softness of the striped beach blanket, sand, and the soft, beautiful woman herself.

Circulation increased, but the numbers did not count the massive number of times a single copy of the magazine was shared and worn out with use by others.

• • •

1956

Still in Europe, I sat at my grandparents' massive table while a pair of heavy scissors whizzed past my head, hurled by a young uncle who meant to spear another young uncle in the eye. It was a memorable day with much fighting, throwing of articles and then threats by an overworked Nonna. However, later that same evening, there was an unusually happy moment when I played hide and seek with my youngest uncle who was only four years older. There, in the kitchen and living room, hung a curtain off a high shelf on the plaster wall that hid a flipped-up Murphy bed. It was where my grandparents slept. The bed had been pulled down, presumably, for my benefit. The curtain had not been pushed aside, and still hung partially over the top part of the bed creating a perfect and comfy hiding spot for me. It was the first and last time I saw my uncle truly laugh. Someone yelled at him to cool it down and emphasized it for good measure by slapping him across the head. In his short remaining sixty years of his life, I never heard him laugh with such joy in my presence again.

This world, I had come to realize, lacked lightness of being. I was eventually motivated to do nothing but fill in the deeper black voids with a sickly-sweet, eternally happy demeanour. I now believe that perhaps I did that more for self-preservation, as I could see clearly even as a child that these voids seemed to be bottomless pits. I sensed my relatives' pain and struggles. I could not bear the thought of them, so I quickly learned how to find ways to put some lightness into their eyes and faces, even if only for a moment.

Though many times I would be told to get out of their faces entirely.

• • •

1957

Along with hundreds of thousands of other citizens over a period of years, our homeland government sponsored my parents, my six-month-old sister, and me with a one-way ticket to North America. We sailed on an old, converted navy ship with nothing but seed money and a wad of hope. Women and children were separated from the men for the nights. So, it was surprising when late one night, over the rumble of the bulkheads, my father woke me. He held me up so that I could press my face against the cabin's one porthole to see an unforgettable sight: a massive woman elegantly draped in cloth holding a flame up to the orange, hazy night sky. She herself was bathed in light, the shadows amongst the folds of her covering created a beautiful sensation for my young eyes. Around her tall base, boats of all shapes and sizes scurried back and forth in the dark. I could smell my breath off the pockmarked glass and was frustrated when a gray, moist film formed between my gaze and the Statue of Liberty. It eventually faded all lights into a series of varying bursts of radiant light. I could no longer focus. To me, she represented beauty and dignity in her womanhood, draped from shoulder to her toes, holding a book and wearing a sunburst for a crown.

My heart had skipped and warmed. Obviously, this woman was held in high regard, which was a completely foreign concept in my brain.

A day or two later, we spent the night on the train. I sat awake with my father watching him slice off a piece of cheese for me while my mother slept with my baby sister on the hard, uncomfortable seats. I looked at the different people from different lands, all immigrating as we were. I could not help but notice one or two swarthy looking men studying my beautiful mother as she slept. I wanted to go and tell them to look the other way.

The next morning, we arrived in Toronto and were met by another one of my father's brothers. He had gone ahead to scout this great new country called Canada and had arranged a flat for us to move into. My sister was ensconced into the depths of a rattan, baby carrier with a plastic window in the lid. I remember checking to make sure she was still in there while the adults spoke about the new world and all its wonders above my head.

Even at the age of three, I had great hopes for her and me in this new land where people seemed to be much happier.

● ● ●

Throughout that year, Jayne Mansfield and fifteen other women had graced Playboy's stapled centerfolds. The magazine's distribution, now at a million, slowly crept outward across the United States and into Canada. The covers were artistic and light-hearted. Cleavages and bellybuttons had not yet adorned the front, but certainly were within. Vintage sports cars, cruise ships, yachts and cocktails, all the covers were designed with an almost apologetic innocence. It was a lifestyle that was celebrated and expounded with aplomb. Every young man gobbled it up, especially now that the focus was no longer on war. The smoke on the horizon of future wars had not yet been spotted. Every man was told they had a right to a job, a wife, a family, and a future. Post-war houses had been built so that every single man who fought in the war would be a king of his own castle. But now that they had everything, most were not entirely happy.

Playboy's underlying message was, "Come on. That's not *really* what you want." The message to men was loud and clear. "Enjoy yourselves! The world and the women within are part of your own sacred oyster."

The magazines were displayed on the lower shelves on magazine racks in markets and drug stores. However, they hadn't made an alarming impression as yet. In fact, they were so nicely and imaginatively created, the art work alone attracted the eye of elderly, retired art teachers or young, prudent mothers. Yes, young boys and men now equated them with objects to be put secretly under mattresses. But, inevitably they were picked up by unsuspecting women or girls enticed by its covers. Once opened, however, the truth smacked them between the eyes. Shocked, they quickly replaced the offending publication, hoping no one saw them touch it. For most women and girls, this would be the first true images of what their own sexuality looked like. The only thing they learned was that it was undignified and suggestive. It was almost too much to bear.

Girls and women were learning from Playboy as well.

• • •

After our arrival in Toronto, my father got up early the next morning to look for a job. Since he was trained as an auto body man at my Nonno's shop in Europe, my father quickly landed a good one. My parents managed to rent a house right next door. For a short period of time, life was gentle and kind.

My mother rented out rooms and saved a substantial amount of money for a pair of poor, war-torn immigrants. The only disruption I recall was an elderly gentleman who rented on the second floor. While I played on the front steps, he insisted on urinating out of his window over my head.

Back in Europe, my Nonno, however, was not happy with the situation. He had lost a valuable and cheap form of labor in my father, so he decided to come and see for himself. He also brought one of my uncles. A few years older now, my uncle had fallen into a bad crowd and begun pimping a girl on the streets. After a while, my Nonno returned to Europe but left my younger uncle in the care of my mother. Nonno also took along my mother's savings including that of my first established uncle. He decided to buy the shop building he had rented for thirty years. He knew he could sell it for a profit.

He and the rest of the circus were coming over to Canada, too.

My mother, who looked like Grace Kelly remember, was left with two children, five male boarders, and a horny, young brother-in-law.

It wasn't long before my uncle tried to force himself on my mother while she was doing the laundry in the basement. She screamed, ran out of the house, and called to my father over the fence. My father dropped everything in the shop and rushed to her rescue. I watched my father and uncle roar mightily at each other like two great ferocious lions on the African veldt. The walls vibrated with their explosions. Then, suddenly, my uncle swept my mother into his arms and held her over the balustrade of the stairway, threatening to throw her down the two stories. I don't remember if the crying I heard was from my own throat or my little sister's. But, after he heard it, my uncle backed down. As a final statement of brutality, he punched the plaster wall at the top landing, leaving a gaping hole. Plaster dust settled on the worn landing below. After the adults dispersed, I walked to the top landing and stood on my tip-toes to place my small fist into the jagged hole. Such power. Such intensity. It seemed like magic.

I went down one landing where I punched the wall with all my might. Just like my uncle did. I accomplished nothing but scraped knuckles. I studied them as a doctor would, measuring the scrapes and droplets of blood to see if I should allow myself to be alarmed. I wasn't.

I had begun to accept aggression to an alarming level. By this time, I was only five.

About a year later, my Godmother insisted I go to a Catholic School. Still very young and obedient, my parents dutifully registered me into St. Basil Catholic School on Hazelton Lanes in a little back neighbourhood called Yorkville. One day, Peter, Paul, and Mary would perform to beatnik crowds in coffee houses here. But for now, it was still a slum.

With no English to my vocabulary except for what I learned on programs on TV such as *Diver Dan* and *Captain Kangaroo*, I entered a school where there was seemingly little tolerance for young people. Although my kindergarten teacher was quite gentle, by the time I entered first grade, I had learned that the nuns were quite another matter.

Fortunately, the nuns liked music and singing. Somehow, they discovered I had a good voice. Singing became my refuge because it pleased my teacher, especially when others couldn't understand the notes. The nun would call me to the front of the class and hold a stick up to the notes on the board. I would sing each one of them, mouthing the English words without knowing what they meant. I would finish and she would nod with approval. She would then turn to the class, tuck her hands into her black tunic and announce, "*That's* how you sing it. Like an angel."

Frequently, our class walked along the city streets, regardless of the weather, either to the library or to St. Basil Church. There would be a nun at the head of the line, and a nun at the end, who was always ready to slap the ears of the stragglers in front of her. During our jostling into line outside the side door into the church, the nuns would check the girls' heads to ensure we covered our *shame* before we quietly and reverently entered. By this time, my world had flipped. With the arrival of the rest of the family, we were not able to afford a hat or school uniform for me because my father worked for my Nonno once again for little wages. Frustrated, the nun would roughly pin a Kleenex to my scalp. Sometimes a pink one. Sometimes a blue. It seemed I was always the only one. I bore that shame daily.

I had learned a new saying in English. I saw this Kleenex routine as my own *cross to bear*. I was proud to have one. For I also found that I loved Jesus and His *cross*.

Was it my natural desire to right the wrong I found in this life? Jesus' death seemed so unfair, unnecessarily cruel and wasteful. All I wanted to do, when I looked up at the statue of Mary, the Mother of God, holding the dead and crucified Jesus, was to reach out and hold Him, too. I tried once. But one of the nuns grabbed me and hissed at me. I couldn't find the English words to explain, so I burst into tears of frustration. In response, the nun pointed to the front of the church and ordered me to sit in the first *pew*.

What was a "pew?" It sounded like a cartoon sound.

"The *pew*," she hissed.

I looked to where she pointed and came to the conclusion that a pew was a bench. So, I dutifully walked to the front pew and sat on the cold, hard, wood. I looked up and over at the beautiful altar. The sun shone through the stained-glass windows. The bejewelled lights glinted off the silver and brass. The fine white linens covering the altar danced with angels' brush-marks of heavenly tints of violets, royal blues, and crimson. Somewhere in the bowels of the church, nuns were singing, sounding like a choir of angels.

Suddenly, I felt this warmth overwhelm me with a peace I had never experienced in my short life. As I sat transfixed and felt the lifting of my heart, a loving hand rested on my shoulder. Instantly, it occurred to me that perhaps one of the nuns finally understood me. It was a tender gentle touch.

I swivelled on the slippery surface of the pew to see what loving smile I might see.

There was no face, no smile. No one was even near. All the other students, their backs facing toward the center of the church, stood silently doing the Stations of the Cross while the nuns stood by watching, their hands tucked into their tunics. One nun closed her eyes. I thought she was listening to the angelic voices as I was.

No one was looking at me.

I looked up into the arches of the high ceiling of the church, then over to the altar again and then up to Jesus on the Crucifix. I got up, walked closer to the altar, and knelt on the pad in front. Were His eyes watching me? But the carved face showed a weakness that was not in the touch of the hand. The face was miserable. Understandable. But the triumphant and brave act of His must surely have been exactly what God intended Him to do. Where was the strength in the suffering?

I came to the conclusion that perhaps I knew better. He was stronger than they showed.

And that to suffer in life was normal.

That night, I created space on half of my bed so that He could rest as I did. I was devastated when, in the morning I found myself sprawled in the center. After that, for years into my young teenage years, I always kept half of the bed empty for Him.

I had a Friend.

Shortly after that day in church, I floated one night from my bed and found myself hovering over the path in the backyard along the side fence. I floated close to the shrubs where I was surprised to discover flowers that looked just like the bleeding heart that was painted on Jesus' chest in church. I put my nose close to them and smelled their aroma. Slowly I steadied myself in front of all the bleeding-heart blossoms, following the path to where it ended halfway up the garden near an old trellis. In fact, I hadn't noticed that trellis until I floated out. It was completely overgrown with branches and wild plants.

At breakfast the next morning, I told my parents I had floated out and smelled the flowers in the backyard. My hard-working father laughed and said it was just a dream. But I knew what dreams were. This wasn't one of them.

I learned afterward the flowers indeed were called Bleeding Hearts. I renamed the bush, Jesus' Bleeding Hearts.

It was a difficult introduction to this new English speaking world. Much did not make sense. For instance, boys played soccer and other neat games in the large spacious play yard in the back where the sun seemed to always shine. The girls, meanwhile, were imprisoned in the small space surrounded by a fence out front of the school. The sun never shone on our heads during recess or when counting for the separate lines of boys and girls. It was sometimes unbearably cold and torturous in the winter. The boys enjoyed clear, dry, warm pavement free of moisture and melting snow, while we still stumbled over the frozen indents in the ice and snow. I think this caused the young girls and nuns to be miserable, tough, and cruel. The light always seemed to shine upon the boys, even the light of the nuns' eyes.

And why did I have to learn that, because I was a girl, I must stay silent and listen enraptured while a boy talked about whatever he liked? And why was I so evil because some woman had eaten an apple? The message was loud and clear at school: women were the lowest kind of animal, just above the writhing despicable snake below everyone's feet. I recognized it as similar to what I was learning at home.

I saw the innate unfairness of it all. I wanted to be a boy—to punch walls, comb my hair back slickly as my uncles did, and walk as if the world belonged to me.

But I was taught that I was an evil little girl. I had to pray for forgiveness because I was naturally sinful. Secretly, after observing my own family, I thought the males were the naturally sinful ones. But what did I know? I even failed at Confession, for I could never think of a thing to repent over. So, at the confessional box I reiterated what I was taught: I was a sinful creature, and oh, by the way, I had taken a toy from my sister and made her cry.

Then I wondered about a girl in a higher class who did nasty things to me. If Jesus was my friend, why would he keep forgiving *her*?

One day she punched my stomach quick as a wink. I was shocked when my body doubled over and dropped without me telling it to fall. I couldn't drink air anymore, and I was reminded of a fish one of my uncles caught at a cottage once. It lay on the raft with its eyes looking wild and its lips and gills scrambling to pull something through.

I remember I jumped off the stranded raft and ran over to collect my metal, peanut butter pail. I dipped and poured water as fast as I could over my new friend. He looked at me and begged me to throw him back into the water. I looked over at my uncle, the one who punched the wall. I pondered which would garner the most discomfort: knowing the fish died because of me, or knowing I disobeyed an adult. Especially a man. So, I let it give up its spirit and use its gills as wings to fly to fish heaven. It took me a long time to get over the guilty feelings of this terrible thing I did. But at least I had something to confess to that priest with the bad breath behind the screen.

I lay there on the snow-covered pavement imagining I had gills on the side of my neck frantically sucking in something, *anything*. I refused to give up and fly away. Just then a nun came out and rang her big brass bell. Fear of being the straggler and getting my head slapped was enough incentive to frantically pull myself into an upright position and stumble into line. Getting a whack on icy, cold ears was a real zinger.

One day I was inadvertently walking in front of this girl and two of her friends. She was also Italian but beautiful. Her curled hair always had a ribbon carefully tied into the mounds of her black shiny tresses. Her hair was so intensely black that it shone blue just like Superman's hair in the comics. It was the color and style I wished I had instead of my straight, dirty-blonde bowl-cut hair.

The other two girls were Irish twins. They had a funny way of speaking. They always wore a thin, green tie in their long red braids. They were the first people I had ever seen with faces full of spots. This fascinated me but turned out to be a hindrance. Whenever they caught me staring at them, they'd throw a snowball at me, or they'd start running in my direction threatening me with something that was 'bleedin'.

One afternoon after school, they and the darker girl, carrying their books, caught up to me quickly. I couldn't go any faster on the narrowly-shovelled sidewalk because my over-boots were too big and threatened to slip off my shoes.

"Do you mind?"

I stiffly turned to the beautiful one with my one eye looking past the fur trim of my hood. By this time, I had acquired a tremendous amount of respect for her, so I made an effort to be extremely polite. I understood her to mean, *are you going to be nice and move out of my way?* I bodily craned to face her and respectfully said, "Oh, yes!" Beaming, I looked eagerly at her face. As I proceeded to sit back on the pile of snow on the side of the path to let them go by, she pushed me over the mound of snow so hard that my heavy boots swung over my head and flipped me backward. My Eskimo jacket's zipper split and the rest of my jacket spread-eagled behind me. I looked like a strange cartoon hero with a thick cape with arms.

That was when I learned there are nuances in the English language.

I collected myself and waited until there was a good distance between them and me before I trudged behind them. When they turned left off Hazelton Lane towards Avenue Road, a tall man, with a gray face and eyes as black as stone pools, stepped out from behind a tree. For the first time I heard the term, *pedophile*.

"There's that bleedin' pedophile agin'!" one of the twins yelled.

"Let's throw snowballs at him," yelled my nemesis. The girls picked up shards of icy snow from the side of the road with their free hands and pelted him before running off.

I stopped.

Why did I feel sorry for him? The way he raised his arms to protect his special eyes?

He straightened up and his dead pools of eyes slowly turned their gaze at me.

I screamed and flew with my cape to the other side of the road. I didn't stop even when the boot covering my right shoe flew off.

Later, Mam dragged me back to look for it. We found it packed full of dirty snow. While Mam dug it out, the snow drifting in over the top of her Eaton buttoned overshoe, I kept watch with my glassy eyes. It had gotten dark and I imagined him lurking in every shadow amongst the tightly-packed townhomes. He was probably eyeing Mam's under-slip as her woolen skirt rose up. I saw it clearly myself because its laced edge hung about two inches from underneath her stretched hem. I shifted to cover her behind to keep the sight from his prying eyes—wherever those black bottomless pits were hidden.

Being an outsider who spoke sketchy English attracted bullying. After too many times of being punched or pushed by her and her friends, I tended to stay by myself in a small corner of the building out of everyone's sight. It was next to the caretaker's door. The wind piled debris high into the corners. Pigeon poop was liberally splattered here and there on the pavement. I played with my red, white and blue foam ball, bouncing it against the wall, letting it bounce back once while clapping my hands before catching it again. "How many times could I clap before I wouldn't catch the ball in time?" I wondered. I never went beyond four, I remember. At one point, intent on reaching five claps, I bounced the ball so hard on the pavement to make it hit the wall higher in order to buy more time that it bounced right onto the roof of the small protruding part of the school.

Upset, I ran to the other part of the front yard to tell the nun. She told me to knock on the caretaker's door to ask the caretaker to go up and retrieve it. If he didn't have the time to do it, he certainly had enough similar balls regularly retrieved from the roof or the grounds to replace mine.

I knocked on the caretaker's green, peeling metal door. My knuckles, still bruised from punching the plaster wall at home, felt tender against the gravelly cold surface. So, instead, I made a fist with the side of my hand and banged against the solid metal door. Suddenly, I heard a scraping of a latch, and the door opened. It was the first time I came face-to-face with the old caretaker. Bending over me in his rumpled work shirt and pants, he listened as I explained in halting English that my ball was on the roof. Just to be clear, I pointed to the roof.

He motioned me inside instead.

Carefully, I stepped over the high, cement threshold, slightly scraping my shin on the sharp edge. It was as if I stepped into a netherworld. The air was dank and smelled of oils, old tools, dirt, and other smells I couldn't recognize. I looked toward my right. I stood almost directly underneath the one source of light, a single light bulb hanging from the exposed rafters blackened by time. Over the old, well-worn wooden workbench hung the largest picture I had ever seen. It was a picture of a completely naked woman in a pose that made me feel queasy. I intuitively knew it was demeaning. It was in stark contrast to the dignified image of the great Statue of Liberty I saw on our way to Canada. And, somehow, I felt ashamed that, if my friend Jesus saw it, He would be upset I had seen it.

Why would the caretaker want to look at a nude woman? I had already learned that any reference to our bodies was bad. Yet, here he was, at a Catholic school which was almost the house of God and with nuns all around him, blatantly displaying this large image.

He must have read my mind, because he quickly gave me a ball out of a stained cardboard box. This ball was not as new and beautifully pure in colour as mine was, but for him, it was good enough. He put his heavy hand on my shoulder and pushed me toward the door. When we got there, he groaned, sat, and patted the spot on the threshold beside him where I should sit.

Obediently I sat beside him while I continued to tally the dents, holes and scratches in this ugly ball he gave me. With so many missing spots of foam, how could it possibly bounce properly?

While I was musing on this technical issue, he suddenly took my right hand and held it between his own. I looked at his gnarly hands. They were as dirty as my father's. Trusting hands that were warm against mine. I thought he was keeping them warm for me. Then, with one hand he pulled my little hand toward himself. Innocently, I thought he wanted to warm my hand more quickly. I couldn't believe someone would care so much for me.

It turned out to be something altogether ugly and vulgar. It frightened me. I felt used. I became alarmed and with a whimper, I pulled hard on my arm.

Perhaps it was my whimper, my mounting alarm, or his fear of being caught, but he suddenly let my hand slip from his. I raced away from the once safe corner. I never returned. I never told a nun. In fact, I never told a soul. More importantly, I never openly admitted it even to Jesus. I believed I had done something shameful. I truly thought what happened was my fault. It was a good reason why I was sinful and headed for Hell.

I had officially come face to face with the relatively new phenomena called a *Playboy Centerfold*. I did not know that this magazine, and its effect on my world, would haunt me for the rest of my life. No one could foresee that by the time I reached seventeen, *Playboy* would reach its peak circulation of over nine million subscribers and it would have singlehandedly ushered in the "Sexual Revolution." This sexual revolution had a devastating effect on my family and me.

I was nicely conditioned to live a perfectly dysfunctional life into adulthood while the men also affected in this environment were perfectly trained and brainwashed to cause it.

TWO

Let the Circus Begin
James Bond and Hefner,
a Perfect Cocktail

1962

Mam peeled potatoes with a small paring knife, leaving thick skin peels on top of the good potatoes in the paper bag. In the background, Walter Cronkite talked about the Cuban Missile Crisis and the stand-off with Russia.

Mam didn't quite understand English but she turned to see the map of possible missile strikes on the TV. The arrows showed them going all the way up to Toronto. Walter Cronkite even mentioned Toronto. I think that's what made her look over.

With devastating fresh memories of bombings, dead bodies and starvation from the last great war, she whimpered and rushed to the window and threw it open. She frantically looked this way and that. Somewhere a truck exploded, and I heard it groaning up the hill. She fell back in panic and screamed.

Her scream didn't bother me. I was on the floor on my stomach reading. I was seriously fretting over a comic book story called a fable. It was about a man who was looking for the perfect wife. His measurement of a woman's perfection came down to one thing: how well she sliced cheese. I never learned how to slice cheese. I knew my mother sliced the potato peels too thickly. In my innocence, I was sure she would fail the cheese test.

Pap roared through the door.

"The Russians are coming!" she bawled at him. "I just heard a bomb explode and I can hear the engines of the tanks! Russian soldiers, marching! Listen, their boots!" She remained rooted to the old, threadbare carpet. Only her shaking head and hunched shoulders swiveled slightly toward the window. "They'll be coming down the street like they did in the war," she cried.

The room we were in functioned as a slapped-together open kitchen and living room with a pull-out couch where my parents slept. My sister and I slept in the little bedroom next to them. The rest of the house was bulging with Pap's family who now had successfully emigrated. We were running out of room.

"I'm going to die!" She sobbed with tight dry hiccups. Her shoulders curled over her body as she held onto her stomach with crossed arms. She was like a little girl again. Littler than me.

I had begun to feel much older than her for a while now. I had come to believe I had to be her protector. That's why I was so unaffected by her daily *moments*. I felt confident I could eventually fix this latest crisis for her. You see, I *knew* things. And I loved her.

"Come here," Pap said, motioning to the window and standing off to the side. "I want you to look."

She was still sobbing like a little girl. Her eyes swiveled in all directions as if she were trying to figure out where to run to. Just then my Nonna came huffing up the stairs, her massive bosom heaving under the effort. "Is she okay?"

"Mam, get out! Mind your own business!" Pap had an ugly look on his face. He felt helpless.

Nonna looked over at me with her massive hazel eyes. I waved at her from the floor and smiled. She waved back at me with a tight smile and wordlessly motioned for me to come with her. Pap saw her do that. I knew if I did I would make him angry so I stayed put.

"Out, Mam!" Pap yelled.

Then Nonno got into the scene from the bottom of the stairs. "Woman, get down here! Mind your own business!" At the sound of his gruff voice, Nonna suddenly twirled and huffed heavily down the stairs. Nonno yelled some more at her and I heard her mentioning my name. He yelled at her again, and then I heard a door slam and their muffled voices rose up from below the floor under my stomach. I could feel the vibrations.

"Look out the window," my father continued, raising his voice. "There are no tanks or soldiers. Just cars."

Mam violently shook her head, her eyes looking inward replaying past blood, gore and bombs of the nightmare that was her childhood.

I got up with a little grunt thinking it was time I quietly got involved and went to the window. It looked right onto Davenport Road. Slowly, as I leaned through the window, the sounds behind me faded and were replaced by Saturday afternoon traffic. I craned over the windowsill and pushed to just before my tipping point. I looked briefly at the dried-up corpse of a baby bird I found in the back laneway and tried to rescue. At the time, I thought I would help it by going up to our rooms on the second floor to throw it out the window.

"Fly, birdie," I had yelled as I tossed it up. It flopped on its thin belly with wings flapping and then it settled on the little roof that covered the front door below me. During the next few days, I tried to entice it with pieces of rusk, butter and bits of chocolate sprinkles. It didn't recognize the crumbs as food. Or the chocolate. At first, it eyed me. Then it just sat wobbling with its eyes closed. Eventually, it died.

Something else for the confession box and more tokens of guilt for my heavy suitcase labeled, "Destination: Hell."

Suddenly, my attention was snapped back to the streetcar hobbling, rocking, and screeching past. A few cars sped from the other direction after revving their engines in anticipation of the green light at Dupont Avenue. I watched as the ESSO sign across from Pepe's went from red to blue and then dwindled to white, then red, then blue… I always felt slightly dulled when I watched it but I didn't linger with my eyes. I had to continue with my assessment of the situation.

Only a few people were out. There were some teenagers across the street wearing white ankle socks and blue and white oxford shoes that I couldn't have because of lack of money. They also wore men's white shirts with long shirt tails. They had pony tails swinging in the cold late autumn air.

I gave another glance all around, even up into the skies. No missiles or bombs. And not a single soldier or tank. How am I going to fix this if they're not here yet?

I heard the door slam behind me. Pulling my body back in, I saw that Mam had run off. Pap loudly knocked things around on the little table where we ate our meals.

I went over to stand in front of the TV where Walter Cronkite instructed us about what to do when the sirens go off. I already knew all this. The nuns told us we just had to hide under our desks. I looked at the kitchen table and knew for a fact that there wasn't enough room for my parents, my little sister and me. So, I decided I should sacrifice myself for them by standing guard.

I was happy now that I sorted that one out, but I was still in a quandary about downstairs. My grandparents and four uncles would never fit under their white enamel kitchen table. Oh no, scratch that. One uncle went back to the homeland to find a wife. I heard Pap and Nonno talking about the woman he found and married within one week. She was a third cousin once removed to Pap and my uncles. They talked about how she was probably as demanding and miserable as her aunt, the one that lived with us when we lived in the attic before we left for Canada. That house with the window and the cold wrought-iron grate. He hadn't returned to Toronto yet.

"I can't see." My father's exasperated voice cut through my thoughts. He was the highest authority in the world. Dutifully, like a soldier, I jumped out of the way and climbed onto the deep, maroon-colored couch cushions. Absentmindedly, I fingered the raised rose pattern while I continued to listen to Walter Cronkite. I felt like a grown up listening while Pap listened, too. Like we were a team.

• • •

My parents fought all the time now. Pap used all of Mam's saved money to bring over the very people Mam didn't want living in Canada. We were poor again because Nonno didn't pay Pap enough at the auto body shop they opened. Pap and my uncles put in longer hours and worked on Saturdays and sometimes Sundays, too. They worked around the clock to pay off the loan they had taken out to buy the business.

One Saturday, Mam, Nonna, my sister Bettina, my youngest uncle, and I got off the streetcar out front of the shop and walked into the waiting room. All the tools and air compressors in the main shop were humming and blasting like a badly-tuned cartoon orchestra. I could barely hear a tinny version of "Let's do the Twist" on someone's transistor radio.

Mam carried a big pot of homemade tomato soup wrapped in a small blanket. I held a paper bag with prosciutto ham sandwiches in one hand and Bettina's hand in the other. Nonna carried a pot of spinach pasta and my youngest uncle—the miserable, sad one—carried the milk and juice we had picked up at the *Igga* on Dupont on our way. (Years later I would discover it was pronounced, *I.G.A.* but all the women called it *Igga*.)

I looked at Nonno's office on the right. The scratched door was slightly ajar, with black smudges forming a donut around the banged-up brass door handle. I could see my uncle (the one who had gotten married in one week during the Cuban Missile Crisis) in his little cubicle on the left behind a high counter. It had one of those push bells perched on the edge of it.

My uncle could see us but didn't act like it. He was talking on the phone

There were old, cracked chairs in one corner with a blackened little table between them. I walked over and sat Bettina on one of the chairs. For the first time, there were magazines on the little table. I liked to read, so I picked one up. On the front was a woman's foot with no shoe or sock on it, but she had a little bracelet on her ankle with a bunny rabbit on it. She was touching a man's foot that had a nice slipper, and I could see a leg clad in a pajama pant. I read *Playboy* across the top. Then, I carefully read all the English words on the page. One sentence caught my attention. "How to Succeed with Women Without Really Trying."

I gasped. I needed to read that. *If only Pap would read this, then he could make Mam happy,* I thought. Anxious to learn, because I *really* wanted them to stop fighting, I opened the magazine, and it fell open to the middle.

My breathing stopped. A woman.

I tipped the magazine sideways and frowned. My heart started to beat a little faster, while I felt this strange urge to run away. She was like the woman above the caretaker's workbench. And I remembered what he did to me afterwards. I quickly closed it and dropped it back on the table. I pulled another one out from underneath. On the cover was the bottom half of a woman on a towel in very tiny panties with strings on the side. She looked brown like I did after being in the sun. Except I wore a bathing suit, not small panties like her. I opened that magazine. Again, there was a naked woman. I think I drooled because I know my mouth hung open. Why did all the women look happy? They were naked.

I don't understand.

"Hey, put that back. That's not for little girls to look at."

Not for little girls to look at.

"Why," I asked.

"Why? Because I said so."

Bettina piped up and said, "Why?"

My uncle broke into a big toothy smile at her. He put the phone against his chest and said, "Because it's not for pretty little girls like you, Bettina. Just big men like me."

I looked over at Bettina on the chair. She did that cute little hands-clasped-together-thing and then twisted them shyly under her tiny chin. Her big brown eyes pulled at our uncle. He kept smiling at her until the voice at the other end of his phone shouted. He returned to the phone and talked roughly.

I watched him. Big men like him. Like the caretaker at school. I was told to love and respect my uncle. He was a man. I didn't want to think badly of him. But …

Now I was really confused.

As my uncle talked, I could hear his irritation. When he started yelling, Nonno stepped out of his office, hollered at him for yelling, and went back in and slammed the door.

I took Bettina and went outside and bounced my ball around her while thinking about those images in the Playboy Magazines. I didn't know why but I felt deflated like a party balloon after the air escaped between my fingers while making funny farting noises. But this wasn't funny.

I walked over to the open garage doors to look for Pap. Bettina followed and stood in the corner at the rag bin. She strained on her tip-toes to look inside. I walked over and tried to tip the big round drum over toward her, but I wasn't quite strong enough. So, I walked around and lifted her up so that she could look inside. Somewhere in the back of the shop above the noise, I heard Elvis Presley singing,

"It's now or never, come hold me tight,
Kiss me my darling, be mine tonight.
Tomorrow will be too late,
It's now or never, my love won't wait."

Love won't wait.
"Wife, shut your mouth for a change," I suddenly heard Pap yelling behind us.

I immediately let Bettina down, while we both twisted around to look.

Pap was perched on the front fender of a baby blue-colored car speckled with spots of rusty filler. His stained white and red coveralls covered in oil stains and dirt. Using a large soup spoon, he ate directly from the pot of soup. Mam looked at him grimly, her face tight.

"Pete, you work like a slave for your father, who doesn't pay enough money. You don't do the shopping or buy milk and bread. You don't know. The prices keep going up."

He roared at her and tossed his spoon back into the pot. A grinding machine in the shop was so loud that no one else heard him except for the three of us. That saved me some embarrassment. I didn't want people to know that he yelled at Mam.

Mam, humiliated, angrily turned and headed toward us, leaving the pot behind. She grabbed my hand and Bettina's, but I hesitated and looked back at Pap to make sure he was okay. Mam yanked my arm so hard my whole body shuddered. My head was the last to snap around. I stumbled, fell, and scraped my knee. Then I got up and wiped myself off of the oil, grease and small pebbles imbedded in the already well-scraped skin.

Another angry three streetcars home. More garlic-smelling men looked at my beautiful mother. One whistled softly, while another made kissing sounds. She pretended not to hear.

"Mam, why do those men ..." I whispered.

"Just ignore them," she said, cutting me off under her breath. She was angry and upset. Her eyebrows knitted tightly.

I was learning how to ignore misbehaving men.

• • •

I began to worship Pap and unfortunately think less and less of Mam. The nuns said that I should see my father as next to God, and that a wife should obey her husband as she would obey God. I found that a very noble concept.

Therefore, Mam was, like me, also less important and she should be obedient. But in my young observation, I felt she wasn't being obedient, ever, at *all*. She was *never* happy and wouldn't do what Pap asked. She got him so angry and loud that my ears would ring. That's when the thunder clouds exploded in the room and the walls started curving in. My sister would cry. Then I would lose sense of the real meaning of the moment and get frightened, too. I'd like to think I didn't but occasionally I heard myself cry, too.

• • •

That winter, leading up to a big European Christmas, Nonno and my uncles fell in love with Hockey Canada. They whooped and hollered at the TV, while the swishing sounds of skate blades cut across the ice. It was absolute mayhem when a fist fight broke out between players. They'd all punch the air, while their grunts of approval echoed off the high ceilings and the tired-looking living room walls cracked with age.

None of the women appreciated the attention that the men gave to hockey games. They were hungry for positive feedback for themselves. In a way, I understood. But from what I was learning, the women had no right to expect any. I thought they were being very selfish.

By this time, there were two new aunts—women brought back from the homeland after short bride-quests. They, Mam, and Nonna, stayed in the kitchen. Sometimes they dragged their feet to the living room to serve the men their beer, cheese, pickles and Dijon mustard. When they didn't come fast enough to check on the men, my youngest uncle, now about 11 or 12 and still in his usual miserable state, was dispatched to the kitchen to get their drinks.

They never bothered me because, I think, they didn't notice me. Bettina sometimes stayed with Mam in the kitchen playing under the enamel kitchen table. She would use her Crayola crayons and draw pictures on the underneath part of the table. No one knew she did, only me.

One night during a hockey game, Bettina and I stayed behind one of the couches. I don't know why I thought to do this, but we took turns sitting on the sharp teeth of a large, metal vegetable grater. We'd sit on one side and then compare the feel of the teeth on the other side. Those were the days when little girls and women didn't wear long pants. So, in our skirts, we'd feel the teeth grab into the skin on the back of our thighs and bottoms, piercing through our skirts, leotards, and undies. It made us giggle. The teeth tickled so beautifully! The men didn't notice what we were doing until there was an unexpected moment of silence on TV. Then they heard us giggling. Everyone turned to look at us. When the sound came back on, they turned back to the TV. Everyone except Nonno, who never liked us around. He told us to shut up and get out of the living room. Dutifully, I took the grater and Bettina and led her out into the drafty front hall to play our giggle game again.

On a similar night, when all the men were together, I saw a news film of a blonde lady with the back of her dress cut off. It was open all the way to just above her bum. The men, including Nonno, made almost as much noise over this as they did over hockey. When I saw her white hair (it was a black and white TV) and lots of make-up on her lips and eyes, I wondered why Pap liked what he saw on this lady called Jayne Mansfield. He wouldn't let Mam wear make-up at all. Not that I thought she should. Even without make-up I thought Mam was more beautiful.

Marilyn Monroe was beautiful. I saw her in the *Playboy* magazine left in the living room. I thought she was a close second to Mam. I was careful not to look between the covers, but this was when I learned the word sexy. I wondered if I would ever be able to be *sexy*.

I think because Pap liked hockey, he purchased skates for Bettina and me. We'd go skating at a nearby arena somewhere above Bloor Street. I loved feeling the cold, dry air on my nose, lips, and chin. Bettina and I fell down often, but neither of us cared. She wore double-bladed training skates, while I wore a used pair of boy's skates. I was happy with mine until I saw an older girl skate and twirl like a ballerina with wings. I noticed she had different skates with jagged teeth in front of the blades to grip the ice. When I tried to twirl, my legs would splay out, and I'd fall onto my icy, wet pants.

One Sunday morning, Bettina and I took our bath before going to skate. I used the plastic soap holder with the holes in the bottom as a toy to make Bettina laugh. Sitting in Mr. Bubbles, I dipped and held the soap holder as high as I could. Delighted, we watched the four or five streams of water flow through and onto the bubbles below.

When it was time to finish and get dressed, my mother toweled us dry. I heard the final gurgle of the drain in the tub.

"What is *that*?!" Mam looked shocked while she studied something in the tub. I leaned over the rolled edge to look myself. At first, I thought there was a hot dog resting on the rusty drain. It wasn't a hot dog, of course. I analyzed it, wondering how such a large object could come from a little girl like Bettina.

"Who did *that*?!"

I looked at Bettina and expected those massive brown eyes to admit guilt. She said nothing. She simply stared at Mam. Mam and I peered at each other. Then she turned to Bettina.

"Did you do *that*?!"

Bettina shook her head. I could almost see the halo forming. "Did *you*?!"

I swiveled my eyes to Mam. She glared at me accusingly.

"No, I didn't do it," I said. "Bettina did." I turned to Bettina. "Didn't you." I always assumed that Bettina and I had an understanding. Sister bonding. I took care of her when I could. We were in this war together. So, I was dumbfounded when she shook her head *again*!

"You lie," Mam said to me. "I will get your father."

Mam disappeared downstairs to get Pap. I turned to Bettina. "You did it, didn't you?" She nodded, her eyes were very, *very* big now.

Pap came into the bathroom. "What is this that I *hear*?"

"We had a bath and Bettina had an accident," I said.

Mam drilled her eyes into mine. "You lie."

"No, just ask Bettina. I just asked her. She told me she did." I felt like I was in a Perry Mason episode. I turned to Bettina again. "*Didn't* you!"

She shook her head *no*.

I don't remember if I was spanked at that point or not. I do remember that I hid in the bedroom for a while and then I sensed time was getting on. Skating would fill me up with good stuff again. It would make me forget the bad feeling in my tummy. I got dressed for skating the way I liked: two pairs of leotards under my skirt and a pair of knee socks over that. Then I ran down the stairs. Pap was in the living room with my uncles and the aunts. I stood in the doorway of the living room and looked at him. I saw that he wasn't ready to go. Then I looked back at Mam, who had stepped into the hallway behind me. She wasn't ready to leave either.

"Aren't we going skating?" I asked.

In front of everyone, Pap said, "No. For punishment, you are not skating anymore. You lied to us. Everyone," he said to the rest of my family in their Sunday finest, "do not talk to her today. She is a liar and is being punished."

Now, I'm sure he thought he was being a proper parent. Strict according to the Victorian principles. But it was painful. The whole world sat staring at me with damning eyes. Cigarette smoke rose from fingers.

I was heartbroken. I always tried so hard to be a good girl. Now all hopes of proving that I was were dashed forever. I was branded. And once branded, once it was tattooed on your forehead like Cain's was, it was all they remembered about you.

• • •

1963

Kennedy was shot. I was watching *As the World Turns* on TV sitting on my parents' bed with the purple Sears cover. We now lived in a small duplex on Lindy Lou north of Toronto somewhere away from the family. Mam rented the back rooms out to a German baker and his shy, French wife who couldn't speak English. She hid in the rooms all day while he was at work.

She tried very hard not to see me through the open door of the bedroom.

Walter Cronkite said Kennedy was hurt and it didn't sound good. I watched another hour just to find out how the President was doing. I liked him. I sensed he was a good man. He kept the Russians from coming down Davenport Road to our old house.

Then he died. The whole world cried. Even I did.

Years later, I learned that he had had an affair with Marilyn Monroe while in the White House. He was such a saint of a man that we all forgave him. That showed me two things: a man was allowed to have other women, and it had no bearing on his morality. But, what of Jackie O? Surely this was a double-edge sword issue.

But I wasn't surprised really. It was like that in our own family. Because I started noticing a difference in the men. And the women they ogled at.

Mam, too. Mam was doing something on her own now. She wanted to make extra money to save for a trip to Europe to visit my other grandparents, aunts and uncles. I think it made her feel like she had more control over her life.

After working awhile, she came home and talked about the women who lost fingers in the pressing machines. There was one woman who had lost three fingers. She had to smoke her cigarette squeezed between two stumps. I got the feeling that maybe Mam would stop working there as soon as she had the money she wanted.

Now I made Bettina's lunch and took care of her after school. I was eight, Bettina was six. We now went to a public school because Pap said the nuns were teaching me garbage. There was no God, and the *church* thing was a bad influence. So, it was public school for us from then on.

But, I already *knew* God. Pap's blindness and inability to hear and understand me when I talked about Him was mildly upsetting. I learned not to talk about God anymore, or of my Guardian Angel. For some reason, Pap made me feel ashamed to have such a wonderful presence in my life. Is he going to take that away from me, too?

One blustery day, I waited for Bettina at the door closest to her class. Then, I took her hand, and we started to walk home. Our route took us across the playground toward the park. Our house was just around the corner. The wind was so strong that day that bits and pieces of branches and old leaves from last fall blew around and hurt our eyes.

I heard a lot of shouting and screaming off to one side, so I stopped to look over at a group of older kids. I let go of Bettina and walked over to see what was happening. There was cheering and whistling. Everyone was taller than me. I pulled at the sleeve of a taller boy and asked what was going on.

"A razor blade fight. Two girls are fighting over a guy." He looked concerned but excited at the same time. He then went right back to watching. I pushed through bodies and spied two older girls with their legs spread, looking like they were about to pounce on each other. One girl, her jacket almost completely off her shoulders, swiped at the other girl's face. There was a guy in a leather jacket standing to the side grinning. My stomach turned. I knew razor blades well after living in a house with so many men who shaved. Just picking one up made my fingers bleed.

I got out of the crowd and went to get Bettina.

She was gone.

I looked all around the playground. I ran past the crowd to look on the other side. Then I looked over toward the park. My eyes still stung and watered badly. I called her but my voice was swallowed by the wind. I started walking toward the park, calling and calling.

I looked up at the sky. The clouds sped overhead, pushed by the cold wind. A piece of newspaper whipped by my face and I followed its track through the sky.

The sky.

Bettina was whipped up into the sky. She blew away!

I started running. I kept running, looking up into the big branches of the few trees in the park but only the odd ruffled black bird perched on branches. They were laughing at me. I prayed to God that He kept her safe but to please make sure she came back in one piece before my parents came home. In the meantime, I had to call Pap.

I ran and didn't even stop when my throat was so dry it was painful to breathe. I sweated in my heavy coat and my face streamed with tears from both crying and the wind. I ran through the front door, straight to the phone on the wall in the kitchen. I knew how to dial the number. Those were the days when phone numbers started with letters followed by a series of numbers. I dialed the shop. The kind lady answered the phone.

"May I please speak with Pap?" I asked her.

She put me on hold. It took a long time of listening to the two quick beeps over and over again. I looked out the kitchen window at the clouds racing by. Bettina would be very cold up there. I didn't doubt that she'd be able to sit on a cloud. She wasn't heavy at all.

"Hello!"

"Pap, I don't know where Bettina is." I started to cry. "I'm so sorry. I was looking at two girls having a razor blade fight and then she was gone. The wind took her away and I don't know how to get her back."

There was a lot of grinding and banging noise behind Pap's ear.

"She what?"

"She blew away!"

"What? Speak up!"

"Bettina. The wind blew her away!"

"The wind?"

"It blew her away!"

"Oh, it's windy!"

"Yes. Bettina went with the wind!"

"Oh, she'll be okay. Just cover her ears with her hat."

He hung up. His presence and the massive bubble of shop grinding and banging noises around him burst and went quiet.

I didn't eat. I fretted and then prayed to God she was okay. Then I felt better. I still didn't eat, but somehow, I knew she would be okay. So, because there was nothing else I could do, I went back to school and quietly fretted in class all afternoon.

After school, there she was, playing with a little boy we knew who lived around the corner. She had gone home with him for lunch, and his mother invited her to stay.

I guess his mother may have tried calling our house, but I was there. I was appalled that no one thought of checking with me first. I was, after all, responsible for *my* little sister!

I thanked God for dropping her off at the other house. Maybe He wanted her to have a nicer lunch than what I was planning to make.

• • •

1964

The twins.

Intuitively, I felt there was a bad seed in them. They were older but I was quite taken that they insisted on calling my house to see if I wanted to come over and play.

We had a problem, however. I wanted to play Monopoly, but they seemed to want to do things I would never do.

One day, while at their house, they led me to a bedroom where the first thing they did was put a finger to their lips. Both of them. I had to be quiet.

"Is your Mom home?" I asked, fearful that perhaps they were sneaking me in. That wouldn't do. That's like lying.

"No, no one's home," said Yanina.

"No, we're just going to sneak into Uncle Dimitri's bedroom," said Salina.

"Oh."

"We're not allowed in here," offered Yanina as she opened the door gently.

"Then why …?" I stopped in mid-breath. If there ever was a real man's bedroom created, this would be a famous one. In a magazine. It was surprisingly clean and organized. It just had a lot of, well, *things*. Models of cars and planes. The same *Playboy* magazines on a side table. There were real paintings on the walls. The single bed looked like it was done up by a soldier.

Salina opened the bi-fold doors to the closet. She bent down onto her hands and knees, and without a word, Yanina stepped onto her back, reached up to the top of the shelf and pulled down a yellowed white box. It looked like one of those special boxes a white Bible comes in.

She carefully stepped down and they both went to the bed and sat down next to each other. Yanina patted the spot next to her. I dutifully went over and scrambled up onto the bed.

Gingerly, Yanina opened the box and took out a massive white book with gold edging and letters. The letters were not English letters. I couldn't tell what language it was. Slowly, she turned to the beginning of the album.

Every page had one large photo. Each photo was only one woman in a garden. The same woman and the same garden. But she was naked and sat and stood in many different poses. She was heavier than the women in the *Playboy* magazines, but there she was. She had all the same parts except that she never sat with her legs open.

I didn't want to see anymore. I got up to leave. Yanina grabbed my hand.

"Where're you goin'?" she asked.

"I don't want to see this," I said.

"There's nothing wrong with this."

I shrugged.

Salina was disappointed in me. She closed the book and put the album back into the box. I walked out of the bedroom. Yanina was right behind me with a human skull.

"Ooooooooooooo," she said spookily while she held up the skull.

Intrigued, I said, "Let me see that!" She handed the skull to me. I looked at it closely in the filtered light of the dark hallway. Then I took it into their living room to the large front window. *Wow. Is that what we look like under our skin and hair?* I thought.

"Come on! Let's get some candles and be spooky!" We played with that skull for an hour. I laughed at the ridiculous sight of a body-less skull held high in the air over a candle and putting funny voices to it. I became proficient in moving the jaw in time to my funny words.

Then it broke apart along the small cracks across the top.

I went home right away. The girls must not have cared about the broken skull because they caught up to me and followed me all the way home. When we got to my place, they asked to come in to play. Usually, I wasn't allowed to be in the house during the day unless for lunch or something. But, I went inside to ask Mam if my friends and I could come in and play. She said yes, but only in the basement.

There were large pieces of cardboard left over from our move lying around in the basement. We built forts with the cardboard and then made up games to play. Yanina got bored with playing Tag and suggested we play a game called, King and Slaves.

"What's that?" I asked.

"I'm the King and you're the slave," said Yanina.

"What about Salina?"

"She'll be another slave but you'll be my sex slave."

Sex. Sexy. Does that mean I had to do something that looked sexy? I thought of Marilyn Monroe and Jayne Mansfield. I thought of the women spread-eagled in Playboy. I had no costumes, no make-up. My hair looked like a boy's. But there was no way I was going to sit or lie down spread-eagled.

She found a small stick along the basement wall and touched my ankle. "There, now you have a leg shackle on your ankle. You are now mine." I looked down where the stick touched my ankle.

I panicked. I imagined a bracelet like the one on the woman's ankle on *Playboy*.

Then she kissed me and said, "Take off your clothes." She started to unbutton my sweater.

As I stood dumbfounded, my sister, Bettina, yelled down, "Can I play?" Then she came into view. She took each wooden step carefully while clinging to the handrail.

"No!" yelled Yanina. "We're busy!"

I wasn't feeling quite right.

"I think we have to get ready for supper," I said as I pushed her hands away. "You better go home now."

"I don't wanna go home."

I turned and ran upstairs into the kitchen where Mam was cooking

"Mam, is dinner almost ready?" I asked, hopefully.

"Yah, almost."

"Okay," I said. I turned and ran downstairs.

I told the twins that supper was almost ready and they had to go.

"I need to use the washroom," said Yanina, eyeing me.

I turned and ran upstairs again.

"Mam, can Yanina use the bathroom?"

"Yah."

"Yes, you can!" I yelled down the stairs. I wanted to get rid of the twins as fast as possible. Yanina trudged up the basement stairs to the main landing. I showed her where the bathroom was. She was in there a long time. Finally, she got out, and the twins finally left.

Later that night, Bettina and I were invited into the back rooms to say goodnight to the baker and his French wife. I guess they were moving away soon after because it was the first and last time we were invited in. It was past our bedtime. Their TV was on. I looked over, and there was a beautiful woman, with dark hair and dark eyes, who looked like a darker version of Mam. It was Sophia Loren in The Boy on the Dolphin. She had been swimming. But she wasn't in a bathing suit. She had been swimming in her clothes. You could see her nipples.

There must be something wrong. She had no brassiere on. But she was swimming so why would she wear one? But she should be wearing a bathing suit. I felt ashamed. I didn't want to look at someone's nipples.

I gave up trying to piece that together in my mind. I said goodnight to the lovely folks. I went to the bathroom where my mother was standing looking into her jewelry box perched on the lid of the toilet tank.

"My jade earrings are gone."

I looked into the box. Her jade earrings were gone.

"*She* took them." I knew Mam meant the baker's wife in the back room. But I knew better.

The next day, I looked for the twins. I knew they were probably in the park at their favorite tree. I saw them in the distance and walked over. They had their Barbie dolls out and they had just gotten a Ken doll. All three Barbie dolls were naked. So was Ken. They were doing vulgar things with the dolls.

I interrupted them.

"You have Mam's jade earrings," I said. I looked at Yanina. "She wants them back." I turned and walked away. On the way, a boy from class came to me.

"You wanna play with me?"

I looked over at my house before looking back at him. "Yeah, okay." We ran off to the monkey bars. As I swung with both hands, I asked, "So, what do you want to play?"

He picked up a branch and touched my ankle. "Here, now you are my sex slave. You have a bracelet you can't take off!"

I went and sat on the ledge that connected one end of the monkey bars to the other end. He ordered me to sit there for so long that I peed my pants. I looked down to see if it was obvious what happened. The sand below slurped up every telltale sign. My shorts were now wet.

"I don't want to play sex slave anymore," I said and I stubbornly sat there until he became bored and walked away. I waited until he was almost out of sight before I ran all the way home.

Did everyone see that Playboy magazine? Everyone's talking about sex slaves and ankle bracelets.

I snuck into the house to change my undies and shorts. When I carefully closed the door behind me, I turned and saw the jade earrings in the jewelry box on top of the toilet lid.

The sense of power that came over me made up for the humiliation of wetting my pants.

• • •

1964

One Sunday morning I was sitting on the floor listening to a Samba LP on the portable record player. I played it over and over again. I stared at that LP cover so intently that the image was burned into my brain for life. It was of a man in a Mexican or Cuban outfit with ruffles of many beautiful colors at his neck, arms, and wrists playing his bongo. Beside him, one on each side, were two women, each one facing away from him. One wore a long, tight white-sequined dress, and the other wore a long, tight red-sequined dress. Their black hair was pulled back creating little curls as a fringe along their hairline and two huge curls at their ears. Massive gold hoop earrings hung from their earlobes. What fascinated me wasn't so much their dark looks or their colorful costumes, it was how the women stood. They had their hands elegantly positioned, one slightly higher than the other. I assumed they were in Samba position. But the location of their back arms allowed you to see under their straps a hint of the top of their breasts. I wondered if they did that on purpose.

It's not that I found them sexual. It's just that the women seemed to go out of their way to give sneak peaks of their bodies. I'd begun to see that everywhere. Women went out of their way to show their figures or cleavages. Which embarrassed me. We were supposed to hide our sexuality.

Before this day, I was at the strip mall. While Mam was shopping for groceries, I went over to the Nickle and Dime store. Nonna snuck some money into my hand while visiting last time, and I wanted to buy something. Maybe a present for Mam. I didn't know what exactly. As I walked between the bins of various articles dumped into them, I found some pens. I could afford a pen. I lifted one up. On the outside, there was a drawing of a woman in a bathing suit. I didn't mind. It was cheap. But when I clicked it to see if it would write into the wooden ledge around the bin, the click made the bathing suit disappear and she was naked. I placed the pen back very carefully. They must have bought a whole shipment from some company who did nothing but naked women. There were playing cards with the same lady. Mugs that when you tilted them, the bathing suits disappeared.

I left because there was absolutely nothing I could buy.

My thoughts jerked to attention when I heard Mam yell at me to turn the record player off and come to the car. We were off to my grandparents as usual. I'd gotten in trouble before for not hearing things fast enough. Pap always thought I was dis-obedient and I was punished many times for not doing what I was told right away. He didn't believe me when I told him I didn't hear at first. When I was deep in thought, I didn't notice anything else in the world around me.

I turned off the record player, but the music didn't stop in my head. It followed me all the way into the car. While Pap drove along the streets, I saw people who seemed to walk in rhythm with the Latin beat in my head. The roads were very quiet on Sundays, so it always had a different feel. People didn't work. There weren't many buses or streetcars running. People didn't seem to be in a hurry to go anywhere. It was Sunday, we still wore our Sunday clothes, got together for the day, and ate sup-per with the family. Why I didn't know. They always argued. But then the Samba music with the bongo drum in my mind faded when I realized we weren't going the usual way downtown.

"Where are we going, Pap?" I asked, concerned. Changes made me nervous.

"Surprise."

I looked at Pap's profile. I loved him with all my heart. Every little crevice and fold in that face were like a magic carpet to me. I could float and fly over each bristle of five o'clock shadow forever. His neck had muscle bulges, and his Adam's apple was manly. He had a way of coughing, a habit caused by working such long hours in that dusty shop and from the dust of his grinding machine that caressed the body filler he slapped onto the cars. The grinder would float effortlessly and gently over the curvature of a car fender or door. I loved watching him work. He was gentle there, at work, but nowhere else. Those hands, already stained by a couple of decades of work, were beautiful. I looked at them as they lightly rested on top of the steering wheel. I wondered what he was thinking. He coughed again. That cough. It was like music to my ears. He'd cough in the middle of the night and I knew that the world was at peace. I felt tears coming to my eyes as I watched him. He was someone so far away. Yet, I couldn't imagine living without the sight and sound of him.

I looked over at the back of my mother's head. Beautiful hair. She was smiling at something. When she smiled, I noticed. Then I looked out the window. We were driving past fields of animals that I recognized as sheep.

"Sheeps, Mam!"

Bettina shuffled over to my side of the car (we didn't wear seat belts in those days). She leaned over me. "Sheeps?" she asked.

"Yes, like Mary Had a Little Lamb! And Shari Lewis and Lamb Chop!" I was amazed. They were real!

Pap slowed down and we turned into a light brown cut into a field of corn.

"Corn, Pap!"

I remembered the first time Pap came home with a crate of corn. I was sitting on the front porch of the big house when he got home from the shop. Mam came to the front door and looked at the crate.

"What is that?" she asked surprised.

"Corn," Pap said. "A customer gave us all a crate of corn." He saw the look on Mam's face. "What am I to do?"

I looked into the crate. They looked like long things of nothing.

"Pig food? They think we eat like pigs?"

Pap deflated and stood back. He raised both hands. "A customer gave them."

"I'm not making pig food."

I tuned out. Pap didn't even get through the front door before Mam started. If I were her, I'd grab him and give him a big hug. If he'd had noticed me, I would've done it. Make him feel better. He worked so hard.

And that corn intrigued me. Everything Canadian intrigued me. Except for maple ice cream.

Suddenly, we were in a big field that looked as dry as a desert. There were massive bulldozers and trucks parked here and there. I thought of my clean white ankle socks. They never did well when walking through dry dead earth in the summertime.

We stopped in front of a make-believe-house with colored flags fluttering in the breeze. They reminded me of the beat of Samba and the colors of the flags matched the ruffles on the bongo drum player. I looked over and saw my grandparents' car parked in front.

"Look, Pap. Nonno and Nonna are here, too!"

Through the windows, I saw my grandparents, uncles, and two new aunts. They must have all come squeezed into one car. We got out of the car, and I ran into the building.

They were looking at a glass case on top of a pedestal. I moved closer and stood beside my new aunt. She turned and smiled at me. I gave her bulging middle a hug and hung onto her dress for a bit.

My uncle, the one who tried to hurt Mam, found a nice lady from New Brunswick. I saw her for the first time when we were still living in the big house and I came downstairs to see them both sleeping on the couch in the living room. After that, I heard they had to get married—whatever that meant.

She was very nice. She actually took my youngest uncle, Bettina and me for an ice cream cone at a park. My youngest uncle smiled that day. However, I didn't know how to act when she gave me the ice cream cone. I felt I didn't deserve it, but I thanked her ever so much. She was beautiful. She had a turned-up nose, pretty lips, and big brown eyes with naturally thick eyelashes. She was tiny, even smaller than my youngest uncle. I loved her. And she wasn't miserable. Not yet, anyhow.

My other uncle and the third cousin he married were there as well. She was blonde, beautiful, and walked like a queen. She was the first woman I ever met who stood up to the men. She didn't get anywhere though. They said they were right when they guessed she would be just like Nonno's cousin. That she was a *cagna*, a bitch. But to me she made sense.

Once, at the Highway 400 Swimming Pools, she wore the first bikini I ever saw. I stood staring at her bottom piece. It looked exactly like that cover on *Playboy* I saw at the shop. Now I knew it wasn't panties. It was part of a bathing suit. A bikini. The new fashion trend started on the French Riviera a few years before. I had never seen so much skin on a woman in real life before. She also put makeup on right in front of us whenever she felt like it. The men rolled their eyes at her.

When no one knows you're there, because you are a child, you see and hear a lot.

I turned my attention back to the glass case. It housed a tiny village of streets and miniature houses with tiny little trees.

Pap came to me and pointed at a little two-story house. "See that? That's our house."

With wide eyes, I looked where he pointed.

"And see there?" He pointed to the one next to it. "That's where your uncle and aunt will live. And see the next one? That's where your Nonno and Nonna are going to live with your uncle. And there?" He pointed a few houses up. "That's your other uncle's house."

"Wow," I said. I thought of Mam and how she would react. We were all going to be close to each other again.

• • •

1965

For the very first time, I thought I'd try cream on my face. It struck me that if I was to be beautiful like the women in *Playboy* I should start early. I needed a lot of help. My friend down the street kept telling me to do different things to myself. I was too plain, she complained. At every glass surface or mirror, she stopped to primp and prime while I stood by averting my eyes. Pap taught me that a woman should never look in the mirror because she would become vain. I guess by not checking a mirror I usually looked terrible. So, I started sneaking peeks into the bathroom mirror, but didn't like what I saw. I didn't look like the girls in *Playboy* or the commercials on TV. I made a bold move and, using my babysitting money, bought the cheapest cream I could find—a blue glass jar of Noxzema.

I was upstairs; Bettina was in bed. Downstairs everyone was having a big party. The music was loud and joyful. I decided to let the cream sink into my face for as long as possible while I listened to the laughter and chatter.

In the family, anyone's birthday provided an opportunity for a massive celebration at the birthday person's house. This particular evening it was Mam's turn. Because we were spread throughout the street, everyone had neighbors they liked. Therefore, it was easier to invite everyone on the street. In fact, the parties sometimes spilled out onto the street. They would do conga lines, dancing from a living or rec room. They'd shuffle and kick through the house, through the kitchen, out the side door, down the driveway, onto the street, and then slither and bounce back through the front door. Everyone drank till they dropped.

James Bond and *Goldfinger*[3] were really big in everyone's mind. The women around me dressed and acted differently. As did the men. Things started happening. A teenager down the street stood at his big bedroom window naked every time we came home from school. He leaned into the glass so we couldn't see his face, but we saw his thighs and upwards.

Then there was that man who asked me to come closer to his car so he could hear me give directions and he had his manhood out.

There was the man who flashed me on the way to school.

My friends, who were all boys, and I built a new fort from wooden pallets. It was a huge, wonderful, and cleverly built space. One day, a new boy in the neighborhood sat in the fort pointing at me and said, "Show us your tits or you're not allowed to be here." I looked at my friends. For the first time, they looked at me differently. As if they woke up and realized I was a girl and not one of them. They stared at the image of Popeye on the front of my top. Where my breasts were starting to bud. I left, upset. There were construction workers who whistled and said crude things to me as I cried on my way home.

It felt like a war out there. My whole life was surrounded by men's penises. Babies' little ones when I changed their diapers were fine and innocent. I couldn't understand the fascination the men had with their private parts and ours, the females'.

During the weekly auto body shop meetings at our house on Friday nights, I was expected to politely say goodnight and give a kiss to all my uncles and Pap before going to bed. One night my boisterous uncle was so drunk that he grabbed my face and put his tongue between my lips. I pulled away with a squeal and looked at Pap for help. He just laughed. Everyone laughed. Then went on with their cigars and their grappa.

---

[3]   Eon Productions, 1964

Another time Pap, unaware of the effect of his words, looked at me and said to everyone at the table, "Look at my daughter. She's starting to look like a pencil with two peas." All my uncles laughed and looked at my breasts. Life was becoming something with a sickening edge.

But, somehow, you go on. You still worship your father anew, over and over again.

At the end of the day, I had my Lord's Prayer. It was my way of checking into something that was loving, kind and gentle. It seemed more real. Then I went to sleep, a space beside me.

Looking back, socially and politically these were fascinating times. People fought for their rights, women wearing topless bathing suits hit us between the eyes, and *Playboy Bunnies* were revered. James Bond made every woman swoon. Bettina, our friends, and I sang the lyrics from the latest Bond film. Someone was playing it now downstairs at the party:

"Goldfinger,
He's the man
The man with the Midas touch.
A spider's touch..."[4]

I thought about kisses as "death for women" as the song described.

Then I thought about everyone downstairs while the cream tingled on my face. The men had changed but not in the best of ways. But who was I anyway to think that way? As my father would say, "You're only a girl, what do you know?"

I felt the men acted more *confidently, brazenly*. Whereas they were once miserable, at these parties they seemed to glow and their hands became freer. I think that, in a way, groping was their compliment to the women who never heard spoken compliments. Perhaps the women were relieved to be noticed at all.

---

4   Written by Anthony Newley, Leslie Bricusse & John Barry, sung by Shirley Bassey, 1964 Film "Gold Finger"

I didn't know. In any case, I'd see the odd gentle pushing away of a man's hand with a polite, apologetic smile. Then the hands would boldly grope again.

I had seen the men work the room. My uncles, Pap and Nonno, would dance with every female—family or neighbor. They were all married by then, except my youngest uncle who never did marry. My third uncle, the blonde one, followed in his brothers' footsteps, went back to the homeland and came back with a seventeen-year-old fiancée two weeks later. He wanted to make sure the family was okay with her first, so she stayed in the downstairs apartment in my grandparents' house. At night, my uncle would sneak down. Then they went off, got married in the homeland, and she came back visibly pregnant.

By this particular evening, she had had her first little boy and was pregnant with her second child. The other two aunts had two each so far, and one was pregnant with a third. Three boys and one girl altogether. Being the oldest of the cousins in Canada, I was the standby babysitter. Sometimes they would pay me and sometimes not. It didn't matter, I loved it.

I noticed Nonno getting drunk earlier, and knew my Nonna was in our kitchen cranking out the finger foods and clean glasses because they kept running out. A wall of cigarette and cigar smoke crept upstairs while a loud effervescent Tom Jones now sang on the stereo's record player:

"It's not unusual to be loved by anyone
It's not unusual to have fun with anyone,
But when I see you hanging about with anyone,
It's not unusual so see me cry,
I wanna die …"

Then, as I stood at the snazzy, black plastic bathroom counter wondering how I should take off the fresh, tingly, urine-smelling cream, I sensed three individuals standing by me.

I froze and let my eyes look to the left toward the shower curtains.

It was the shower curtains, surely. With dabs of cream half off my face, I turned and looked toward them. There was nothing.

I looked into the mirror again.

Once more, I sensed three forms near me. They were observing me more than anything. They had nothing to say to me. But I "heard" one, the taller form, say to the other two that I would continually have problems with men throughout my life.

I stood frozen though I felt a soft trembling inside of me.

Suddenly, the pandemonium downstairs turned from laughter to screams over the loud music. I heard Mam screaming at Pap to stop.

"Stop!"

Men shouted.

"STOP!" she screamed again.

I forgot the forms, stepped out of the bathroom, and pounced down the ugly, green patterned carpeting about five steps. I sat down where I had a view slightly into the living room, the front hallway, and the front door.

Pap was viciously kicking my uncle in his chest. He was literally trying to kick him out the door. My uncle had a grip on both sides of the door frame. His hands, like Pap's, were big and strong and he wouldn't let go. I eyed the screen door that strained behind my uncle's head.

Pap then kicked at the right door frame to loosen my uncle's grip. My uncle laughed.

The screen door tore off its long, solid hinge and bent back, now attached only by its metal spring. The glass cracked.

Pap now kicked my uncle in the face. My uncle released his grip on the door frame and fell out onto the front stoop.

I sat enthralled. It was like witnessing two massively, strong, beautiful roaring animals. One so drunk he didn't feel the pain. He just laughed. It was all he could do in his stupor. Pap must've had some drinks, but he focused intently on this particular thing. I saw it all in slow motion, and I found my heart skipping beats. He approached it like an engineer. First this side.

Then that side.

Pap straightened in the doorway and kicked at my uncle's knees. My uncle slowly inched past the stoop and slithered into the dewy grass.

Pap tore the rest of the screen door off, stepped out and threw it at my uncle. Then he came back in and slammed what was left of the front door shut.

Apparently, my uncle grabbed a guest's breasts and my aunt saw it happen. She yelled at Pap to kick him out.

Pap simply complied. Literally.

And I was proud of him. And thought my uncle was neat.

My view on what was normal was so twisted now.

And that the beating had been fun to watch.

• • •

1967

I begged my father to let me come with him every Saturday to the shop. I was so hungry for his presence as he never seemed to be home. During the week, he'd come home after nine at night. Though she was sick every day now, Mam would hold supper until then so we could eat as a family. I wished she wouldn't because they always argued anyway. Pap's fist would pound the table. Mam would throw something at him. Once, she hurled a bag of sugar at him but missed and it burst hitting the bird cage instead. That was when she screamed so loud and long that she fell limply on the floor on top of the strewn sugar, bird-shit and feathers. She silently screamed even after there was no air left in her lungs. She was gone for a couple of weeks or so after that and stayed in the hospital making baskets. I had to take care of Bettina again. Actually, I did that a lot. And she wasn't a nice, sweet, little girl anymore. She felt the strain, too. Whenever I told her it was time for bed, she would go after me with a knife.

One angry wintry night, in a rage, Pap hurled Mam out the door into the snow and locked the door behind her. She didn't even have slippers on her feet. I heard her cry and scream then bang at the door for someone to let her in. I hurried to the door and was about to unlock it when Pap roared. He threatened to throw me out as well if I let her in saying he'd never let me back into the house for the rest of my life.

Time slowed down then. I felt an inner black energy rise like a thick, dead mass of magma, thick at the bottom and pointed at the top. Slowly it solidified around my ribcage. I don't remember actually opening my mouth, but I think I screamed because of it. I don't know what I said, but the pain in my heart made it feel like a heavy piece of lead. It threatened to sink me along with the solid magma into that bottomless pit I so feared. With this kind of hellish weight, I was afraid I would never get out and see the sun in God's face again.

In the meantime, Mam kept being sick with different things. She'd continue to have "nervous breakdowns," a new medical term I had learned. Mam would be in the hospital again doing other crafts. Bettina and I weren't allowed to go to the hospital to her, but we'd wait in the car while Pap went up. Then we'd keep our eyes focused on the windows of the tenth floor until our eyes watered. Finally, we'd see a little figure hidden behind the reflection of the dark early spring clouds on the glass windows, and we'd wave frantically.

● ● ●

Mam got pregnant. Pap was upset. He wanted to leave her but couldn't now. In a moment of weakness, Mam bounced down the ugly green carpeted steps on her behind to try to lose the baby to make him happy but my little sister hung on for dear life.

Within the next few months, Mam's mother, my other Nonna, came over from the homeland for a visit. We actually went out as a family again. We took her to Niagara Falls, to Wasaga Beach, and to Toronto Island. We walked through the gardens where men made kissing noises at me.

I looked over the first time because I naively thought it was a bird. Then I realized it was a man again. He made a lewd gesture at me. It made my guts churn; I had to find a ladies' room.

Somehow life went on. Pap was rarely home now. He and my uncles still worked most Saturdays, so I would come along. They'd let me sweep the grimy, oil-saturated dirt on the shop floor. I would take the hose and spray down the cement, watching the neon colors of the oil slicks writhe down, seep into the central gutter, and meander along the cut out into the grating just outside the big shop garage doors.

My friends, the ladies in *Playboy* magazines, smiled back at me every time I lovingly rearranged them. I felt bad for those whose teeth were blackened by someone's pen. Drawn eye-glass frames weren't too upsetting, but I sure wanted to know who it was that would put the odd, curly moustaches on a woman's face. Or draw rude protuberances into their mouths. Or their private parts.

There were years' worth of them now. I would read the headlines on the covers and recognize their content as it was reflected in my own life: *Nudist Camp; The Plight of the Married Man; Pious Pornographers; Nudist Peter Sellers and Elke Sommer; The Topless Craze; The Provocative Art of Body Painting;* and, upsetting to me, *Hugh Hefner Exchanges Views on the Sexual Revolution with a Priest, a Minister and a Rabbi.* They reflected the new ideas Pap would bring home. Once he said we should all belong to a nudist camp. Then he went out, while I tagged along, to buy a Super-8 camera. The first thing he filmed was a young woman in the store. He started at her feet, slowly went up her nyloned legs, over her skirt, onto her blouse and ended up on her breasts. Then he talked about topless bathing suits and dared Mam to wear one.

One day he announced something that was incongruous, even coming from him. He already kept telling me there was no God, that only weak people relied on something they imagined. But this time he used a new phrase.

"God is dead. Don't waste your time."

That quote came directly from a headline in *Playboy Magazine*.

I still had no idea that I didn't know the full story about sex. I thought you kissed and then had a baby. I stopped seeing two girlfriends because they told me they had learned all about "the Birds and the Bees." In my mind, they were being vulgar just to bother me. Just like those men who drew on the *Playboy* images.

"The man puts his little weewee into the woman's hot dog bun."

"That's disgusting!" I said.

They usually went out of their way to tease me, so I thought this was just one more insult. The winter before they locked me into an old stone farm shed that stood like an afterthought in the middle of the vacant fields between our subdivision and our school. I sat in the near darkness watching my breath float past the shards of light that shot through holes in the heavy wooden door. I was so very happy I had God. I stopped the rising panic and simply asked Him to help me get out before night fell. He showed me I needed to put something small and sharp into the ancient lock and jiggle it around a bit.

I instinctively knew the perfect object would be near the back, stone wall. The freezing ground hurt my fingers as I dug, but I had to take my mitts off to feel for the object. I found an ancient square-headed hand-hammered nail under the frozen dirt and pebbles

I jiggled the nail into the large key hole and unlocked the door. I thanked God.

How could I tell Pap that God wasn't dead at all?

In the meantime, we discovered Nonna had leukemia. I went with Pap to visit him. While I sat unnoticed, he bragged, with a sparkle in his eyes, to Pap that he wanted the nurse to tell him while she bathed him that "down there" was beautiful. I looked over at my father for some explanation, but he forgot I was there, too. He laughed hard.

After my Nonno died, my youngest uncle was forced to take over my Nonno's share of the business. He didn't want to. He was an artist. He wanted to study art. They said he had to whether he liked it or not. He took his hunting gun up to his room and threatened to kill himself. I heard about it through the other younger cousins. I ran through all the yards to the back of my grandparents' house, now my Nonna's house. I called up to his window. I could hear him yell and scream and cry. I wanted him to know that someone loved him. That I understood. Somehow, he heard me and stopped crying.

The tip of the hunting gun shot out of the window and pointed down at me.

"Get outta here, or I'll kill you!" I backed away. Then I heard him yell at Nonna inside the bedroom. She was at the bedroom door. He had locked it.

Suddenly, an ear-splitting explosion shattered the air around me.

THREE

Living like Punch and Judy

1969

That day my youngest uncle fired in the general direction of Nonna who was on the other side of the door begging him not to hurt himself. He missed her by a hair and blew out the side of the doorway.

After that, he also went to the tenth floor of the hospital before coming back to train for his partnership at the family shop. Over the years, so many members of my family went there that the nurses threatened to name that ward after our family. I think my relatives laughed at that.

My youngest uncle, who felt like a brother to me, was entirely under the dysfunctional wings of my *Playboy* uncles who were now his partners in business.

By now, with the sexuality of Tom Jones and Elvis Presley gyrating their groins, the Beatles vibrated them in other ways with their "Sergeant Pepper Lonely Hearts Club Band" and "Lucy in the Sky with Diamonds." One uncle started wearing Nehru collars, and stayed cool on benzodiazepine, bought a race horse, and a single-engine plane. He would leave for a small airport north of Toronto for the weekend and would show up weeks later. One November, he flew south and missed Christmas and New Year's altogether. He woke up in the Bahamas after a two-month binge. My stately and longsuffering aunt didn't miss his usual endearments of "drop dead, wife" anyhow. She and her two sons had a somewhat more peaceful holiday. Only somewhat because they still had to be with the rest of our dysfunctional family on Sundays, Christmas Eve, Christmas Day,

New Year's Eve, and New Year's Day. We also celebrated Pap's birthday as well as two of my aunts' and two of the little cousins'. The crazy beat went on.

My other boisterous uncle, before he embraced AA, had a problem with alcohol. He lost in the races, lost at the tables, and lost doing the numbers. When he needed more money, he'd simply take more money from the till at the shop and start again. Sometimes, he'd hit the jackpot. Then, out of guilt, he would shower it on his tiny, crumpled up once-happy-but-now-miserable New Brunswick wife. He'd scatter the rest elsewhere, and with his amazingly massive heart he would spread droppings of $50 dollar tips here and there. One night at a bachelor party, he was so drunk, that after the cake and the girl came and went, he sat his solid, alcohol-expanded frame on a folding chair without noticing the glass of hard stuff on the seat. The chair with the glass crumpled under his weight. Everyone laughed as they combined their strength to help him to his feet. After a while, someone noticed he was trailing blood. The glass was embedded into his buttock cheeks. An ambulance ride with jovial paramedics later, he leaned over the hospital table, his pants down, with a nurse holding long tweezers, focusing close at his behind. As the blood pooled into his crack, he briefly forgot where he was, grunted, and passed wind spraying a bloody Niagara Falls all over the nurse.

The female portion of the family peanut gallery thoroughly enjoyed giggles and laughter-laced coffee hour about it the next day. I thought it was neat. Couldn't wait to tell my friend at school. In fact, I started bragging about my family. They were all heroes. They were all beautiful.

Pap and my blonde uncle discovered a new, healthy outlet: sailing. Another female play object but this time made of fiberglass, wood, and sail, into which they invested every spare moment and dime they had. They had their *Playboy* yachts, however small at first.

The women, in the meantime, thrived during the coffee hour which usually lasted about four hours. In the summer, they sat outside on lined-up foldable patio chairs on the front lawns. The kids got into their own trouble soiling their pants and peeing into window wells as they were left to go wild. One day, I was bringing out more cookies for Mam and my aunts, when I heard them laugh about what happened the night before between my boisterous uncle and his once happy wife. While she was lying in bed, he had come home, picked her up by her nightgown and slammed her body against the bedroom wall. She got up, ran to the kitchen, grabbed a wrought iron pan, and smacked him over his head, knocking him out cold. Thinking she had killed him, she ran to the phone, called the police and said she had killed her husband. Then she took a bottle of pills. When the police arrived, he came to and laughed as they carried him out to the ambulance. She had her stomach pumped. She never let him back into the house after that.

But the police had laughed. The paramedics we were told had laughed. My mother and aunts laughed. My father and other uncles laughed. The only person who did not laugh was Nonna.

I laughed, too. My uncle was a movie star to me. He had a heart of gold. He was generous, talented, a genius in many ways. But something had gone wrong. Somewhere.

No one had heard of the term, *wife abuse* as yet. It was so much a constant in my early life that it was only logical to assume that it would become a major presence in my adult life. It was a given. It was perfect, precise programming.

But it would take more than sixty years for me to recognize how thoroughly it had been ingrained within me, my thoughts, my expectations of men, and my psyche.

• • •

I thought my family was the most amazing family in the entire world. The men were breathtakingly handsome and the women beautiful. They did amazing and outrageous things. They grabbed life by the horns. I didn't connect the upheaval, neglect,

abuse, violence, and bi-polar mind-states around me to what
was going on inside of me at the time. For a few years, I had
begun to fight internally to stay alive. I was thirteen or four-
teen, and mornings were difficult because it meant I had to live
another day. Breathing was an effort. I rarely brushed my teeth,
took a bath, or washed my hair. Mam was sick every day, a legacy
we now understand to have been left by the war, but it left us to
fend for ourselves.

Bettina and I had to share a bed now, for what reason, I do
not recall. We had a spare bedroom. I think Mam liked the idea
of a *guest room*. She bought white furniture with brass handles
and gold motif from Simpsons-Sears. Then she set the room up
just like in the catalogue photo. Like most of the house it was
out of bounds for Bettina and me.

Bettina continued to exhibit mounting aggressive behavior which she funneled toward me. Lots of fun when you have
to squeeze together into a single bed at night. I didn't find it
very pleasant at all. I couldn't say the Lord's Prayer for fear of
ridicule, and I started to feel the difference. I didn't make this
connection, though, because I wasn't aware I was in emotional
and psychological dire straits.

One day, finding myself alone from cousins, sister, and
neighbors, I sat on a swing at a little cousin's house. I swung
gently with my feet planted into the rough, bare patch of the
grass. I was having a conversation with God. I suppose I told
Him I missed Him. I prayed then. If there was one gift I could
ask for in life, it was the gift of wisdom. I thought, perhaps, with
wisdom I could handle more than I did. Help people. Perhaps
even figure out why the heck we had to stay on this planet.

The image of a bike came to mind and I had a thought.

The next Saturday, while sweeping the floors of the shop and
after saying hello to all the *Playboy* centerfolds in their birthday
suits over the workbenches, I asked Pap for a bicycle. Pap was
carefully hand-sanding a beautiful curve on the back fender of a
Plymouth Barracuda that had been tail ended.

"Pap."

Sanding, sanding, caress, caress, sanding, sanding.

"Pap."

Sanding. "Yah."

"Can I have a bike?"

Sanding, caress. "A bike? We're not in the homeland where everything is close and flat. It's dangerous here. Why would you want a bike?"

"So, I could get around."

Caress. Pick up a rag, wipe. "Don't be stupid. You get around walking okay."

"I'd like to go farther."

Sanding, sanding, caress, caress, sanding, sanding.

"Pap."

"It's too dangerous."

"I would be careful."

He impatiently sat back on his haunches, his eyes on the fender. "They cost money."

"I don't need a new one. You can get really cheap second-hand ones."

I forgot about it until Christmas, when I was told there was something outside in the driveway for me. I grabbed my worn, thinly-quilted ski jacket and stepped out through the side door in my bare feet. There, covered in a sprinkling of newly-fallen snow, was a second-hand bike! One straight from the homeland. A bit old, a bit big. But it was mine! I had actually learned how to ask for something. Regardless of the road blocks my father seemed to stand by, somehow it was possible to get my humble wish come true.

Even though there was snow on the sidewalk I immediately climbed on top and rode two doors over to Nonna's house. I had to show her. She hobbled on her stiff legs to look out, saw that I was in my bare feet, and insisted I come in quickly. She was very happy for me as I stood there huffing and puffing with excitement. Her eyes sparkled into mine. I loved her so much.

That bike was a God-send.

I used that bike for everything. I rode to school on the sidewalk. I explored and discovered new streets. I compared each house with another. I wondered how these people lived. Were they happy or were they sad? I salivated over those with a pool at the back and those with a garage. I loved to see who cared to garden.

One day, I rode all the way to the Dairy Queen five miles away where they had five cent soft ice cream cones. With cone in hand, I stepped around to the back of the Dairy Queen to sit in the sun and enjoy it. It was a glorious early summer day.

I stopped.

My soul jumped. It felt like a tiny hand or elbow slipped past underneath the tight skin of one of my aunt's bellies.

I slowly, gently, stepped forward. My eyes widened and my breathing slowed. From my feet to the horizon lay a thick bright carpet of tightly packed fully-bloomed yellow daisies. I took three steps forward.

I looked to my left and to my right and there was nothing but daisies. Blossoms so thickly grouped together they seemed to fight to face the sun as if they worshipped the golden globe. I dropped my cone and watched it disappear between the blossoms. I took another step and stretched out my arms. I tilted back my head and looked up at the sky, the endless blue dome with clouds that reached so high they looked like they touched the bottom of heaven's floor. Below them, there were more gigantic, brilliant white thick clouds slowly sailing by. They, too, worshipped the lofty one. But I sensed they weren't reaching for the sun. It was God's face of love.

I floated further into the daisies and felt myself sink as if to my underarms, bees buzzed gently around me, celebrating my visit, as if ... I stopped. The daisies. They were for me. They were a gift from God. Why did I think that? Because I *felt* it.

My heart slowed, my breathing stopped as if I didn't need breath. I moved further into the yellow depths and heard the angels call me. They sang, almost like the nuns in St. Basil church when I had first felt His touch on my shoulder. I allowed myself to swim through the blossoms until I sank into a gentle low depth that hid a small wooden shack. I knew I was to meet Him there. The closer I came, the larger it grew until I found myself resting inside. I drew my knees up to my chin, my skirt carefully tucked over and under. Sitting on a bed of straw.

The sun came through the slats in soft laser beams, landing softly on my brow and head. I closed my eyes as they caressed my face. I sat, inhaled, and contained the love that swept into me and expanded my soul. I felt a tear trace down my cheek that quickly dried under the heat of both the sun and my hot skin. I stayed and listened to the choir and heard the story of forever. And I understood, once again, I was not alone after all.

• • •

Out in the rest of the not-so-sane big world, things were turning upside down. Five years before, two U.S. destroyers sitting in the Gulf of Tonkin in Vietnam had allegedly been shot at by North Vietnamese forces. President Johnson requested permission to increase the U.S. military presence in the interests of keeping peace and security in Southeast Asia. Thus, almost nine years of slaughter in a horrific war began. Waves of American draft dodgers overflowed the Canadian borders. Flower children and women's libbers, miniskirts and psychedelic music, a fight for global peace, and equality between the sexes and races took hold of everyone. Things were drastically changing. *Playboy*, films, and the sexual revolution took on new forms. *Playboy* boldly began a new trend of younger sexuality with headlines such as "Sex on Campus." Hugh Hefner almost unilaterally gave male students, teachers, and professors permission to see young female college and university students ranging in age from 17-22 as their own form of personal entertainment and toys. Hughie began to refer to his *Playmates* as "sex toys."

By this time, my youngest sister was born. There were many complications, but she was an incredibly bright little girl. Unfortunately, this brave little girl was hampered by a barrage of continual epileptic fits. She spent an inordinate amount of time in emergency rooms or downtown at the *Sick Kid's* hospital.

With each episode, Mam cradled my little sister's pulsating, jerking, stiff little body and cried out as Bettina and I watched helplessly. Mam died a bit each time. She carried the weight of the whole ordeal while we were at school during the day. Pap rarely came home till 9, 10, or 11 at night. Many times, Mam had to rush downtown in a car provided by the shop held together by nothing more than rust and spit.

Bettina and I eventually learned how to read the signs of when a convulsion was brewing. Our little sister would first lose her sight and then panic and call for us. Then she would vomit. And then her eyes would roll back. That's when we quickly put a wooden spoon between her tiny teeth so that she couldn't bite her tongue. All we could do after that was keep her warm and hold her tightly. I would pray with unshed tears, staying strong for my mother and Bettina.

School now became an outlet for me. I acquired a great love for it and did well for the most part, though I floundered in the depths of depression. When I finally moved on to ninth grade at the neighborhood high school, I found myself in an entirely different environment and mentality. For a while, my spirits lifted because of the new challenges and distractions that lay ahead. The older students seemed like adults, and the school felt like a well-run government. I became Ninth Grade Representative on the Student Council. I was given one duty: keep in touch with a child we had adopted through a charity.

I was in the 'browner' class in the five-year program of Arts and Science. There was one thing that didn't work to my benefit, however. Both my Math and English teachers believed that girls had no right to be in Math and English classics. In Math class, I was the only female student. In English, one of three. Consequently, whenever I put up my hand to answer or to ask a question, I was ignored outright. Consistently I received a 54% in both, ensuring that I would not pass into their tenth-grade classes, but not fail outright.

They were closed doors for me.

I didn't have the power to complain. I hadn't learned yet how to. That wasn't unusual. Women were barred from many things that women today participate in. And we felt we could only accept it, however unfair it all seemed.

But it was not all bad. Football games and school spirit buoyed my temper and once a young man from eleventh grade invited me out for the day. We went dancing at the Electric Circus in Toronto. We both looked like we stepped out of a 1950's novel: he in his white ankle socks and glasses and me in my loafers and shift dress. New *hippies* surrounded us. Psychedelic lights flashed and formed multi-colored blobs on overhead slides while trapeze artists swung from one end of the cavernous building to the other during a strobe light show. A fire eater walked amongst us as we writhed to the Moody Blues and *Sgt. Pepper's Lonely Hearts Club Band*. We walked through blue lights and checked out little nooks. One room had strobe lights where people threw soft balls at each other. You couldn't see the balls coming. Then there was a room full of carpeted tubes where people lay and lounged and smoked sweet-smelling tobacco. The lounge chairs that looked like waves were all covered in cigarette burns. It was all so colorful, crazy and exhilarating. And still so innocent.

At school, we followed the times. The female students had a sit-in outside the school demanding to wear pants to school. Miniskirts weren't made for Canadian winters. We wanted to wear bell bottom pants. We tested our young voices and we actually won.

Being athletic and not wanting to go home as long as possible, I stayed later playing basketball and volleyball. I also was a member of the gymnastics team. I won the right to compete in Floor and Parallel Bars at the Ontario Provincial Competition, but on the day of the meet, my period, a fairly recent and uninvited guest in my life, started full force. I don't know if tampons were available yet, but I was too afraid to compete with a sanitary napkin. Embarrassed to even talk about it, I took two steps onto the bus and then got off. I think I walked away toward our street, which was miles away, without a single word or apology to my gym teacher and coach.

That's when depression hit me in full force. I wanted so to fly in certain directions but my wings were clipped. I started to suffocate in depression. I never wrote that poor child even though the vice principal reminded me it seemed every single day. I got a 100% in Public Speaking for my speech about Spontaneous Human Combustion in class and was invited to present it to the 13th grade English students, a true privilege. However, I put off re-memorizing the speech. By the time I found myself—in rumpled clothes, un-brushed teeth, and un-washed hair—standing in front of a huge crowd of older students and teachers, I simply stood mute. Eventually, the vice principal cut short everyone's embarrassment and excused me. I silently walked out of the hall feeling like a real loser.

Because I was a loser.

Then we moved.

FOUR

Teacher's Pet, Puppy Love and Jesus in my Heart

My father and blond uncle kept their boats at a yacht club on the other side of Toronto and that meant a tremendous amount of driving from the West end. So, without conferring with my mother and aunt, they decided to sell their houses. We moved to an area East of Toronto to be close to their boats. At the same time, the family business bought a building and opened another branch just a short drive from both new houses and boats.

We were suddenly uprooted and plunked into a style of life that was overwhelmingly intimidating, one month before the end of the school year. Now, instead of walking to school, Bettina and I had to take a school bus. We died a thousand deaths trying to fit in. Standing at the cluster of trees waiting for the bus with other kids who stared us down was almost unbearable.

The school was interesting. The first time I sat in the cafeteria, next to me were hippies counting different colored pills. It slowly dawned on me that they were drugs. I looked around. Nearby stood a smiling, chatty teacher serving as monitor. He ignored what was going on. At the other end of the cafeteria, rough looking kids in leather jackets played with pocket knives. Two entirely different groups of students.

I was overwhelmed. I didn't fit in either group. But my English teacher was really nice. He was polite to me and introduced me to the class as the new student. He did it in such a way that I felt dignified. Perhaps the other students would look at me with respect. Some did. It was the first time any adult treated me that way. However, I had already been snickered at that first day. I wore a purple and pink straight shift and a white blouse with ruffles at the neck. I sewed the shift in Home Economics at the other school. It was what everyone wore there. I wanted to look like Paul Revere and the Raiders. These students were into Creedence Clearwater Revival or Hair.

There I stood at the front of the class, a dirtier classroom than those I just left west of Toronto. My hair was already white blonde from the early sun, my skin slightly tanned from walking to the other school and back. I looked squeaky clean and nerdy.

And one of my teachers seemed to like what he saw.

From then on, I looked forward to my English class. Each time it was over, he would ask me to stay a little longer. It was the last class of the day. I enjoyed the chats, and I didn't want them to end even though I would miss my school bus home. He asked me about what sports I liked to play, what my favorite hobbies were, and about my family. I think he understood the struggle I had with depression. He went out of his way to make it a lovely class just for me. He started showing films on art and music, things I loved, but they had nothing to do with English. At one point, a student had asked why we were watching so many films. He said it was because school was almost over. There was nothing more he could teach unless he started an entirely new subject. So, whenever he put on a film, one or two students would look at me with disgust. They knew the attention he gave me was abnormal.

But I didn't.

I looked at them apologetically and squirmed under their gaze in any case. But, at the same time, I was thrilled that someone paid me so much attention to me. I wanted to cry.

• • •

I needed to find a summer job but I was too young for a Social Security Number. I didn't know anyone with children who needed babysitting and there was no public transportation except for the new Go Train into Toronto. I felt helpless without pocket change. My mother decided that perhaps Bettina and I could keep our Family Bonus each month and with that we were responsible for all our clothes and other items. It was $22 per month so it really wasn't enough. But it was something.

While I pondered this predicament, my English teacher began calling me at home. If Mam answered the phone, he would hang up. So, I found myself staying indoors or within hearing distance of the phone. Sometimes I caught it, and we would talk a very long time. He asked me to come for a visit to his place downtown Toronto. He said he had a swimming pool so I could swim. He knew I loved swimming. I didn't have enough money at that moment and I had never tried to go downtown from where we were.

I pondered this predicament for a while.

In the meantime, nights were bad. My bedroom was at the back overlooking the ravine. The back of the house had a walk-out basement with a rock garden on both sides of a patio. I would look down at the rocks below and wonder anew why I had to keep living. I kept asking God to please take me away.

Pap and Mam fought just as much and loudly. Though now there was a more desperate edge to Mam's reactions. As time went on, I would over-hear Mam and my aunt talk about a newly-hired receptionist at the shop. Both my uncle and Pap stayed behind at work till midnight, but they didn't come home dirty and sweaty. In fact, they would come home showered. Mam thought they went for a sail at the yacht club and then showered. But my aunt had a sense that there was something more going on.

One Saturday, while Mam was under a hair dryer at the hairdresser's, she overheard a woman talk about two guys she worked for. She said she would have sex with them. One wouldn't pay but the other one did. Mam glanced at the woman. Then, the next Monday, Mam drove by the shop pretending to drop something off for Pap. The woman was the new receptionist.

There were terrible, awful fights and I would lie in my bed and cover my ears. I'd stare at the ugly faded mauve paint on my walls. I couldn't stand them.

One day, while shopping with Mam, I saw a metal basket with rolls of paper at the front of the hardware store. I walked over and looked. It was wallpaper that was on sale. I had just enough money to buy one roll. It didn't necessarily have a pattern I liked, but anything was better than what I had. When I got home, I put up the wallpaper. It only went two and a half strips—halfway across my wall.

I slept with that half-papered wall the entire time we lived in that house because I could never find a matching pattern or price that worked for me.

The house was on a heavily-treed, dead-end street that ended at the raised railroad tracks which followed the shoreline of Lake Ontario. There was a worn path from the gravel road down to the bottom of the raised hill where you could pass under the bridge to a little beach. I was sitting on that beach sunbathing after a quick swim in the freezing waters listening to my transistor radio. Roy Orbison was singing *Pretty Woman* when a group of young people came trudging by through the soft sand. It was the first time I saw African Americans outside of movies. I politely kept from staring and suddenly a voice sang, "Pretty woman sitting on the beach …"

I turned and looked at the young man who appeared to be my age. He had a massive smile and he was beautiful. He literally shone. Two young women around my age and two older men were walking with another boy. I knew he lived next door to us, but we'd never met.

I smiled and waved at him. He waved back. Then the eldest of them said, "Paul, we'll be late."

Once more, Paul smiled brilliantly at me, turned, and caught up to the interesting group.

I turned towards the sun, leaned back on my hands, and listened to Diana Ross singing, *My Baby Love*. Somehow the sun shone a little brighter in my heart.

Days later, I was out on the front lawn waiting for the phone to ring when I heard singing.

"You and I must make a pact
We must bring salvation back,
Where there is love, He'll be there. (He'll be there)
He'll reach out His hand to you
He'll have faith in all you do.
Just call His name and He'll be there. (He'll be there)"

They were singing Miles Jaye Davis' song but with *He'll* as in God. My heart jumped and I skipped down the stairs of the balcony. I saw the family of five walking down the driveway next door. The two girls wore pink sponge curlers in their hair. As they passed the bottom of our dirt driveway, I sang along.

One of the girls looked and smiled. The eldest young man motioned for me to join them. I came closer and followed them on their slow meandering walk down to the railroad tracks and back. We kept right on singing. Then they invited me to come with them to the next-door neighbor's home.

● ● ●

Pap mentioned the minister next door once. He said the minister was a hypocrite because Pap heard him swear at something in the driveway. I wasn't sure what a minister was. At that time, I only knew about priests.

So, when I met these neighbors, it was a new experience for me. In the house, I met the minister and his wife. There were books everywhere, something that was missing from our home. We sat at the dining room table and Paul explained to me what they did. They sang music for God traveling from city to city to sing at different churches. There were five brothers and sisters ranging in age from 14 to 19. The eldest was like a father to them on the road. When they broke out singing around the table, I sang along if I knew the words.

At one point, Paul stopped and looked at me with a funny look. "You sound like an angel," he said. He was taller than me. And his eyes were soft and surprised. "What do you like to sing?"

I thought of the hymns I sung at school but my favorite song above all was from Wizard of Oz. "Somewhere Over the Rainbow," I said, shyly.

"All right," he said, "You choose the key."

I stared at him while I imagined Judy Garland looking up at the sky. I opened my mouth and closed my eyes.

"When all the clouds darken up the skyway[5]
There is a rainbow highway to be found
Leading from your window pane
Just a step beyond the rain ...

I paused and opened my eyes. I sang the first note of the next line and Paul joined in.

"Somewhere over the rainbow
Way up high...

Paul's sisters joined in and harmonized.

Then Paul's older two brothers joined in.

The minister and his wife came into the room, and watched and listened as we all continued to sing the song. They let me finish the last lines on my own.

I had completely forgotten about that phone on the kitchen wall.

• • •

Mam let me go to the various churches with Paul's family and the minister. I loved going with them, squeezed into the back of the car with Paul and one of his sisters. His eldest brother drove

---

[5] EMI Feist Catalog, Inc., written by Yip Harburg, 1939.

and his other sister and brother filled the front seat. The minister, his wife and one son, led the way in another car.

These churches were different. It amazed me. I was so full of wonder at these people who came, smiled, laughed, and spoke differently. They stood proudly singing and clapping their hands to the funky, swinging sound of the player-piano style music Paul hammered and knocked out of those ivory keys with such beauty and simplicity. It was so different from Catholic church where we had to be quiet and cover our heads in shame.

Here women wore hats or not. They wore dresses in colors I had never seen put together before—deep purples, oranges, blues, greens, hot pinks, and whites with black trim. Men wore brightly-colored ties, and some had colored shoes. Suits of stripes and checkerboards, purples and reds. They praised God with all their hearts, standing and swaying as a group. Bodies jerked and writhed as the spirit moved them. Each and every one was beautiful to watch. Some danced in the aisles. I couldn't sit still on the hard benches. I clapped along and joined them by raising my hands and face up to God. I felt at home. Finally, I met people who felt the same love for God as I did. They talked to Him like I did. Here was a family of strangers where I was finally free to be myself. It was the first time I heard people call, "Thank you, Jesus" and then burst into strange sentences. They cried tears, but these were tears of happiness.

One day, at the Stone Church in downtown Toronto, not far from where I went to Catholic school and St. Basil church, I actually listened to the sermon after Paul and his siblings finished singing. Before this, I only had ears and eyes for Paul and his family. My heart clung to them desperately.

Suddenly, my ears perked up, and I straightened my back. Like a burst of energy, the fire went up from my tail bone to the back of my neck. The top of my head tingled. I listened closely to the minister's passionate speech.

"Little sister, are you lost, feeling like no one cares about you, not knowing where to go, wondering why we are here on this planet, and not wanting to live?"

Someone yelled out, "Thank you, Jesus!"

"Well, Jesus is calling you today."

"Yes!" someone yelled.

"And he's knockin' at your door!" cried the minister, knocking the air with his fist and then dropping it down like a dead weight. His body doubled over before standing straight again. This time he started shaking. "And Jesus is calling you, giving you His love, His saaaaaving Grace!"

"Praise the Lord," someone else cried and more followed.

I felt he was talking to me. He even seemed to point at me while he cried. And then he said something that I desired with all my heart.

"You might know God. You heard of Him. But you can't get much o' nothin' without Jesus in your Heart. Hear him knockin'?"

"Yes! Praise the Lord, thank you Jesus!"

"You need Jesus to come into your heart today. Know him as your personal savior. He's knockin' and waiting for you to open your heart and let Him in! Do what Jesus had said in the Bible.

"Jesus answered, and said unto him, Verily, verily I say unto thee, Except a man be born again, He cannot see the kingdom of God. Chapter 3 verse 3 …"

Paul started playing a soft melody in the background. He looked over at me and smiled.

I cried. I bawled. All the poison came out in rivers of tears.

"Come on down. You know who you are, little sister. Come and meet Jesus as your personal savior …"

I got up. People celebrated each of my steps as I went closer and closer to the front of the church. They looked over as they saw me out of the corner of their eyes. Then the minister pointed at me and said, "Thank you, Jesus. Come little sister. He is waiting. Come and be saved today. This is your day …"

I kept walking, this solitary little white person in a purple taffeta mini dress and white stockings, young and crying, with white blonde hair covering her tears. At the front, the minister placed his gentle, soft brown hand on my head and closed his eyes and prayed,

"Thank you, Jesus." And he whispered, "A little lamb has come home."

Home. He, *Jesus*, was my home.

I had found *my people*.

• • •

I came home with a booklet given to me by the minister's wife entitled, *Now That I Believe*. I read it but didn't entirely understand it. I wanted to ask someone for help. Paul and his family left after the service to go back to the States. I could've asked the minister next door, but, of course, I still had the same fears and timid conditioning. I was afraid of men. It would take some time for me to shed these layers and layers of poisonous dirt and tar that kept me back from finding my voice.

• • •

My aunt and mother both caught a sexually transmitted disease which resulted in hysterectomies. At this point in her life, Mam looked more beautiful than ever, yet she carried an even darker cloud that slowly etched permanent wrinkles between her beautiful brows. The ugliness between Pap and Mam shifted in intensity. But they had their lives to live and I had mine.

I felt quite happy and relieved, however. Paul and I wrote to each other every single day. Our letters were thick. We talked innocently about marriage and children and their names. He would draw a candelabra on a baby grand piano and say that one day he would be as big as Liberace. We were such sweet babes with no idea about life, no idea about sex, relationships, or the world. He was who I lived for every day.

One day, no letter came. I wrote thinking I'd get two the next day. Nothing the next day. I mentioned that in my letter. Then nothing again. I wrote, wondering if there was something wrong. Five more days without a letter. I wrote, beseeching him, asking if he was sick, begging him to please write because, otherwise, I would think he was dead. That without him in my life, I thought *I* would die.

Then, finally, a letter arrived that indeed made a part of me die. His letter was covered in watermarks, tears dripped over the ink, but much was still legible.

"I can't write to you anymore. It breaks my heart. My Mom and Dad heard about how short your dress was, and people complained about it. They didn't feel it was dignified in church. Also, and this is the hardest to bear, they don't want me to fall in love with a white girl."

White girl. I had forgotten about skin colors. I was stunned.

However much I was aware of the riots in the U.S. and the African American's fighting for equality, that was *there*. In a country where they lynched and hung, where they were forced to drink from separate water fountains and to sit at the back of the bus. But, I lived in Canada. I knew of no such prejudice in Canada. When I had introduced Paul to Pap late one night, he said what a nice polite boy he was. And the closest he said that could've been said about anyone with a dark tan was that, at first, all he saw was a bright white smile in the dark.

In the States, Paul was not allowed to write to a white girl. I lost my Paul. Once again, I felt stamped *Worthless*.

I never wore a mini-dress after that. And it would be six years before I went to church again.

FIVE

Teacher's Cast-Away

Listlessly, I hung around the house once more waiting for that call. It didn't take long. Now my English teacher was someone to whom I would cling for comfort. He did call, finally. Once I told him exactly where I lived, he told me I should be able to take the new Go Train into the city. He said, because I was looking for a summer job, he fired his housekeeper and the job was mine. If I wanted it. Every Saturday. And, I could go swimming each time.

I was determined to not only make money, but also to be close to someone who seemed to care about me. Now that I lost Paul's light and love, I craved the attention. So, I went through the entire house looking for change. I found some under the cushions of the couch, in a jar in one of the kitchen cupboards, at the bottom of one of Mam's many purses. I found enough to cover a return ticket. The next Saturday, I walked the mile along the tracks to get to the new Go Train Station with a towel and bathing suit rolled up under my arm. It took over an hour and a half sitting in a rolling, rocking train car watching the slow rolling waves of beautiful Lake Ontario as we sped by along the shoreline. I was reminded of our trip from New York through Montreal and to Toronto so many years before. Here the sun was shining brightly and I was so excited. I was grown up. Sitting on a train alone, headed for a new adventure. A new discovery. I looked around the car. There were only four of us, so there was lots of room. I moved closer to the window and leaned my forehead against the glass, letting the sun bake the top of my head and forehead. I looked up at the clouds and wished that I could just float up *there*.

I was so naïve and unaware of where I was heading. No one taught me anything or equipped me with the tools to navigate this world. And Toronto was a big, bad world of strip joints with many traps for a barely sixteen-year-old girl/child to fall into. I equated the Electric Circus and Malabar Costumes on Queen Street as Toronto. I thought I knew it all.

Finally, the train jolted, stopped and started, and slowly pulled into Union Station. My heart pounded hard as I made my way to the subway. My eyes were glued to the subway map over the door until finally I was able to get off at the right station. I followed his directions and found his tall round apartment building on one of the side streets off Yonge Street. I went into the stifling, hot lobby and searched for his name on the directory. I felt an ache in my stomach just before nervously pressing the buzzer. I felt lightheaded.

He buzzed and let me in. A man stared at me as I walked past him to the elevators.

It was the first time I had ever been in a tall apartment building with so many floors. I followed the carpeted hallway until I found the right apartment. I buzzed and waited.

It never occurred to me that what I was doing was wrong. Walking into a single man's apartment didn't faze me. He was going to smile and be so happy that I finally came.

I heard the chain come off as well as two locks being unlatched. He opened the door, and my heart leaped. He had let his hair grow since the school year. He was so handsome with his long curls and his tallness. He looked at the towel roll under my arm.

"Good, you remembered you were going to swim. Come in, finally!"

He let me in and locked the door behind me. I stopped to see what looked like a perfect bachelor pad taken directly from one of the *Playboy* magazines: white shag rug, black couch, black coffee table, a massive set of stuffed dice on top of it. Black paisley wallpaper. Smoked glass wall with smoked glass chandelier over a glass dining room table.

"How do you like it," he asked as he watched me take it all in. "As an artist, can you appreciate how it all fits together?"

He called me an artist. "Yes, it all matches. It's beautiful."

"I hired an interior decorator. I wanted something beautiful for people to sit in."

"People?" I asked.

"Beautiful people. Like you."

I felt embarrassed but pleased. I must have blushed because he touched my check and then brushed my waist-length hair back over my shoulder. He motioned around the apartment.

"Don't look too closely. It's very dusty." He pointed towards the dining room. "I caught my last housekeeper drinking the booze and filling the bottles up with water so that I couldn't tell. Some people, huh?"

"Huh," I laughed softly and nodded.

I looked around and my trained European eyes spied thick dust everywhere. It confirmed he was in dire need of a housekeeper.

I put my towel roll down beside the door and took off my shoes.

"Oh, you don't have to do that."

"We always do at home." I looked down at the white carpet. It had a worn, dirty path directly from the door which spread out somewhat into the rest of the apartment. "If you take off your shoes, you would never have a dirty carpet like this."

He looked down to where I pointed. "Good call."

"Where are the cleaning supplies?" I asked, looking towards the kitchen.

"Hey, what's the rush?" he said. "Wouldn't you rather go for a swim first? You've had a long trip. Why don't you put on your bathing suit, and I'll put on mine, and we'll go for a nice swim, all right?"

I looked at him and blinked. It never occurred to me that he would swim with me. That embarrassed me somewhat.

Then I looked around at the dust and calculated how much time I had before the last late afternoon train left for home. If I swam first, I needed to know how much time I had. I hadn't told anyone where I was going just like he asked, but I wouldn't have anyway. Nobody cared. Who cared? I nodded. "Ok. A quick swim now or later, I guess. So long as I have enough time to clean and still catch the last train home."

"Great!"

"Where's your bathroom? Up here?" I pointed to the hallway. He nodded. As I walked into the hallway I looked around at the dust and noticed he had a piece of paper taped over the mail slot. I guessed it let in a draft. I didn't think much more about that and went into the bathroom and changed. While there, I opened the medicine cabinet to see what secrets he may have. What shaving cream and toothpaste he used. I was curious about this man who showered so much attention on me. I looked at bottles, medicine jars. And I found a bunch of hairpins.

Hairpins. Other women. Or one woman.

Then, with bathing suit on, and excited to take a dip in a nice, warm turquoise swimming pool instead of the cold lake, I left the bathroom leaving my clothes draped over the edge of the bath.

I can't believe my luck, I thought, as I snuck a peek into his bedroom on the way back to the living room. *I get to clean for someone who really likes me, make money, and swim each time.*

For a change, I had it altogether, I thought.

"You don't have your bathing suit on," I said as I came back, noting that he was just sitting there in the black armchair with the white pillow and black dots. I noticed a big stain on the cushion. I was starting to see more dirt the longer I was there.

"No, I thought you'd help me change."

"Pardon?" I asked dumbly. As he got up and slowly walked towards me, I remembered all the clothes and diapers I had changed on babies and little cousins, and I laughed out loud. Then I thought that perhaps he had a problem with his arms or back, like Pap did. Pap always asked to be pulled up from his chair, which I did gladly.

He reached out. I had no idea what he was going to do. But I stopped laughing. He completely and physically overwhelmed me. I thought I was strong. But I felt completely helpless.

I said no many times. I tried to free myself. I tried to run. Anywhere. I was like a little puppy or kitten easily controlled, pushed, pulled, and played with. I saw dead eyes. As I felt myself being bruised and scraped, I looked up at the mail slot from upside down.

I understood the paper taped to it.

In shock, I suddenly escaped from my skin. I felt tremendous turmoil and intense fear. I waited outside my body until the monster finally went away.

I thought back to the dancing and singing in the church. I heard the clapping to the music, the rhythm. And, I heard the words, *Thank you, Jesus, for your savin' and deliverin'. You brought me as a witness. You brought me from a very long way. Oh, thank you Jesus for your goodness, thank you. For your outstretched hand. You've been so good to me, thank you, thank you. Thank you, Jesus.*

● ● ●

I stood in the kitchen. He said he had to go and do something. He told me to clean myself up, and I could leave anytime.

But I thought I heard him wrong. As I numbly watched his back disappear through the door, I went into auto-pilot. I didn't understand what had happened to me. I hurt inside and out. I rubbed my arms where there were red welts and then, like a brainless robot, I unloaded the fridge and freezer to clean it. I took a floor mop and mopped the floors. There were more hair-pins stuck in the massive balls of dust. I opened drawers out of curiosity to see his clothes and to touch them. In one drawer, I saw *Playboy* magazines. They were in better shape than the ones at the shop. But there they were. Like family members checking in on me. I began to understand what sex was.

I stood for a very long time. I remembered moments where I forced to allow being done to me what the images implied, called for, demanded. There was something terribly off balanced. I came innocently with purity of heart. He planned to act out an episode in the ongoing Playboy mantras.

I looked at the door, then out the window. *When is he coming back?* I looked at the clock many times as I went through the motions, and finally saw that I had to leave right away if I was going to catch that last train.

He didn't show up in time to say goodbye.

He didn't call during the week. To make sure I didn't miss the call, I didn't leave that phone. The following Saturday I had my baby bonus money and I dutifully walked the mile to the station and got on the train again. An hour and a half later I was at his apartment door. Someone let me in downstairs at the front door. I buzzed the apartment. No answer. I tried to look in through the mail slot. Just the paper. I wanted to run away so badly but at the same time, I had made a promise to him and I didn't dare break it.

I didn't dare let him down.

I didn't dare not obey him.

I didn't dare have him leave me. Because now that I put two and two together I finally remembered the disgusting Birds and the Bees story. Now I knew we were going to get married. And this was the man I was duty bound to love and obey like he was God for the rest of my life.

He never showed up.

I sat on that floor next to his door for six hours. I didn't know what to feel or think.

I left an awkward note slipped through the slot and just barely caught the last train home. I sat frozen, frightened. Could people tell what happened to me? I slouched in a corner and hid my face behind my hair.

No phone call during the week. No money to go downtown the next Saturday.

I waited for the rest of the summer to end so that I would finally see the man I belonged to at school. I truly believed we most probably would wed.

• • •

Finally, the first day of school arrived. By this time, I looked forward to standing at the tree to wait for a school bus. I felt superior over the other girls because I had found a husband. I was going to finally see him at school, where I would run into his arms, he would grab me, hoist me up, laugh, and smile.

But, I didn't see him anywhere. I went through the motions of following the shortened day schedule until the final assembly. Surely, I would see him there.

During the welcoming school assembly in the gym, I craned my neck to see him. I saw lots of other teachers from the year before but not him After everyone else left, I went up to another teacher and asked if he knew where my teacher was.

The teacher told me he wasn't teaching there anymore. He had moved away.

It felt like a battering ram knocked the air out of me. It was as if someone yanked on my back and pulled me away as quick as lightening. I watched this teacher shrink in size and felt myself about to drown in a dark abyss. I turned and blindly stumbled through the darkened gym. I went into the girl's locker room bathroom and stared at myself in the mirror.

I did not please him. I did not slice the cheese the perfect thickness. I did not say or do the right thing. I was not sexy enough like those Playboy centerfolds. Perhaps I should have worn make-up. Perhaps it would have been better if I said something special. Or maybe looked a little less nerdy. Maybe he didn't like my bathing suit.

Oh my God, my Father, my body wasn't beautiful enough! What was I supposed to do now?

To me, it was obvious I was not good enough and was now ruined for this world. But even worse, I committed an ultimate sin. I was ruined for Jesus and for my God.

• • •

A month later, on a hard-raining thundering afternoon, I dove out of my bedroom window with my head aimed at the rocks in the garden below.

Blackness.

… drops.

Gentle drops on my face.

Caressing.

Was I alive or dead? I couldn't tell. I didn't feel pain inside. In fact, I didn't feel anything at all. Not my arms, my legs, my head. So, I must be dead. I kept my eyes closed. I felt peaceful.

So, I was *happy* dead.

But the rain was real. I had that lingering feeling that someone sprinkled it gently on my face to wake me up. When I finally opened my eyes, the gentle rain I felt turned into a biting rain pounding my face. A flash of lightening etched across the skies and, seconds later, the rumbling thunder vibrated the ground beneath me.

The ground. The rocks.

I tried to move my head. I couldn't. Every muscle in my body hurt as I moved a little this way and that. There was a rock under my one knee, another under one shoulder and elbow. Eventually, I understood why I couldn't move my head. It was pushed into the deep, wet mud and tightly stuffed between two huge rocks.

I got up slowly in the rain, tripped, stumbled through the remaining rock garden in my socks, and carefully slipped and crawled up the grassy side hill to get to the side door. As I looked over to where I had been, I saw the indent of where my head and body was. Even if I tried a million times, I could never plan to land the way I did. My body was practically laid out specifically around the individual rocks. When I looked up at my windowsill, amazed that I hadn't been able to kill myself, I saw my mother standing holding a cloth against the patio door glass below and holding a can of window spray in her other hand. She didn't move. I continued on up the little hill and once inside the house, peeled off my muddy socks and hid in the bathroom.

I told her it was an accident and I laughed it off.

• • •

I floated through the next few months, not brushing my teeth, not washing my hair, until one day a teacher I did not know came up to me.

"Hi, I hear you like to sing," she said, smiling at me.

I responded, came to life a little bit to be polite, "Yes, I used to sing in Catholic School."

"How would you like to audition for me? I'm directing a play called the *Fantasticks*. I want you to try for my *Louisa*."

I had never heard the word *audition* before. "You mean you want me to sing for you?" I was surprised anyone noticed me in particular. How did she know?

"Well, yes. Could you come right after your last class tonight and quickly sing a song for me? In the music room. It won't take long."

I thought of the school bus. But there were two of them after school. One for right after class and one to allow for all the extracurricular stuff. "Okay."

After class, with books held against my chest as other girls did, I found the Music Room. I walked into the gray room with chairs and musical instruments everywhere. The teacher was sitting at the upright piano.

"Hi there," she said. "Come over here. Do you have any songs you like to sing? Perhaps I can play it for you. If I can't, just sing acapella."

I thought *acapella* was another song. "I don't know that song," I said.

She smiled. "It means, without music."

"Oh," I said, not really understanding. Then I thought of Paul, his brothers and sisters. "Somewhere Over the Rainbow," I whispered.

She grinned, turned and started playing it.

I sang it. I sang like Paul was there. My eyes were closed. I imagined the harmony of the others. And then I felt the twinge of shame and abandonment. My voice broke but I kept on singing. I sang like an angel. I was transported and uplifted, listening to the words as I sang. I, too, wanted to fly over the rainbow. Into Heaven. But I no longer belonged there.

When I finished, she turned and clasped her hands together. "Oh my," she whispered. "I want you to be my *Louisa*."

And so, music and theatre came to my rescue. I did not see God's hand in it as yet for I was too far into the abyss of shame. And, as with everything else distasteful, I managed to create another layer of black tar and dirt to cover it, hard and thick enough that no one could see through. For a little while even I forgot.

• • •

"Hear how the wind begins to whisper.
See how the leaves go streaming by.
Smell how the velvet rain is falling,
Out where the fields are warm and dry."

I sat on the stage facing the character named Matt.

We sang and acted well together. Leading up to the performances, we had fun with the entire cast and our drama teacher. The director was like a parent to us. I found that the rehearsals were not enough for me. I needed these new family members around me more and more. So, some of us got together every single day to say good morning and crack jokes before classes started. We laughed, hugged, and wished each other well. Matt was in Grade 13; I was in Grade 10. He had a girlfriend from California who lived downtown Toronto. He had first met her at his first rehearsal for the musical production of *Hair*. She was also in the cast. He was the youngest member and had to hide his role in the production from his parents. They thought he worked the night shift at a grocery store.

Instead, he sang and bared his body eight times a week to packed audiences.

On stage, I continued to sing. The lights were bright and warm, and the audience was quietly listening.

Matt kept his eyes on me. Looked over at the make-belief walls when I motioned to them. He joined in, and we sang. The play seemed to go on forever, but it sped by too quickly. During the adrenalin, the stage kiss became a real kiss. I could tell the difference. I smiled at him when we did our bows to a standing ovation.

Thus began a few years of true happiness.

SIX

A Ham, A Near Death Experience and the Last Attempt

1972

Matt and I were together for almost three years. We never had actual sex—even if we wanted to my body couldn't allow it—and he respected that, amazingly. He had broken off with his girlfriend from California and stuck with me. After we did *The Fantasticks*[6], we spent the years with weekends together and summers filled with laughter, picnics, swimming, Friday nights at a local pub or at the *Gas Light* on Yonge Street.

In the meantime, Matt went through university and got a Bachelors of Arts while I continued through high school getting top marks and starring in every school production that was launched.

One day, during what was to be our last summer together, we went to a provincial park for a picnic. It was overrun by a *Progressive Conservative Party* gathering (before the party was simply called the *PC Party*). Its leader Robert Stanfield was there campaigning. There were competitions, flags flapping in the wind, bands playing, and children squealing and crying.

A woman came up to our group of friends while the band played a version of Elvis', *Now or Never*. My friends and I had just skinny dipped in the river below, we were as hippie as can

---

6   The Fantasticks, written by Tom Jones and Harvey Schmidt, 1960

be, and we thought we were getting into trouble. Instead, the woman asked me if I would go into the beauty contest. They didn't feel they had enough contestants. I looked at the other girls. They looked at me.

"I don't have a bathing suit with me," I said, which was true. I didn't like the attention solely on me. It seemed so impolite.

"Oh, we can find you a bikini somewhere."

I panicked. I didn't want to traipse across that big stage just to be ogled at by men. I thought of the men at the shop who stared at *Playboy* stomachs, breasts, and buttocks. "I'd rather not. I'm so sorry."

"Do it," Matt piped up, grinning.

I looked at him, frightened. To be on stage in a play was one thing, but to be almost naked in front of strangers? I felt sick to my stomach. The other friends encouraged me as well. The woman boldly took my hand and lifted me from my cross-legged position on the blanket. An Elvis impersonator continued to sing his song.

"… Kiss me my darling, be mine tonight,[7]
Tomorrow will be too late,
It's now or never, my love won't wait…"

I mutely followed her to the back of the big stage.

"We got one," said the woman, "but we need a bathing suit. She didn't come with one." The other women gathered there looked at my half-dried hair while the woman looked through a box and fished out a light green bikini. She held it out against my body.

"That should do. You can change behind the curtain here." She moved a make-shift curtain over and waited for me to pass through then closed it behind me.

No mirror. *How the heck will I be able to see if I look okay!*

---

[7] "It's Now or Never", Elvis Presley, 1960, originally "O Sole Mio," lyrics by Eduardo Di Capua and Alfredo Mazzucchi.

"How's it going in there?"

I looked at the bikini in my hand.

"We're already behind schedule. Can you hurry up?"

I quickly slipped off my shorts and t-shirt. I didn't wear a bra or underwear. All my hippie friends went without. I struggled with the clasp on the top, left it hanging and pulled on the bottoms. The suit was a bit large for me. I thought of those two Samba dancers on the cover of the LP—how their straps buckled so you could see the tops of their breasts. But I was still young. My breasts were still on the humble, tomboyish side. I stepped through the curtain.

"I need help with the clasp," I mumbled.

One of the ladies turned me around and hooked the clasp. She turned me to face her. She looked at my tanned face, pulled out a comb and combed my long, white-blonde hair. Then she turned to another box and rummaged through women's shoes. She pulled out a set of sandals with a little heel. I looked at those little heels as if they were stilettos. I had never walked on any kind of heels. I put them on and hobbled around a bit.

"There you are. Pretty as a picture. Now let's go."

She maneuvered me to the back of the stage where five other girls and women were standing. They eyed me up and down. I smiled and nodded, anxious to be less threatening. I looked at the closest one's bathing suit. "Nice suit," I said, smiling tightly.

"Thanks," she mumbled. The others tore their eyes away from me.

"It's now or never
My loooove won't wait."

"Ladies and gentleman, a big hand for our band and Elvis!" People clapped and cheered.

I felt somewhat lost. I turned to the girl with the bathing suit I had complimented. "What are we supposed to do?" I asked, with a touch of desperation.

"Now it's time for that favorite pastime!

Judging beautiful girls in a big beauty contest!"

"Just strut your stuff," she said. She was chewing gum and smacked her lips. She shook her head. "And smile."

Men clapped and whistled somewhere out in the crowd. Music started playing. A Samba. I groaned inwardly. Suddenly I was pushed up a set of make-shift stairs. My loose shoes clunked and wobbled on the wooden steps while I held tightly to the wooden railing. A splinter slid into my right hand. I hesitated at the top but the next girl kept pushing me. I looked back and saw that all the women and girls were packed together and I was holding them up. Their looks could've killed. I turned and led them onto the stage.

The funny part of this entire ordeal was once I was up on that stage, I felt fine. I straightened my back, walked in rhythm with the music, and smiled. I looked at the women, children, babies, and the emcee but not the men. There were catcalls and applause. I went to where the emcee motioned for me to stop and I stood in a pose I had seen so many times in *Playboy*. Right foot slightly into the left, knee bent inwards, shoulders back, head and chin up. Tummy in. I was 18, never strutted my stuff before, but with all the conditioning, I was a natural.

I won the beauty contest. The emcee later told me I was a natural ham. I was devastated and told Matt, about to cry. Did I look like a pig, snort like one, walk like one?

"No," said Matt laughing. He was used to my lack of understanding English slang terms. "It means you are a natural. You glow. You look comfortable, and people feel you connect with them."

"Oh," I said, not seeing how on earth ham came out of all that.

I was a natural ham.

Unfortunately, this began my hunger to be a ham continuously, but it also kept putting me in front of the wrong kind of men. At 18, I still did not have the brains or experience to make that connection.

• • •

My uncles and father stopped working on Saturdays. By now the loans on the first shop were completely paid off. The new shop, where Pap and my blonde uncle worked, was paying for itself. The draw of sailing kept them on the water during the sailing season or in the shop itself during the winter where the boats were stored to work on them. More time for leisure and less for exorbitantly long work days.

So, I was given a key to the old shop. This time I had a paid part-time job cleaning the worn-out offices, lobby, and the disgusting bathroom. I couldn't understand how disgusting things could end up on walls and toilet seats. What the heck did these men do?

I made the mistake of complaining about it to Pap the first time he brought me there. This was just before I got my own car. Pap was standing at the counter talking to someone who had dropped by asking about a quote for work on their car. Pap was shooting the breeze when he heard me complain. He pointed at me and said, "That's my daughter." He looked back at the man who was eyeing me too closely. I was on my hands and knees and looked back.

"I hire her to clean the offices here, but she does nothing but complain. I'm trying to teach her what real work is all about." They both looked at me.

New brand on forehead: *Lazy and spoiled. Does not understand hard work.*

Pap left to go to the bank or something and left me to finish cleaning. I made the mistake of organizing the desks. I had become a neat freak since the teacher and somewhat obsessive-compulsive, so I filed the papers into little piles according to subject matter and date on all the desks.

My *Playboy Playmate* friends were there, of course. I organized them in order of newest to oldest editions in piles of years. There were almost eight full piles, the older ones frayed and torn at the edges, the newer ones in not too bad a shape. Almost every single front cover that displayed women was again doctored up with a moustache and goatee over their beautiful faces. Sometimes I would stop and read an article or two. I still stayed away from the nude shots, and especially the centerfolds, but I noticed that some of the *Playmates* were getting younger and younger looking. There was a set of *Playmate* twins that I could swear looked sixteen. In a March edition, it featured *Girls of Italy*, and someone had written, *delizias*. Italian for delicious. I found myself comparing my looks with theirs. It frightened me. We were fruit for the picking, devoured and cast aside. It made me wonder if there were actually nice men who looked for life-long partners and loyally stuck to them. *Was* there such a thing?

Soon afterward, Pap gave me my very first car, a Volkswagen, and went out of his way to get it painted at the shop in a color I wanted: neon orange. It was old, but I loved it. I noticed it had stretched-out old belts for seatbelts. We never wore seatbelts in those days, so I never gave it another thought. However, I excitedly made it my own by taking my paints and painting beautiful, psychedelic designs on the back window-ledge and on the front dashboard. I was proud and felt privileged. Of course, with transportation, I was able to spread my search for work further out. I found a summer weekday job waitressing at a Holiday Inn in Scarborough.

It was hard work. I called it slave labor. Parents didn't like how you made chocolate milk for their children, or the coffee was too strong, or the toast too burnt. But if I was gentle, kind, and diligent, I made good tips. I even shared my tips with the busboys and cooks as required even though one or two of the girls refused.

Our manager was a woman who never had time for us, only time for one of the hotel owners. He would come down, sit in a booth and watch her every move. She had teased hair in a high French roll, wore large, dangling earrings with a two-piece light gray dress suit, but she had a bit of a gut according to what I considered to be my well-trained "*Playboy* school of sexy-looking bodies" mentality. He didn't seem to notice. His hands were all over her. The rest of the girls and I would make comments about it, and keep each other up to date as he became bolder. From where we stood in the main dining area, we saw everything going on under the table.

Finally, the two of them would disappear during the afternoons. "Isn't she married?" asked one of the waitresses.

"Yeah, but so is he!" said another. We'd giggle and keep working.

One day, someone must have said something to him, or his wife, because he came in with our manager. She looked upset and withdrawn standing behind him. She didn't look too well. It was 7:30 in the morning, and it was unusual to see him there so early.

"Who's da one who's spreadin' all dese rumahs 'bout me 'n her?" The few who were there with me all looked around. No one said a word. He touched the side of his nose and said, "I'll fin' out, jes' wait."

Later that day, he came in and pointed at one of my friends who came in for the overlapping and evening shift. She looked at the rest us before mutely meandering between the fully-occupied tables. I heard her start to cry, then plead. She ran out sobbing and knocked a tray of dirty dishes off one of the racks.

Our manager came over and motioned for me to come to the side of the dining room. I finished writing down the order I was taking. After pinning the order up in the kitchen for the cook, I rushed over to her.

"You're working the next shift," she said stiffly.

I looked at her blankly. I quickly figured out how much more money I could make. "Till what time?" I asked.

She checked her schedule. "I've asked Doreen to come in two hours earlier than her usual night shift for the bar. You can go home at 8:30."

I nodded. I didn't know how I was going to do it. My feet hurt, my back hurt, and I was looking forward to getting off at 4:30. I was exhausted, but as Pap always said, *mind over matter.*

I worked the next four-hour dinner shift. As tired as I was, I covered another waitress' section after she cut her hand on a broken glass. It was crazy. At one point, the busboy and I collided when I smacked through the swinging door with a platter of Spaghetti Primavera and Spaghetti Bolognese. My entire platter crashed to the floor. Some of the patrons clapped and cheered. I blushed, hot with embarrassment. Red sauce covered my nylons, and cream sauce dripped from my outfit. I quickly tried to clean it up while the other waitress stepped over me in a hurry to get her orders through. It was the most intense part of the restaurant's day.

While I was serving another table, the owner came to me his face like a thundercloud. *Oh no,* I groaned. My legs started to tremble. An angry man always took away what strength I had. He bent close into my face. I could see his five o'clock shadow. *He must have a hairy back,* I thought for some reason.

"Finish here 'n den come to the cashier's counter. I need to talk to ya."

I finished with the table and hurried over to the cashier's counter. He was leaning on his elbows, the shoulders of his satin suit bunched up around his thick hairy neck. As I came closer, he stood back up and shifted his shoulders. Then he tugged on his sleeves and adjusted his satin gray tie. His expression went from disgust to anger while he poked his finger into my shoulder.

"How da frig can you serve people lookin' like dat? Are you stupid or somethin'? You know what you're doin'? You are makin' me look bad here. This is a business. If I didn't need you so badly right now, I'd kick you outta here."

I looked down at my uniform. It was gross, I knew, but when would I have time to clean it properly? I started crying. "I'm sorry, I didn't have time. I'm carrying two sections on my own right now, and I'm covering for someone else you fired this morning."

"You didn't have da time? What do you t'ink dis is, some slum? Get cleaned up first!"

I rushed to the washroom and quickly scrubbed the front of my uniform with wet paper towels. It did very little, but at least I was getting the cream bits off. The other waitress ran in and hissed at me, "There are people waiting for their orders, and they're complaining! Some are threatening to walk out. And you've got orders ready for pick up!"

I dropped what I was doing and ran back out.

It was truly hell that entire evening. I pushed, smiled, and apologized continuously. By 8:30, when the other waitress/bartender finally came in, I was more than grateful and ready to go home. I filled up a glass of chocolate milk quickly and downed it in a second. Then I clocked out and ran to the car. If I hurried, I might still be able to see Matt. He wasn't very happy with me lately. Not making actual love was starting to wear him down. He was really pushing me now, but I would burst into tears each time he brought up the subject. I really wanted us to have the nice time with friends we'd planned over a month ago. I needed our usual easy laughter and fun.

The traffic going East on the 401 was stop-and-go because of an accident. I was tired, hot, and filthy. By the time I got off at Pickering, it was still barely daylight even though it was just after the summer solstice. In my daze, I missed the last turn home, so I continued on to the next side road which was a more roundabout way to get there.

They had just dumped gravel onto the road that day but hadn't finished spreading it out or rolled it down. However, I was committed and stubbornly continued on through the loose, crunchy gravel. My eyes were heavy and I was listening to Diana Ross singing, "Ain't No Mountain High Enough," on the radio.

"Ain't no mountain high enough,
Ain't no valley low enough,
Ain't no river wild enough,
To keep me from you…"[8]

---

[8] "Aint No Mountain High Enough," Diana Ross, written by Valerie Sim and Nickolas Ashford, 1970.

I started daydreaming, thinking about my inability to love and my *problem* and how that affected Matt and my relationship. I thought of my teacher, who still in my mind *owned* me.

The music started to falter and crack due to bad reception. I reached for the radio knob but fiddled around a bit too long. When I looked up, I was heading straight for a bridge abutment, too close to the side of the road. The loose gravel sucked the car sideways–BANG!

• • •

Emptiness.

Long emptiness.

Nothingness.

Bright, bright light and lightness of being.

Then I came back.

I came back feeling absolutely magnificent and alive with music in my soul. I was happy beyond measure. I had come back from Light, Love, and Hope. It was so real, that it took me a while to realize I had a body and needed to open my eyes.

When I opened them, the first thing I saw was a shattered, jagged, broken windshield with long blonde hair hanging from the sharp edges, swaying gently in a breeze. It was elegant, beautiful. Slowly I realized the hair predominantly hung almost upside down. I moved my head and looked to the driver's side window. I had the windows completely open to let in a cool breeze in the stifling heat. I saw blue sky and red clouds. Then I realized I was actually looking *up* through the driver's side window. My head was hanging freely, and it felt good. I could feel the back of my body resting touching the front seat. I tried to move but realized I was stuck under a now bent steering wheel. There was something under my kneecap that kept me hanging. I reached behind me, but my arms barely moved.

I had had an accident. After the initial attempt to right myself, I simply gave up. I felt the happiest I had ever been in my entire life.

Then a soft voice, ever so faintly, said, *Wait. Rest. Someone will come by and help.*

So, I happily waited and reveled in the amazing feeling of wholesomeness and lightness of being. I heard music in my head. I had no doubt. I had come back from someplace amazing.

Eventually, I heard one car pass by. Intuitively I knew this wasn't the right person. Then, as the clouds turned crimson and the sky a deeper vermillion blue, I heard a slower car come close. It went past, stopped and then backed up. I sensed this was a nice man before I heard the sound of a door open. Footsteps crunched through the loose gravel, and then, quite suddenly, a kind face looked down. The eyes widened, and I heard an English accent say, "Oh my GOD!" and he let out one choking sob.

• • •

My mother had stayed home after Matt and my friends, who had already gotten together for our planned evening at Matt's, said they'd immediately come over to take me to the hospital. Matt decided it would be faster if they all took me to the hospital instead of waiting for an ambulance. We were so far away from a paramedic station and it would've taken a half hour before they arrived.

The kind man who picked me up had a stiff drink at our house before he moved on. After initially choking when he saw me upside down in the car, he completely averted his eyes from me.

Mam helped me hobble into the washroom. My darling little sister followed. She was curious. She didn't cry like Mam had. She couldn't keep her eyes off the blood on me. There was barely a spot that was not bloodied on my uniform and body though I could still see the orangey stains of the red sauce.

I sat on the toilet to take off my white nylons which were soaked in blood. After struggling with one hand (my left was crushed and swollen), I saw the nylon was completely imbedded into the bloodied, congealing, mess underneath the bone.

I found that fascinating.

"Wook, see dere?" My lips wouldn't move but she somehow knew what I mumbled. I pointed to where the nylon was stuck.

She bent over with her little body and peered very closely. I loved those freckles over her nose and cheeks. I loved her to pieces, and at that moment felt like squeezing her into a tight bear hug. She touched where the material ended and the knee-cap bone started. That was good. I wanted her to learn to not be afraid. I didn't want her to grow up like Mam, frightened of every imagined thing.

"Doesn't it hurt?" she asked amazed.

I shook my head. I tried to smile. That one thing, of all the injuries, was the only thing that hurt me a little.

I decided to carefully and slowly take off what I could and left my leotards on. I slowly put on a housecoat that Mam handed me earlier. It was then I caught sight of myself in the mirror.

I didn't recognize myself. In fact, there was very little of me in that grotesque image. The nose was flattened and swollen about the width of my face. My lip was split to the bottom of the nose. The gums of my teeth had torn away. The front part of my hair was missing, and there was glass sticking out of my swollen, pumpkin-sized face. My eyes were almost swollen shut. I was amazed that I didn't get glass in my eyes. I tried to touch my face, but my arm couldn't move very well. My left hand was crushed. My chest felt like there was a cracked rib or two.

It wasn't at all what I felt in the deeper depths. I felt won-derful and healthy, so I ignored what I saw. I looked down at my little sister. She was staring with wide eyes. I ruffled her hair.

I shuffled out carrying the bloody mass of clothing. Mam averted her eyes, quietly sobbing while wordlessly taking it. She immediately put the bundle in a garbage bag. Matt and our friends sat in the living room. He saw me, covered his mouth, and broke down into tears.

I raised my hands to let him know I felt great. That I wasn't dying. In fact, I felt the happiest I had in my entire life. No fear, no pain, no remorse and I knew there was something more beautiful beyond this life and this planet.

On our way to the hospital, I couldn't help but find everything funny. People in other cars. A joke someone shared. I spent the entire evening at the hospital giggling and laughing. I wanted to tell everyone that I was okay. That it was only an image they were looking at. It wasn't all there was. It was an illusion. But everyone, even the nurses, found it difficult to look straight at me.

Later, sitting in the operating room, the doctor shakily looked me over. He pulled and yanked gently at glass shards. He stuck needles into all the open wounds. Someone liberally soaked me in iodine and then he started to stitch. He talked, and I tried to answer. My shoulders hopefully passed on the message that I was not at all distressed. In fact, I found it very fascinating. I motioned that I wanted to watch what he did under my kneecap. He got the message and patiently sat back as I looked at my knee cap, the fat, the skin, the bone. I watched him cut away dead skin, fat. And he sewed the jagged edges together. The whole time, his hand shook.

• • •

Months later, I still walked with a limp. By then, Pap sold the house from under us again and moved us into a slum house closer to the new shop. He took the remaining money and bought a bigger boat. Of course, that made Mam angry, upset, and even sicker than normal. Matt and I took my little sister into the backyard for a bit so Bettina could continue helping Mam unpack inside. We blew bubbles with her, and once in a while, I looked at the neglected property.

That feeling of internal peace and happiness had waned. Life took over again. Pap and Mam continued to fight every time they were together. Sail Past was coming up at the yacht

club and he wanted new brass buttons on his blue blazer. He
kept on her and on her. It was such a simple thing to do, but she
dragged her feet. One day, he was desperate to find his blazer.

"Where is my blue blazer?" he yelled.

"Pap," I gently said.

"Where is it!?" he yelled at Mam. She was hidden in the
kitchen and he was standing in the doorway. I was sitting on
the orange-red couch with teak arm rests looking through a TV
Guide. I swiveled my eyes in his direction. My tentacles went
out. Somehow, since the accident, I had begun to feel people's
emotions and thoughts. I stopped double-guessing why. I just
accepted the impressions as they came into my mind. They
seemed to always be relevant.

I heard Mam quietly say something.

Suddenly, he stomped to the front door closet which opened
right into the living room. He angrily yanked it open and everything stuffed inside tumbled out. "God damn it! This is a pigsty!
How can you live like this!? Do you not have any sense of order?!"

Mam scurried into the living room. She was shaking as
she stopped and leaned over the things that had tumbled out.
Pushing metal hanger after metal hanger to the side, she pulled
out a wrinkled blue blazer.

"There! There is your blue blazer!" She looked at him angrily.
She had aged since Pap tore us out of that other house and put
us into this box.

He looked at the front of it. "Where are the brass buttons?
And where is my crest!?"

Mam dipped her hand into one of the pockets and took out
an embroidered yacht club crest and some brass buttons. "Here!
Here they are!"

"I need the jacket now!"

"I'll sew them for you, Mam," I offered.

Pap's thick finger pointed straight at me. "You stay out of
it. I ask very little of Mam. She owes it to me to do this simple
little thing."

I hadn't heard the phrase *passive-aggressive* yet but it was precisely what Mam now used with everything. That and being sick in bed with one thing or another.

Pap didn't know where his underwear or socks were. Mam dressed him for all occasions except for work. She ironed his shirts, pressed his pants. When we sat at the table to eat, all squeezed into the tiny kitchen, Pap would sit at the head of the table with his back to the silverware drawer, and Mam sat at the other end.

"I need a knife. Where is a knife?" he'd say irritably. The knives were in the drawer behind him, practically touching the back of his chair.

Mam would get up from her end, walk over, wait for him to shift his chair some more to allow her to open the drawer to take out a knife. She did this mutely, obediently, out of rote.

The house was very small. Smaller than the last one on the ravine. Instead of the Lake at the end of the road, this time there was a nuclear power station.

Most importantly, there wasn't enough cupboard or closet space. Mind you, Mam did have an inordinate amount of clothing to squeeze into every nook and cranny she could find. How could she not have so many clothes? Her whole sense of pride was her beauty, clothing, accessories, and jewelry. These tools kept her pride afloat.

She reasoned that with Pap spending so much money on sailing and women, she would just spend it as it came.

Mam secured Pap's brass buttons, and I attached the embroidered badge. Another drama over with. I took many drives and walks just to get away.

One day, I took a shortcut walking along the train tracks near the shopping district where I had been looking at wallpaper again. A reporter drove by, spotted me, and asked to take a photo for the paper. Surprised and amused, I pointed out the areas of freshly healed stitches, the raised bulges, the scars, and the missing hair.

"I don't care. I don't see it. You are one beautiful young woman." He took several photos of me walking towards him on the tracks and it appeared on the front page of the local paper.

Perhaps he saw the glow I felt. For, though I was starting to get pulled down into depression again, I never felt far from God. I had my own room and prayed the Lord's Prayer every night. I slept deeply knowing there was life outside the box we lived in.

I changed after the accident. Instead of wallowing in deep black depression, I learned how to stuff it even deeper and adopted a mask that wasn't me. Photos taken a year apart looked like two different girls.

I lost weight and grew my hair even longer. I started to curl the front sides inwards with a curling iron every day. My eyes were larger and expectant all the time. I was manic. I thrived on making a schedule in 15-minute intervals each morning that listed my chores all the way to 10:00 p.m. I was a robot following a program. And I crammed it in in a super human fashion.

The schedule had 15-minutes for sit-ups and 100 shimmies in the morning. Fifteen minutes to dress and do make-up and hair. Fifteen minutes for toast with cottage cheese and sweet tea. Fifteen minutes to drive to school. Fifteen minutes to go to the locker and get my papers and books.

Even the classes were broken down into slots allowing teacher time with rushing to finish work and any homework given so that by the time the bell rang, I had finished that night's assignment for that class. Study periods were spent in the Art room where, with classical music in the background soothing my inner beasts, I worked on perfecting something due for Art.

Then I would prepare for a Student Council meeting since I was President. I would also finish correspondence and phone calls organizing snazzy dances. I was the first student to organize a mass tri-school dance with a big-name performing group. By the time we covered all the costs, we split what was left three ways. At the end of the school year, we had money in the bank. Apparently, it was the very first time that ever happened in our high school's history.

I also used my new, old car, a convertible MG sports car from Pap. It was white, with rust and holes in the top, I had Pap's old underwear ready to stuff the holes in rain or snow.

With the top down, all the cheerleaders sat on and around the edges while I drove back and forth in front of the bleachers to get the students all riled up and cheering, my horn honking away. It was like light and life poured through me. I was always in the *flow*.

But there was inevitable trouble brewing. Matt's patience with me waned even further. He was now 21, and I was not quite 19. He finished his Bachelor's Degree, and I was in my last few months of the five-year program of Arts and Sciences. I knew I wanted to go to the same university. I'd study Fine Arts with a major in Visual Arts and heavy on the sciences and languages.

One day he insisted we *try*. It was a fiasco. My body was a steel trap and he hurt himself badly. I left him sitting in a hot tub almost crying. It was while I stood there dressed, looking down at him, that something inside of me died. I wordlessly, coolly, turned and walked out.

Then one night, Matt and I visited his brother and sister-in-law. They had to get married the year before because of an unwanted pregnancy. Now they were dealing with a second newborn. She made supper, and I helped her by changing diapers on both the toddler and newborn. As I rinsed the cloth diapers in the toilet, she said how wonderful it was that Matt had a role in Toronto's on-going production of *Hair*. I looked up at her. I thought no one in the family was to know.

"How'd you find out?" I asked her, surprised.

"Well, he's in the cast photo at Ed's Warehouse in Toronto! How can you hide *that*?"

That sounded logical. "What about Matt's Mom and Dad?"

"They don't know. They'll never go to Ed's Warehouse. They're too cheap!"

I laughed. They were as Scottish as they could get in every way.

On the way home, Matt and I were chatting, and I mentioned how his sister-in-law was so proud of him being part of the cast of *Hair*. I was driving the old Volvo Pap had given him.

Matt was drunk. I always could use mind over matter and see straight even after the same number of drinks, so I drove after a night of drinking.

Suddenly, he turned and swore at me with a vengeance. Stunned, I just continued driving as he lambasted me for breaking my promise and discussing his role in the production. I explained that I hadn't brought it up at all, that his brother and sister-in-law knew all along.

"You lie!" he screamed. "You're a f--- liar!" He continued to throw the accusations, angrily, vehemently.

He was not the Matt I knew.

Part of me already died the day of the bath incident, and there wasn't much left over. I lost hope that he still loved and accepted the damaged me. I stared at the full moon that hung on the horizon looking at me, as if waiting to see what I would do. I felt life liquefy and ooze out of me. The branded words burned anew.

Liar.

Loser.

Corrupted.

Damaged.

"And I'm sick and tired of hearing about your rape! It's a lousy excuse for pretending to be sexless. You kiss like a nun. You act like a nun! You probably secretly asked for it! Isn't that what you Catholics do? F--- say, ooooooh no, don't, don't! and then you're the worst of the lot!"

Whore.

Killed. Me.

I pushed all vestiges of emotions deep, deep into the abyss where I was heading. Inside of me, I was packing up and leaving *town*.

Wordlessly, with no expression on my face, I continued to drive towards my friend, the moon. We had a silent conversation as Matt kept yelling.

I told the moon I would be right back and slowly turned right onto Matt's dark street. All the lights were out at his house, except at the side door. His parents, older than mine and devoutly Protestant, were evidently fast asleep in their own cocoons. The very people who were not allowed to know he stood naked briefly in the soft lights of the stage, baring all to an audience over and over again for almost three years.

Finally, out of verbal darts and hand grenades, he wordlessly got out and slammed the door. I watched him stumble up the driveway in the moon light. My spirit looked into God's face to try and read it and then back at Matt's back disappearing into the house.

God, what happened?

Matt had picked me up earlier, so I had to drive his car back to my house. I already knew it was a logistical problem for the next day. I sensed where I was going with my conversation with the moon. Oh well, they'd have to figure it out. *They* being Pap, Mam, Bettina, Matt. Normally, I didn't want to impose on others, but I had no choice this time. They would see and inevitably understand why.

I put the car into gear and slowly crawled through the abandoned streets to the main road that was well lit by the moon. I left the headlights off and drove by the softness of the full moon. It felt like I was gently strolling hand in hand. I knew the moon saw the beauty in me. It knew the broken shards that were there. It knew I could not help it.

I followed the Bay Road feeling the street lights pour over the car and caress it as it passed. I felt the wheels gripping the pavement, the grooves each digging in and letting go. My breathing was very shallow. As if I were ready just to stop.

The moon said good night at our ugly driveway. Before Pap bought the box, years and years of heavy trucks had indented and bulged the cracking blacktop. As I got out of the car, I stepped into the bright moonlight. I looked and waved with my heart at the moon. I then walked onto the harsh, gravelly grass at the end of the driveway and started to cry. I bent over from the pain. The pain in my heart and my gut. That teacher who used me and threw me away.

I am not worth keeping or loving. *God, this is wrong. I want to go home. To You.*

No voice.

I went inside, especially quiet because I didn't want anyone to stop me. I gently went up the gold shag carpeting on the staircase and into my room. The carpet there was blue shag. I could see the pattern of the wallpaper I had just put up. Pap paid for it, but he didn't let me buy what I really wanted. He said I had expensive taste. So, I bought the cheapest version of blue-bells and leaves. Something delightful and uplifting. But now it only looked gray and white and sad.

I went into the bathroom and took out my bottle of anti-tuberculosis pills. Mam was exposed to someone dying of it while she was pregnant with me, so pills were part of my routine. I had monthly lung exams at the Oshawa Hospital.

I went back to my bedroom and took them all.

Slowly the layers I formed around and around me turned into arms that let go. Another set of arms lifted and disappeared. Then another, and with the lifting of each layer, I felt lighter. The light above me grew from a tiny gray speck to a general lightening around me. Then it became brighter, and finally, I could touch the face of God.

But then God quietly said, *Look.*

I looked and saw a vision of two people I did not recognize. They held each other. The clouds of loss hung over their heads.

See, God said softly.

Then I saw. They were softer, older versions of my parents perhaps in their 80's. I saw clearly that their spirits were grieving. I wondered what had brought them together. What had broken their hearts so?

They grieve for you.

For me?

The concept of me having that much of an effect on those who had never truly seen or heard me, was like a lightning bolt.

"I would cause them to grieve like that?" I asked God.

I did not need to hear the answer. I felt it as if a bubble of warm love formed inside of me for them. And then, suddenly, I realized I could not do this to them. I could not *live* like that for eternity knowing I had caused so, so very much pain. I could not bear it.

Go.

The lightness disappeared, and I felt gravity pull strongly on my limbs. At first, I could not bring my body to answer. But then I learned anew to crawl, head heavy, stomach flat on the shag rug that went from blue, to red in the hallway, and then gold in my parents' bedroom. Gold shag and purple walls. I gave up just inside their door. I saw the moon watch me from the large master bedroom window.

Speak.

I opened my dry, parched lips and a hiss came out. I found a muscle further down my throat and squeezed it with some air. "Keep going," the moon said as it shone its light on my face. I pressed my chapped lips together and came up with the sound of "P".

"P--. P--."

I heard him snore somewhere up on the bed. Then he did that cough I so loved.

"Pap."

I could feel my father jump awake in his minds-eye. He was not happy about something.

"Pap." It was a gentle, raspy voice. A voice full of love for a man who did not know he helped to create my damaged soul.

"What!" He was gruff.

I could only whisper now. I laid my head down on the golden, scratchy, thick woolen threads and breathed out, "I took pills."

"God, God, God *damn* it!" He was upset. How could he not be?

From the carpet of cloud, I felt the vibrations of a big man getting out of bed after whipping back the covers. Next, this big man who spawned me, lifted me up bodily and swore as he dragged me down the steps.

Next, I watched the moon look down lower to where I was laying in the back seat of the car. My one eye opened with a slit. The moon gave me comfort as I felt my body toss this way and that with every curve on the road. It bounced in slow motion when the car went over bumps. And finally, I settled into a black sleep.

Ah, my soul said.

• • •

I lay in a darkened corner behind a heavy curtain. It wasn't the usual bed with paraphernalia surrounding it for the support of one who was ill or in distress. No, it was a curtain, three feet from a wall, hiding unwanted objects: an old tray on wheels, a chair, me, a bed. A large cement stone wall painted thickly. A vomit cream color. No light. No plug in the wall. And memories of the night before.

I lay in the dark. It was what I felt. Shame a curtain separating me from love, guidance, understanding, and forgiveness. Arms that said, come. Just come. Because God didn't want me to come yet.

I didn't dare reach out to Him today. I know that He saved me, but not for me so much but for so many more. Somehow it was indeed my responsibility to prevent harm to others, especially harm to the hearts of those who forgot I lived because of them.

I was ashamed. A lesson. It's never just me. It's the others around me. God didn't stop me because I decided I wanted to die and come back home. He was more concerned about how that would affect His plans for the others.

Ah, others, my soul said.

Black.

Me. No, others. Not me.

I could see the odd nurse's squeaky white footwear that gripped the highly polished linoleum of the ward from under my curtain. I knew that I had a face with mascara smudges caused by tears of a lifetime ago. My previously white top covered in running make-up, spilled liquids, and vomit from the night before. Still stained by words cutting sharply into the abyss that was my wound.

"Why are you here to waste my time? Why should I deal with someone like you? Are you on drugs? Are you pregnant? Who do you think you are to waste my time? I'm the best doctor in the world with the best talents for saving people, ensuring they live in spite of their discomforts and desire to die in dignity." The doctor never stopped hitting me with his words. I came to with them and it sharpened my senses. Just to scatter under the verbal punches.

Well, doctor. I wanted to die because I HAD no dignity. If you are saving me, then save me with a bit of love, of dignity for the soul pain that writhes throughout my mind, my limbs, my thoughts, and my tears. I demand to know why you couldn't see that last night. How could you, the amazing doctor, not see the child who was rendered in half and couldn't find a way back or the glue to piece herself together again? Perhaps give me a glimmer of hope that at least God would forgive me.

Forgive me.

Forgive me, doctor.

Forgive me, Mam.

Forgive me, Pap.

Forgive me, dear, dear, dear God.

I waited hours to be picked up. I was ignored by all in the hospital. I dared to slink from behind that curtain slashing my purgatory from the light of the people who dimly shone in this world. I was to face the dimness. Gather the strength.

Pap and Mam didn't or wouldn't ever know it was for them that I returned.

I walked through the slush along the highway one wet, soaked sneaker step in front of the other. People stared as they drove by. No good Samaritan asked why a young woman walked like the dead along a winter's road with sneakers, stained sweater, stained face, stained soul, and stained heart.

Eventually, as the day dimmed along with those who filled it, I recognized a face in one of those cars. This one was aching to pass right by. I could feel it. But my slashed eyes followed its tail lights and watched as it did a U-turn. I crossed the slush between passing cars, all slowing down for fear of what I might hurl at them. *"She must be a drug addict."* They saw the stamp that the doctor put on my head in neon lights. *"Shame, shame, shame."* I ignored them as I must.

The car stopped along the pile of snow. I climbed, then slipped into the snow, and somehow opened the passenger door to squeeze through. Mam didn't say a thing. Didn't know what to say. So we silently drove back, into the early winter night.

Neither Mam or Pap would dare ask.

Dare ask.

I dare you to ask.

No, please, I dare you not to ask.

• • •

High school ended and I became Valedictorian. Pap, Mam, Bettina, and my little sister almost didn't come. Pap said it was just a piece of paper. He didn't understand. Never had the time to know he should. Bettina was upset at me getting award after award and a chance to shine on that stage in my homemade gown with every teacher, vice principal, and principal smiling, glowing over my clever words in my speech. I was a ham. Bettina knew it. Sensed the double face of all that weight of pain deep inside, yet so much light on the outside. I was good at duping people. What she did not realize was that the abyss within me had gotten so deep, that she would've shown some mercy and gladness perhaps for having a slightly shallower abyss.

It was all relative. And she was too blind with depression to even sense we were trying to survive in the same personal hell.

I moved on to University where, because of my fear of preying teachers, I became withdrawn. This negatively affected some of my grades. Ironically, I fell into blind promiscuity. I forced it upon myself. To prove I could be a functioning woman. And not just for a gentle touch, but only with boys who knew nothing of selfishness. Yes, some forced it upon me, but the physical touches that came with it all were like tiny vitamin pills. Another little bit to go another long and bleak day.

Needless to say, I no longer wanted to see Matt, though after the hospital he came to the school twice with an engagement ring.

The person he had once known was no longer there inside of me.

That girl had checked out.

BOOK TWO:

The Stumbling Years

"To the woman he said:
I will increase your labour and your groaning,
and in labour you shall bear children,
You shall be eager for your husband,
and he shall be your master."

(Genesis 3:16, NEB)

SEVEN

As the Clay is in the Potter's Hand

"Women again must dress in becoming manner, modestly and soberly; not with elaborate hair-styles, not decked out with gold, or pearls, or expensive clothes, but with good deeds, as befits women who claim to be religious. A woman must be a learner, listening quietly and with due submission."

(1 Timothy 2: 9-14, NEB)

1973

I sat, watching the world as if on a distorted TV screen. The one and only time I tried *some* illegal substance. I didn't even know what it was. I befriended an unthreatening friend from one of my massively-attended first-year lectures who happened to live along the same route I drove every day from Nonna's house. He wanted to thank me for taking him to campus every day. He had gone on and on about some mind-opening drug. I don't know. I trusted him. And then I sat back. People came into the room, looked at me. They saw that I was in there somewhere. I was in control of the TV inside my head, and they were in a movie. My friend would say something to them about me, and then I would hear canned laughter like on *M.A.S.H.*

But that something didn't make me feel any better.

I now lived with Nonna. It was a short drive from her place to university. She was years older, and it worked well for both of us as she needed help in a general sense. I helped her shop, sew the special shifts she preferred to wear over her bulky body, and this way she wasn't entirely alone. Yes, she still had two sons and their wives and families on the street. My cousins, who belonged to the two couples, were still there as well. But they had graduated from peeing into the window wells to shooting pellet guns in her house into the ancient paintings hanging on the walls. These were painted by an ancestor who was a royally-appointed portrait artist in the 18th century. Holes went through beautifully-painted little fishing boats laid out at low tide on the North Sea, shepherds in mountain valleys, or through the pupils of a remake of Renoir's portrait of his own wife. Pellets went through the tiled ceiling of the rec room downstairs or through the curtains at the windows.

As I did at their age, they pretended to be spies and snuck around the adjoining family backyards to peer into everyone's windows. Sometimes, as I lay in bed, I heard the rustle of grass, and clothing and the whispered *shhhh*. Then, the profile of a head with a woolen cap would slowly rise up from the sill at my bedroom window. I saw the raised hands cupped against the glass. I saw who it was every time. I stayed frozen, looked from under my lids, and thought, *that one was from stately aunt, the other was from my blonde uncle.*

They were very disappointed. I never brought anyone home. I just slept or studied, burned a candle or two while studying, and listened to Moody Blues or Chuck Mangione. Sometimes, I played Ravi Shankar, and my mind swayed to his twangy slide dance on his exotic strings. My idle thoughts floated away with the beautiful bubbly notes that seemed to form a ladder to Heaven.

Jacob's ladder.

I wrestled with those same angels every day, but I had yet to win like Jacob. I kept trying over and over, but the abyss of depression sucked the energy right out of me. I was not in a good state, and it seemed anything could tip me further into an inability to function normally.

Giving in to the darkness, which was now so familiar, I stopped washing and brushing my hair again and covered it with a large woolen hat I had found at Lost and Found. I wore a large, hooded coat whether it was winter or summer. It screamed, *don't look at me.*

On that rare time when I did want someone to look at me, I went to Nonna's after a day of classes, cast off my hat and coat, washed my hair, put on make-up, and became one of those centerfold students *Playboy* magazine consistently glamorized.

The magazines were spread all over campus as were other publications of sex and mild pornography. *Sex on Campus. Sexy Girls on Campus. Hottest Girls on Campus. Jesus Christ Super Ham. Sex, Sex, Sex.*

Sex on campus was as much a part of the university as academia. Comic strips put out by the Engineering students were explicit pornographic images of super engineers being catered to sexually and crudely by females with breasts and behinds that were grossly exaggerated. These materials lay all around the lobbies, especially near the cafeteria where all the Engineering and Geology students hung out—who with very few exceptions were all male. They, too, habitually drew moustaches and beards on the beautiful faces of those who had sold their souls in magazines.

Every once in a while, a budding Feminist would tear them up, or burn them with her cigarette lighter. She'd go into the men's room and throw them into a toilet or in the men's urinal to sizzle to shards of floaters in the small remaining puddles of urine. Most of the male students missed the point and simply flushed them away or left them there for the cleaners to clear out of the drains.

One evening, I watched Dean Martin's Celebrity Roast[9]. Hugh Hefner was his guest and as usual, the jokes were actually quite funny. But I couldn't help but feel resentful. Torn.

---

[9]   Dean Martin, Celebrity Roast Hugh Hefner, NBC, September 21, 1973

"(Hugh)… started off with only two bunnies! But you know how bunnies multiply…"

"As a boy, he picked himself up out of the gutter, but unfortunately he left his mind there."

"…he gets so much action his is the only water bed with white caps…"

Guest comedienne, Audrey Meadows made wisecracks that in reality hit the issue on the head.

"Now the Women's Liberation Movement claims that Hugh Hefner portrays females solely as sex objects. They say he presents a totally false picture of what a woman is. Well, that's poppy cock. Hugh shows women as they really exist in the mind of every red-blooded American pervert."

Females were a commodity. As a girl went from class to class, these messages never ceased their underlying insidious humming. If I hadn't gone into hiding behind that bulky coat, greasy hair, and massive woolen hat, eyes would have lingered on my breasts, on my waist, and my lips. I would've been propositioned continuously. My behind would've been compared to the latest *Playmate* of the Month, rated between 1 and 10.

However, I took the risk of spending a night with three separate young men that first semester. Unfortunately, and surprisingly, each one of them came back afterward asking why I dropped them so quickly.

Didn't they know? I was *afraid* of them.

You see, I didn't want them in particular. It's just that they seemed nice. I just needed their touch, a kiss, or a look that said, "you're all right after all." Then I was gone before they found out how damaged and corrupt I was.

Life somehow continued on. But, it was so empty and so dysfunctional that, after exams at the end of the semester, I was so depressed I couldn't talk. At Christmastime, I left Nonna's for my family's box house east of Toronto. Why I thought I would get some positive feedback there, I don't know. I took my brooding soul back to Pap and Mam's. Two days in, Pap said, "Why are you here again. I thought you left."

Mam said, "Oh, don't say that."

He pointed at me and said, "Well, is she or isn't she out of this house?"

I ignored him. I loved him. I worshipped him.

This time I let Mam pour her own choice of sin over me. She took me shopping every single day buying this and that. Nothing too expensive, for if she did, Pap might notice it. On almost daily shopping trips, she spent hundreds of dollars a week on cheap clothing and knick-knacks that he'd never notice. She'd bought things at the Salvation Army, Goodwill, consignment shops, and flea markets. She packed the cupboards and closets full, and then she gave them away to make more room so that she could start all over again.

I wondered how Pap didn't complain about that.

But then you'd have to be around to notice.

One day Mam bought me a wig.

"Here, you look a mess. You should wear this wig."

It was red and shorter. I had been wearing a hat for so long that the sun hadn't touched my hair for months and it had turned dirty blonde. Mam didn't like it. I supposed a change would be nice.

I took that wig and bought some material to sew a Granny top. It was red with white trim and tiny white hearts. Not at all reflective of who I really was, but it reflected the wig. One day, while wearing the wig and the top, I bumped into an old classmate of mine on whom I'd had a crush. He was of tough farmer's stock, always wore a leather jacket, was older than I, and a jock, like me. Once while in the gymnasium getting ready for a basketball game, I decided to weigh myself. He sauntered over with that cockiness of his, a basketball clamped under his muscular right arm, to look at the numbers on the scale.

"A piggy I see. Look at those thighs." He pinched my left thigh. I wanted to clobber him. Another male measuring my body, cutting it up into dimensions to try and fit the *Playboy* model. I no longer had a crush on him.

Well, here he was, right in front of me, a few years later, attracted to me because I had a red wig on and a cutesy Granny top.

"What happened to your blonde hair?" he asked flipping one of the curls.

"It's a wig. My Mam bought it for me."

"It looks great on you."

We dated just for that Christmas holiday. He made me keep that red wig on all the time.

Just after Christmas, he went on a hunting trip with three of his guy friends. I insisted on going because I refused to be delegated to second class. I was getting rebellious against the norms of the day, and was sensitive about how I was being treated as a woman. I liked camping and hiking, why not have the decency of asking me at least?

"Am I just a little lady to push aside when you don't want sex, and you want to hang out with your guy friends?" I had argued. He gave me the stink eye but gave in.

We set out for the weekend, driving in a big truck to a campsite about four hundred miles northeast of Toronto. Once there, we slept with the woodstove going after enjoying a pan-fried dinner over a campfire outside. Everyone behaved like a gentleman for my sake. I told them to relax and just have fun as if I weren't around, as if I were a guy. We slept in four bunks between the five of us. I hardly slept because my red-wig loving guy was big. I was squeezed between him and the cold exterior wall. But that was my choice. I was the one who insisted on coming.

The next morning, we woke to a beautiful sunny wintry day. The sun was warm enough to melt the ice away. Water dripped off branches and the edge of the low roof of the cabin. We walked around only in our boots, sweaters, and caps. I didn't wear the wig but wore my hair bundled up under my woolen hat.

I walked around with a pellet gun while they carried shotguns. We slowly and carefully made our way deeper into the forest. They were hunting anything they could catch.

Along the hike, I spotted a porcupine up a tree. No one had fired a shot as yet, so I was proud to have found something. I aimed carefully and fired.

I hit the bulbous rump. The porcupine squealed and jumped, but hung on to the tree for dear life.

It sounded like a human being. I lowered the gun. *For crying out loud, what was I doing?*

I really thought that shooting a gun would ease my pain. That if I acted as aggressively as a guy, I might have the same confidence and respect from others. It hadn't worked as a girl or young woman. And there I was pretending I had it in me to kill a defenseless creature.

Well, if that was what hunting was about I wanted nothing to do with it. That porcupine had a voice, a heart that pumped blood, a brain that thought and knew fear. It knew pain. And it knew how to cry.

I looked closely at the gun. It was just a pellet gun. How much worse were other guns? I silently prayed, apologizing to God, and with a humbled heart, sent a prayer up to the porcupine. I promised I would never hurt another creature if I could help it. I promised to even stop along the highway and pull road kill off the pavement.

I followed the guys for the rest of the day. But I *accidentally* made a noise when a creature was in sight of their shot gun barrels. They figured out what I was up to eventually, and must have had a talk with my friend. They cut the weekend short, returning Saturday night. Along the way, he broke up with me. He didn't try to hide what he was saying from the others. And they didn't react except to sit stiffly looking ahead.

I knew they knew.

I went back to going with my dirty blonde, messed-up hair.

It was hard to find a niche as a woman, one where I felt comfortable. I refused the drug route and decided the free sex prescribed by *Playboy* certainly wasn't it. Pretending to be one of the guys didn't work, and ultimately didn't harmonize with my sensitive female energy. And it hurt my spirit that I was no longer in line with God.

I couldn't figure out how to get back.

• • •

1974

After New Year's, I returned to Nonna's and to campus. One morning after class, I saw a notice about modeling lessons. I thought that it had something to do with clay sculpture as I was studying sculpture and pottery. I stepped closer to read the notice. It was about fashion modeling.

I thought back to being 14 when a friend of the family had asked me to model and work at a couple of hairdressers' conventions in Toronto. They needed hair models, and I had, at the time, waist length white-blonde hair. Once, I went into an elevator to go up and get ready for another show when someone from the last lecture asked me what color my hair was.

I looked up at him, confused. I still had somewhat of a European accent. "Blohnde," I said, surprised.

"Yeah, but what is the name of the color."

"Blohnde. Just blohnde. But it gets lighter in de sun."

His jaw dropped, and his eyes had widened. "You mean that's your natural color? It's not a dye?"

I shook my head wondering what the big deal was. Many in the homeland had blonde hair, and so did Mam, Bettina, my little sister. No big deal.

But I learned that modeling in whatever form was extra money for me and a tremendous amount of fun. It was that *ham* in me again.

So, I called and made an appointment.

It was not as simple as I expected. I went all the way downtown Toronto one evening straight from campus and spoke to a gorgeous woman with perfect skin. She said that I would have to take lessons to learn how to care for myself. She eyed my hair, my nails, my skin. I was in bad shape. I never knew how bad, however, until I saw and studied her in comparison.

Like being as beautiful as the women I saw in *Playboy* magazine?

No, because she was dignified. In control. With perfect hair, perfect nails, perfect teeth. She demanded respect. There was no cleavage, no thigh, no come-hither looks. She was a lady. Something in me said, "I want to be like *that*."

I didn't have the money or time, so, I went back to my dysfunctional days at the university and finished the last semester of the first year.

My father didn't believe in girls attending the university. He had only agreed to give me a $1,000 towards tuition, but that was all he would give. "The rest would be wasted money," he said.

There were no student loans per se in the 70's. Loans depended on the combined income of your parents, and my father made too much money, so I wasn't eligible. I worked two jobs in the summer in preparation for the first year. I continued to work part-time at K-Mart evenings after class. But it still wasn't enough. Facing another summer of two jobs only to fall short in the fall, I decided to look for a corporation with a Commercial Art Department I could get into or work up to. Then I would continue my degree part-time evenings.

I discovered that Ontario Hydro or Bell Canada were the places to work. They had great benefits, paid well, and had a Commercial Art Department. One of my older friends managed to snag a job at Bell as a junior in the Commercial Art Department. I applied to both. Ontario Hydro called me in for an interview. I was told that I had to start at the bottom, as a mail clerk, but that I could work myself up the ladder and eventually they'd find a spot for me in their Commercial Art Department.

Great! I was ecstatic. I continued to live at Nonna's and worked at the main office in Toronto not far from my old church, St. Basil's. I climbed my way from mail clerk, to filing clerk, and to the photocopier, which, at the time, demanded a two-week diploma course to learn how to use the monster of a Xerox photocopy machine.

Then I happened to be sitting next to a young man at lunchtime. He had been hired straight from high school and was placed four levels above where I was.

I went to the Human Resources Department and asked to speak with someone. I could never get in. But the lady who managed me said that they always did that with the men. She agreed it was the right way. I looked at her in silent amazement.

"But I'm in my second year of university, and I'm still taking classes at night. I have more qualifications."

"Yes, but he'll more than likely make a career out of Ontario Hydro whereas you may not. After all, you're only a girl." She looked at me from her gray desk, through her gray horned-rimmed glasses with her gray eyes from a gray face surrounded by her gray hair. I remember looking around the office. We were surrounded by gray filing cabinets and gray walls. "You keep at it, it will be worth it," she added. "The benefits are incredibly good until you get married and want to leave."

Benefits. The magic word. So, I put my nose to the grindstone and continued to get up 6:30 in the morning to get to work at 8:30 then left at 4:30 to get to university for a 6:30 class. Then I waited up to an hour for the once per hour bus that dropped me a few blocks from the street. I got home around 11:30 at night. Then it started all over again the next day. I realized I was of no use to my Nonna but I felt I had no choice.

I did this for a year and a half, and then, suddenly, I fell very ill. The flu hit me so hard that I had to lay in a bath of cold water with ice cubes. After that, I lay in bed for days while Nonna struggled down the stairs with bowls of her magnificent homemade chicken soup. She continuously asked why I wanted to work so hard. That it wasn't natural. I couldn't explain. She really didn't understand.

I realized, however, that something had to give.

So, I had to give up university.

Temporarily, I promised myself.

It worked. I was slightly less overworked, got more sleep, and somehow, I worked my way up a few more levels at Ontario Hydro. Then I became a cashier at the Credit Union. No computers, just adding machines, and we counted the money with spit and fingers. Every Thursday was payday. Every single Ontario Hydro employee would come at some point during the day to cash their checks. And I would say that out of the thousand or so people I served each payday over the next year, none of them said they loved their work. They stayed for the benefits and a pension. But they were dying inside.

By this time, I felt the same way. It never occurred to me that we had a choice in life. A job was the ultimate goal for everyone. Security. Benefits. Savings. Pensions. I felt guilty wishing I didn't have to work in a corporate setting. I prayed for forgiveness for being so ungrateful and thanked God all over again for the work. Wasn't that what life was all about? Work you didn't like?

But it didn't feel right. So, I thought I'd add a challenge less demanding than classes were. I returned to that place where I had the interview with that perfect woman with the perfect hair, the perfect nails, and the perfect teeth.

I drained my account and signed up for a full year's course in Self-Improvement and Modeling.

It was a risk and, at the time, it was a very large investment. It proved to be one of the best things, and one of the most painful things, I ever did in my life.

• • •

I found I looked forward to the walk from College and University to just below Bloor and Yonge, regardless of the weather. It's what got me through the long, grinding day. The place became my hangout. Students were welcome to come and fool around with different make-up techniques or hang with the other students anytime they wanted.

I lapped it all up. I learned how to walk, stand, and sit. I learned that I had no idea what dressing well meant. I learned how to care for my skin, my hair, and my nails. I learned how to think positively, how to help a gentleman with his coat, how to get out of a car, how to walk down the stairs, and up the stairs.

I learned how to be a lady.

By the end of the year, I was back on track spiritually, mentally, and physically. I started going to an Episcopal church downtown Toronto with a co-worker. I also went and joined lunch time Mass at St. Basil's. I was starting to find a closer connection with God.

At the same time, I was well into my night classes. I loved my life. And now, near the end of the year's lessons, we learned how to model. We needed to know how to pose for a photograph, how to walk a runway, and how to speak in public. By this time, I had evolved into a bright, happy, confident young woman. I lost weight. I was proud as I walked and felt as if I now knew how to portray an image of a woman with respect. I rarely received the sleazy come-ons anymore. Oh, I still got attention, but it was no longer of the lower, cruder style.

I was still so naïve.

One day I saw a notice that a favorite performer of all time was taping a show up at one of the hotels north of Toronto. I don't know why, but I was intent on catching this man as mine. The woman in me wanted to nest, to love, and to be loved. It was like a disease over which I had no control.

So, I put laser beams on him. On the day of the taping, I called in sick (the one and only time I ever lied about sick time) and showed up on set an hour early. While I sat alone on the bleachers, he came in with his agent and sat a few rows up from me. It was like magic. I didn't have to do a thing. He came straight to me, asked me what I was doing there. I told him I was a big fan and reminded him of our meeting at a New Year's Eve dinner years before. He said he remembered, but I knew better. That person was long gone. I was a new version, and there was no resemblance.

I ended up being on camera with him. In all the episodes they taped that day, I was the woman he kissed before getting up on stage to sing next to the grand piano.

His voice was like an angel's. His amazing voice was a cross between Frank Sinatra and Tony Bennett. I told him I thought he was the most amazing male crooner. He wanted me to join him each time he performed in Toronto. He wanted me to come to Las Vegas with him. He wanted to do a lot with me.

It was tough staying up every Thursday, Friday and Saturday night until four in the morning. Especially difficult were Fridays, when I had to get up at 6:30 a.m. to get to work. But, I persevered. Until one night, he took me to his car and we talked.

"You know, you're very beautiful."

I smiled and blushed. I found it difficult to believe someone thought I was beautiful, especially someone as wonderful as him. I thought he was going to ask me something special. I was so much in love.

"You know you're smart, don't you?"

"Well, I'm well read, I guess you might say."

He leaned back. "Yes, but you're pretty stupid, too."

I froze. "Pardon?"

"My wife is having a baby."

"Your wife?"

"Yes, my wife."

"You never said you were married."

"Well, that's where you're stupid, right?"

I gathered my things and shakily got out of the car. It was winter, and I had left my coat in the nightclub, but I had my purse and keys with me. I went straight to my car and drove home. I was so distraught that I ended up driving so far under the speed limit that a police car did a U-turn to check me out. He flashed his lights at me to stop.

"Did you know you were driving under the speed limit." He could see that I was crying and softened up.

"Yes," I said.

"Well, don't. There's a limit as to how slow you can drive, too. Did you know that?"

"No." I looked ahead of the car and around the eight lanes. "But I didn't think it would matter. There's no one else on the road."

He let me go with a warning.

EIGHT

Like a Greek Christmas Tree

"I am under obligation to Greeks and non-Greek,
to learned and to simple."

(Romans 1:14, NEB)

A s graduate students, we were ready to do our first series of fashion shows. We were going to hit the runway for real!

Coincidentally, a hairdresser had called me for a Hair Dressers' Convention. He did my hair in the new full-perm look. I had to walk in the middle of this massive convention hall surrounded by people and shake my head and flip my hair back. It was big hair!

So, my hair was amazing for my first runway show. These shows were booked on weekends because almost all the students, like me, worked full-time. The first was way uptown. Early in the day, we were all getting ready with our make-up and hair.

One of the male volunteer stylists suddenly said, "So, who wants breakfast with me?"

I thought that was very nice of him, but I think I was the only naïve one there. Suddenly the excitement of the moment disappeared and there was tension in the air.

"Anyone?" he asked, looking around expectantly.

"I will," said the girl right at the end of the make-up table.

I turned to my friend next to me. "Does he mean just one of us?"

She leaned into me. "It means who wants to *sleep* with him?"

I looked at her askance. "Just like that? He'd take anyone? Why would anyone want to sleep with someone like that? That's so sleazy."

"It's what people do now," she said.

I was glad he didn't have to do much with my hair.

The show was amazing. The music was happy and bouncy and we twirled and strutted, showing off the clothing. I found, being the natural ham I was, that it was like a duck to water for me. I thrived on it.

One day, I read the notice on the bulletin board that the graduates were doing a paid gig for a *Greek Festival Fashion Show* up on the Danforth.

Money! I was going pro! Excitedly, I prepared for the Saturday evening festival and showed up at the appointed time to get ready. I found the address, but there were no unlocked doors. No other graduate showed up. I stood wondering what to do and looked for a phone booth when someone finally opened the door. A slightly buck-toothed, balding man poked his head out and looked at me. I explained what I was doing there and he motioned me inside. He led me through narrow halls and then through a larger one where there were banquet tables and a stage and runway set up. It seemed so dead. Then he led me into a small office.

"I'm very sorry, but we canceled the show."

I looked at him and blinked. How did the others get the update and I didn't? "Oh, that's too bad. Could you tell me why?"

He shook his head. He had a very thick Greek accent. "We didn't sell enough, you know, these little paper …"

"Tickets?"

"Yes." He clasped his hands together and watched my face.

"Oh, okay." I knew I would get a minimum honorarium I was to get if the show were canceled. I debated whether to ask him or wait to ask at the agency when he suddenly interrupted my thoughts.

"You know, you are like a beautiful Christmas tree with beautiful things hanging. Beautiful colors." He smiled. His cheeks wrinkled up. I looked at his stretched sweater and the comb-over on his head. Suddenly, something overwhelmed me that was so devastatingly tragic. Grievous. Heartbreaking. It came up like vomit. I broke down in tears and bawled.

I was embarrassed, but I couldn't stop. I saw him stiffen, mouth drop open, and his eyes widen. He pushed back his chair so fast that it fell backwards, and he lunged at me to hug me.

If I hadn't started crying, I would have been saved from another eight months of heartbreak. But this phase of my life was set into motion as if someone had pulled a switch on the railroad track and redirected my engine car.

He insisted on taking me on a horseback riding weekend.

I loved horseback riding. I wanted to do that. "I'm not interested in having any, you know. Otherwise, I won't go."

He covered his heart with his right hand as he was kneeling on one knee in front of me. "I give you my word I will be a gentleman. We will go to Sarnia and have two separate rooms. No funny business."

I looked through the tears and studied him. Could I trust him? And I so much wanted to go away for a weekend, to go horseback riding in the fresh air. Being cooped up in the Credit Union office one floor below ground from 8:30 to 4:30 was almost torture. During the shorter daylight hours in winter, I went for months not seeing daylight except for weekends. It was getting to me. A little jaunt to look forward to would get me through the next week.

I nodded and blew my nose.

It was set. I met him downtown the next Saturday morning and he drove us to Sarnia. When we got there, I spotted a horseback riding sign.

"Oh, there's one!" I said excitedly.

He shook his head and scowled as he drove.

"Are we going to another one?"

"We are not going horseback riding. I don't have enough money. I didn't have the show. It was the way I was going to make fast money. Now I only have just enough for gas and the motel. Maybe some breakfast."

I looked at him and my insides sank. I didn't know what to say. He was a man. I had to weigh my words carefully, respectfully. "Well, it's a beautiful day for a nice drive," I numbly offered, trying to cheer him up.

So, we drove around a bit and finally found a motel. "Are we going in already?" I asked.

He motioned with his hand towards the motel. "Yes, we drop off our things and maybe we sightsee some more."

So, he checked us in. I had never gone to a motel before in my life but knowing that he was getting two rooms made me feel my dignity was covered. The man at the check-in counter would see that I was a lady.

He came back, and we collected our overnight kits. I followed him to the rooms and walked into the first one that he opened. I put my little suitcase on the bed, surprised when he put his on the floor. He started taking his coat off.

"Aren't you going to your own room?" I asked, getting a little nervous. *My goodness, what will that gentleman at the check-in think of me?*

He raised his shoulders and hands and looked perturbed with me. "I don't have enough money. What do you want me to do?"

And so, he forced himself on me. Could I call this rape? I came out of my own free will. But I trusted him and took him at his word. I came on the condition there would be no "funny business." I walked right into the trap. I had made my bed.

Now I felt I was claimed and had no choice. Those three one night stands in university had left me feeling dirty. I no longer could bare the feeling.

Pretty soon, he wanted to move in together. He found a one-bedroom apartment in Malton. I was able to take the Go Train from there to work. He told the landlord that he had twenty years' experience as a carpenter.

"Good. That's what we like to hear," he said.

So, we signed a lease. A lease I would pay along with a commitment to a man I would support. A man who went from loving my beauty to claiming I was a painted whore. He molded me into an overweight, depressed blonde version of a Greek mate.

At work, I told the girls of the weekend, and they anxiously followed my romantic story. I lied to them. I also lied about moving in together. I said we had eloped and gotten married. I was so ashamed that we were living together. I went so far as to change my name to his.

In the meantime, he took my money and bought gifts for my family to charm them. He schmoozed them to the point that my Dad gave him a car when his was repossessed.

We were having coffee at Pap and Mam's when suddenly we saw two men in the driveway. My Greek friend went out to talk to them. Then I heard arguing. Pap, Mam and I looked out the window in time to see the one man pulling out of the driveway with his car. The other man was in their car in the middle of the street with the engine running. My friend stopped the car from leaving by standing in front of it, holding it back with both hands on the front hood. The driver got out and held a gun at him, threatening to shoot if he didn't get out of the way. He refused and banged on the hood of the car. Then the two of them got into a fist fight. I watched that gun, my heart pounding, and I heard myself say, "Please, God, don't let anyone get hurt."

Then the other driver got out of their car. The two of them punched, kicked, and then threw my friend over to the side of the road. Then they both hopped into the two cars and burned their tires on the road.

I watched my friend struggle to his feet. He was covered in blood from a bloody nose and he had a cut over one eye. He laughed as he flipped his comb-over back in place. I thought, *good for him. He's a scrapper.*

When he walked back into the kitchen, Pap slapped him on the back. "Hey, you took it like a man!"

• • •

A few days into that work week, a check came through that he had forged my name on drawing on my account. I happened to be hand-filing checks and there it was. A check of mine I hadn't written. My heart skipped a beat. I went over and checked the massive print-out books to verify my balance. There were several withdrawals on it that I hadn't made. *Goodness gracious!* That evening, I asked him about the checks and about him forging my name.

He got angry. He threatened to punish me because I was being selfish.

"You are my woman," he yelled. "You shouldn't question me, I am the man. I need money, too. What do you expect me to do? Sit in this small apartment all day?"

I looked at him confused. Yes, he was the man. Yes, I shouldn't question him. Yes, I should obey him. But why did it feel so wrong?

I made the mistake of raising *that* subject. "It would be so much better for you if you had a job."

Oh, Lordy. He bunched his fists and stomped towards me. I took a step back. He put his face into mine. "If I were in Greece, I would show you what a man does when his woman talks back."

At least he didn't hit me.

But then, he told me he wanted me off the pill. He wanted a baby. *A baby!*

Let me interject here. In this day and age, no one seems to blink an eye when people decide to live together, or even have a baby before marriage. As Bettina and I grew up, Pap always told us to live with someone for at least six months before getting married. He got that logic from reading an article in *Playboy*. Then he taught us something which I thought I understood at the time.

"You have to see if you are sexually compatible, first. Your mother and I, well, we never were. But we were so young, what did we know? Now, if we had lived together, I would've found out in time."

Bettina and I blindly took it as sage advice, not fully understanding what he referred to. Never mind about what that meant for Mam. And us. We would never have been born.

So, I was living in sin with someone for the first time. But Pap's advice about the six months was not done yet and this guy already wanted a baby. I really didn't know that much about sexuality. My focus wasn't healthy enough to face the subject in any way. It was so easy to pretend and act as if there was no such thing in this world.

So dutifully I stopped taking the pill.

Then my Dad gave us some money as if we had gotten married. We put a down payment on a fifty-acre farm near St. Catherine's with a dilapidated old farm house. We celebrated a Greek Easter weekend with a lamb roast and about forty members of the Toronto Greek community.

Land. Real estate.

I must admit, I thought I was in it for the long haul. So, I bought right into it. I walked those fifty acres and thanked God for them. I could almost kiss the ground.

Then my friend said that he found a job near the farm, and that he was going to stay in the old farmhouse during the work-week as it was closer than our apartment. Then I saw checks come in from a lumber yard, a hardware store, and then … my account was overdrawn. I waited until the weekend for him to come back to say we'd run out of money. And where was the money he earned?

"Are you questioning me again? Me, the man? What do you think I live on? I need to eat and keep warm."

"Yes, but what did you buy at the lumber store?"

"What? You are now a detective? Is this a police state, now? I *le*ft Greece because of that!"

"I thought you left because you did something bad?" Sometimes I was so naïve I had no idea what I was saying. I didn't mean to be sarcastic.

He became really angry, and that familiar thunder came into the apartment. I started crying and apologized. Then he threw up his hands. "Why am I being dragged down by this woman, who does not respect me or want me to have a nice life? I am building something special, woman. Do I have to tell you every single little thing I do?!" He grabbed the collar of my blouse. "Now you ruined a surprise. Are you proud of yourself?!"

Guilt. I had done the wrong thing again.

I pulled away, ran to the bedroom, and cried. I heard the door slam. I knew he would go back to the farm.

I got on my knees by the bed and prayed. I prayed for forgiveness for being such a klutz. For being so picky and questioning. And I also prayed to God to fix the situation because it was getting out of hand and I had no money left. Then I prayed asking Him to show me what was to come because I needed to know there was light at the end of the tunnel. Then I would be content.

All of a sudden, a baby cried outside my door. My heart dropped. It was a direct answer to me from God. I knew that if I stayed I was going to have a baby.

I knew there was no future with him. How was I to care for and support a child and this man on my own? There was no pregnancy leave at work at the time.

That week I had to force checks through from my account. Now I was officially overdrawn. I thought about it and realized I could simply carry it as an *IOU*, a minus on my tally sheet at the end of day. But by the end of the week, I owed over $2,000.

Finally, someone noticed it. I was called into the supervisor's office.

I sat there shaking. I had gained forty pounds and looked weary from worry and lack of sleep. My supervisor gave me two choices: either they charged me, and I was fired, or I pay them back within three months.

I looked askance. I was now a criminal, and I didn't see it coming. How had that happened?

I called Pap and explained. And that Saturday, when my Greek friend returned from the farm, Pap was waiting for him in the little kitchen of the apartment, sitting beside me.

He walked in and saw Pap. He stopped, and his demeanor changed from "the man of the house" to groveling in front of an elder. He went over to us and I slid over a seat to make room for him.

"Now," Pap started, elder-like. "I understand that you've been spending a lot of money. Money my daughter didn't have. She was threatened with being charged with robbery. What do you think about that?"

My friend sat, eyes-wide. He fiddled around with his comb-over. He shook his head and shrugged. "I didn't know."

Pap motioned to me. "My daughter has been trying to tell you that there wasn't enough money."

My friend wouldn't even look at me. "I didn't know it was like that."

I jumped in, "Yes, you did!"

Pap put up a hand to shut me up. Then he looked over at him. "My daughter is in trouble because of you." My friend pursed his lips.

Pap looked at me. "What do you want to do? Do you still love him?"

Love him? I never loved him. "No," I said simply.

My friend looked over, but I didn't meet his look of pain. I would feel guilty again.

Pap straightened up in his chair and looked at me. "Well, then. I'll help you move your things. You're coming home."

And that was that. I took all the furniture, except for what he came with, because I was still paying a loan on it all. He complained later that I only left a few sticks of furniture. Then he called to say he wrote a sad letter to his mother, and she would be heartbroken. She was looking forward to meeting me, a new daughter-in-law.

Daughter-in-law? He never proposed.

• • •

I had gotten off the Go Train and was about twenty feet away from my little Kay car when I heard running behind me. I turned to look to see who it was. I immediately turned right around and held up my free hand. My heart jumped.

"What are you doing here?" I yelled.

My Greek friend lunged at me and grabbed one of my arms before I could pull away. "You are my woman. I have nowhere to live. You expect me to live on the streets."

"You have friends, stay with them." I looked around to see if people would help. Most had arrived at their cars; a half a dozen people were on their way. Only one young woman looked over. She turned away.

He raised his other hand, palm up, and shook his head. "Nobody wants me to stay more than a night. I have run out of friends."

I forced myself to calm down. I said a quick little prayer but wasn't sure if God would hear me. I hadn't prayed, not since leaving that apartment. Part of the shame of it all. Tough to face my mistakes once again.

"Why did you have your father come over? It was important to me that he liked me. I deserve respect. You don't. You are nothing but one of those ladies at night."

"A whore?"

He shook his head. I saw that he hadn't shaved for a long while.

"You mean a prostitute?"

He nodded. "A prostitute."

"Then why are you here? Why did you come all the way out of Toronto like this if I'm a prostitute? I'm not worth it. You're lucky to get rid of me." I finally felt him relax his grip.

I yanked my arm away from his grip and raced over to a phone booth. I slammed the bi-fold door shut and picked up the phone. I needed change. "Oh my God," I mumbled as I searched the bottom of my purse. I looked up in time to see him a few feet away.

I swung around and pressed my body against the bi-fold. I found a dime, put it into the phone, and dialed the shop which was just about four blocks away.

My Greek friend pounded at the bi-fold door and then at the side glass of the booth. I stared at him while I listened to the ring on the other end.

"You calling your father?" He shook his head in a circular way and placed both palms up on the glass and leaned in, resting his forehead onto the dusty glass. "What can he do, huh?"

He slammed the glass with his right palm. "In Greece, they would let me beat you because you are not faithful to me."

"Majestic Auto Body, how can I help you?"

"Hi, I need my Dad, quick!" She knew who it was right away. "I haven't been unfaithful. I'm not seeing anyone," I yelled at him through the doors.

"No, you went to bed with me. You are mine now. Women like you, their husbands tear every piece of clothes in their closets. To make a point. You don't do this to me."

"Hello?"

"Pap, he's here!"

"He's here," my Greek friend mimicked.

"Who is?"

"HIM! I'm at the Go Train station in the phone booth, and he's right outside in my face."

Pap hung up. I looked over at deep brown and black eyes staring at me. His overbite made him more comical than dangerous.

"Pap's on his way," I croaked.

"You know you are not pretty at all? You think you are beautiful. You are only a prostitute with make-up and hair and clothes and high heels." He straightened up and stepped to the bi-fold and pushed it in the middle with his forefinger. I put both hands on the inside of it. He rattled the door.

The early evening sun burst through the clouds and bathed his face in light. He squinted his eyes and stood up. He grabbed a package of cigarettes from his denim jacket and lit one. He pointed it at me. "I will talk to your father. He will understand me." He pointed to his chest with his other finger. "I am a man, and men understand other men."

I looked over at the road and saw Pap's rusty car racing into the parking lot.

My Greek friend read my face and looked over.

Pap pulled up to the phone booth and got out. He left his door open and came towards my friend chuckling. "Hey, man. What are you doing here? Go back to where you came from."

My friend turned his back to me, but I stayed in the phone booth. "I want to talk to her. This is not right. She is my woman and she must come back."

"She doesn't want to talk to you. Man, you gave your best shot, and it didn't work. Move on. You're a Greek playboy. There are a lot of fish in the sea."

My friend didn't like that. I think because it hit the nail on the head. He stepped up to my father and pushed him with his chest. Pap laughed.

"Ho, ho, ho. You think you frighten me? You can't intimidate me. I'm not that easy. Go, man. Just go." Pap stood in his coveralls, his hands, and part of his face covered in grease. He looked around the lot. "Where's the car I gave you, man?"

My friend pointed towards the middle. There were few cars left. Pap turned and motioned to his car.

"Go, and leave my daughter alone."

My friend shook his head. "She's mine. She comes with me."

"No, she isn't. She's going back to my place." Pap stepped closer to him. My Greek playboy took the last step, almost touching Pap.

I picked up the phone and called 911. In the meantime, Pap grabbed him by the arm and dragged him toward the car.

The police answered, and in my frightened voice, I explained what was happening. The community was small, and in those days the shop got all the business from the local police squad. My uncle and Pap had been fixing their police cars for years now.

"Is he hitting your father?" asked the constable.

"No."

"Does it look like your father needs help?"

Pap was cool as a cucumber. "No."

"Okay, just keep us posted."

"Oh, okay," I said. I hung up. It took another twenty minutes, but my friend finally gave in. He came towards me, but when Pap grabbed him, he put up his hands.

"I just want to say one last thing," he said. So, Pap let him come to the phone booth. He put his face right to the glass and stared at me like he wished me dead. Then he said, "Because of you, I don't have the farm."

"I signed it over to you."

"You need to pay the mortgage payments."

"You only wanted me to be your cash cow. You work for a change."

"You are an ugly woman."

I drilled my eyes into his and said, "I know."

He stood back surprised.

"I know," I repeated.

Slowly, in the setting sun, I watched him walk to his car again, taking out his keys. He got in, looked back at me, then glanced at Pap before starting the car and drove out of my life.

Years later, I saw a hair transplant ad in the *TV Guide*. It was him.

• • •

I spent the next many months in the familiar abyss of severe depression. I couldn't breathe. I had to force my eyes to stay open, and I wanted to fade away. I knew there was something wrong with me but I didn't know how to fix it. One morning, I numbly watched the waters of the lake go by while riding the Go Train. I prayed to God that I just wanted to die. "Oh, God, you must be so tired of my prayers," I whispered to my reflection in the glass.

That's when I heard that Voice again.

Look up, it said gently.

I looked up. I saw the sky. I saw how blue it was and I noticed for the first time the beautiful grand puffy clouds. It was a brilliant summer morning. The water sparkled, and the lights tickled the back of my eyes. I felt a grace start to pour through and whisper something that gave me hope.

You don't belong here. You are from up here.

I was both startled and calmed by the Voice. I continued staring at the sky.

What did that mean?

You will bump into someone at the station who you think does not like you. You must start a conversation with her.

I thought it was a very strange thing for the Voice to say. I was briefly tempted to think I was crazy? I thought of medical conditions I read about hearing voices, but these referred to unhealthy voices, at times extreme. But how was a gentle loving Voice unhealthy?

At Union Station, I felt an urge to walk to the other car before exiting. There I stepped off and bumped into a tall redhead. I worked with her, believed she gossiped about me, and that always distressed me. I had a lot to hide, many lies about getting married and divorcing my Greek friend, almost being charged with a criminal offense. She intimidated me and was one aspect of the job that made each day a grueling ordeal for me.

"Hi, how are you? Fancy meeting you here!" I said.

She turned to me in surprise. Then she responded so delightfully.

"I'm fine, how are you!?" She smiled broadly.

We chatted all the way to the subway and to the door of the Credit Union. And then she said something that shook me.

"I always thought you didn't like me."

I looked at her. "I thought you didn't like *me*!"

"Why would you think that?" She looked surprised

"Well, because sometimes I'd see you talking about me with the others."

She giggled. "Oh, no! It's because we're all dying to know how you do your make-up. You look so beautiful all the time. You're so elegant in all your movements. And your skin is so perfect. We all feel like plain Janes compared to you!"

I learned a valuable lesson that day.

Not only did I learn it's too easy to imagine negative things that simply weren't true, but also, when you hear His voice, He always follows up with something that confirms it was Him. Something tangible. Something you can't dispute. And however insignificant a *chance* meeting on a train station platform and conversation may seem to another, it proved to me that what God had said just *before* that also had to be true.

The concept of not belonging *here* put my life into a perspective that was livable. Depression finally lifted, and things started looking up.

NINE

You're Just a Girl

1976

I found a new Buddy. He had a 23-foot Shark, the same sailboat that Pap had when I was young. He was a member of the same yacht club, too. So, my bud and I raced Wednesday nights and Sunday afternoons, sometimes against Pap. After a few months, I moved in with him. We had a healthy social life. Thursday nights became our night for a few drinks at the small Waldorf Hotel not far from where we lived on the corner of Bloor and Huntley Streets. Friday nights, after packing for the weekend, we would drop by a liquor store for a bottle of rum and then have a *Frank Vetere's* Chicago-style, deep-dish pizza for supper before heading out for the boat.

I loved my life. It was clicking along very nicely. I lost over 40 pounds and felt great. I even bought a small cottage lot up near Parry Sound with plans to eventually build a chalet-style home. I wanted to live off the earth, what we now call, *living off the grid*. I had plans.

One day, I happened to be in an elevator at Ontario Hydro with someone who normally took the executive elevator. He was very high in the chain of command. He looked down at me and said, "Who are you?"

I told him who I was. "And I work at the Credit Union, but I'm still waiting to get into the Commercial Art Department. I was promised when I was hired that, eventually, I'd get a position as one of your artists."

"You'll never get in there."

I leaned back against the elevator wall and gripped the hand bar. "Why's that?"

He looked down at his $500 shoes and smiled. "Well, first of all there are only 14 artists in that department and no one leaves unless they retire or die. Then there are others who are more qualified than you. And, next, you're just a girl. We wouldn't waste our time and money on someone who will get married and leave to have children."

I handed in my two-week notice that afternoon. Pap needed help to take their 42-foot Yankee Clipper down the Intracoastal Waterway to the Bahamas anyway. He'd already asked me for help, so it was a no-brainer. I was going to take some time off to rethink this life of mine.

You see, I felt God tug at me, telling me that being with my bud was not what He preferred. But stupidly I argued that my bud was such a nice young man and I loved our life together. I felt it wouldn't be right to break his heart. We were bound together forever now. Wasn't that the way it worked? I told God I felt He was asking too much, and I didn't want to hurt him.

I was so naïve about the depths of God's love and His intervention in our lives. Who was I to say no to God, right? So, He literally yanked me out of a dead-end job and plunked me into a form of boot camp laced with exhilarating and mind-blowing interventions. He would shake me till my teeth rattled and stretch me to my limits. He'd frightened the heck out of me in order to make me more receptive to His voice.

Which is *exactly* what He did.

TEN

God's Nautical Boot Camp

"But Jonah set out ... to escape from the Lord.
...But the Lord let loose a hurricane, and the sea ran so high
in the storm
that the ship threatened to break up."

(*Jonah 1:3-5. NEB*)

1977

We left Toronto far later than was considered safe, but Pap had no choice. He had committed to delivering a boat, a center cockpit, from the Toronto International Boat Show to Nyack, New York where he then would pick up his own *Yankee Clipper 42*.

The day after the boat show ended, the September winds picked up. Pap, Mam, my little sister, and I, loaded everything onto the boat. By the afternoon, we had the masts lowered and strapped down along the length of the boat. The winds continued to increase.

We left Canada just as the winter storms were brewing.

The first leg was crossing Lake Ontario's relatively shallow waters which can become some of the roughest sailing in the world. The difficult chop put a tremendous amount of stress on us and the boat. The crazy, harsh, cold whistling winds cut into our eyes and face. Up in the center cockpit our bodies were arcing and bouncing insanely.

After hours of grueling motoring, we finally made the cluster of lights at Oswego.

The rain wouldn't stop, but somehow, we managed to grab a bit of shut-eye before registering to go through the Erie Canal lock system.

As the gray, wet day wore on, we went from one lock to another, slowly rising in altitude, travelling deeper into New York state and further away from Canada.

Soon we got into the rhythm, hooking our lines around poles embedded into the cement walls and watching the boat rise slowly while the Lockmaster let in the waters through baffles. Then the lock doors would swing open into another lock, close behind us, and we'd start the whole process again. Up and up into the land of New York State towards Lake Oneida.

Once we were enclosed in the final lock, something didn't feel right. Even the roar of the rushing waters was different. I stood holding the line at the stern and as we rose, I felt a different tug on the line. I looked down and saw a rush of water swoop and twirl angrily between where I was standing and the wall. Slowly it pushed the stern back and back. I knew that the more the stern pushed away from the wall the closer the bow spit of the boat, 42 feet away, was pushed towards the wall.

This was not good.

I looked over to the gate and saw roiling waters bubbling up from only one baffle. The Lockmaster wasn't aware. The rushing water spewing from only one side created a whirlpool affect with such strength that the boat totally overpowered me. My line started to tighten like a vice grip around my hands. It started scraping and tearing at the skin as I let go of it little by little. I stood with my feet glued to the toe rail and leaned back with no effect. Again, I looked over at the bow spit and saw it slowly rocking towards the concrete wall. Instinctively I knew if the bow came in contact with the wall it would buckle like dry match sticks. The crews on the other boats stood by helplessly watching.

"PAP!" I screamed. He was somewhere down below. Then I yelled at Mam. "GET THE BOAT HOOK AND PUSH!" She dropped her useless bow line and frantically looked for the boat hook. I looked over to the other side of the raised cockpit and saw the end of the boat hook sticking out along the other side deck. I motioned with my chin. "THERE!"

At that moment, Pap's head poked out of the companionway and looked over at us. He saw that the boat was at a dangerous angle and quickly jumped out.

"Pull at the line," he instructed.

"I am!"

He shuffled along the deck toward me and grabbed the line. "Here, give it to me." He was confident that he would be able to pull the stern back toward the wall and straighten the boat out. Then I watched his face go from quiet confidence to alarm.

I looked up to the housing where the Lockmaster was sitting, still unaware of what was happening. I yelled, jumped, and waved my arms. He wasn't looking over at us. He was watching further up the lock system.

"JESUS!" I cried loudly. Mam ran to the side of the bow spit, I hurried over to help. The two of us pushed on hook and broom. The broom snapped and the boat hook slipped off the slimy concrete wall and bent. The bow spit railing was inches away from the wall when I looked back at Pap's purple face. He couldn't do it. The last bit of rope now looped over his strong, thick baby finger. He leaned over the water so far I thought he would fall in.

Suddenly, I saw what he saw. The boat he's delivering ruined. Smashed and twirling free in the contained lock, swiping at and destroying all the other boats imprisoned with us in the small lock, twirling like a crazy destructive corkscrew.

All those boats.

Pap screamed. Something came out of his mouth that sounded like it had come out of a primeval jungle two hundred thousand years ago.

The soundwave of his jungle cry bounced and echoed off those four concrete walls, the other boats, and their watching crew. It shot up through the lock, curled over the lock gate itself, and finally jangled the ears of the Lockmaster. His face swiveled toward us. His eyes widened, and his mouth dropped open. Suddenly I heard bells ringing. Slowly, the angry, dangerous monster of a whirlpool settled down.

That was day one.

There must have been a lesson here. I saw my idol, my father, finally meet his match. He was human after all and I saw him suddenly in a slightly different light. Something was shifting.

• • •

I watched the shores of Lake Oneida go by. The rains had stopped. We now headed to the other end of the lake, and from there we would continue on along the Hudson River. It would be a simple journey, following the river's meandering shoreline to Troy, Albany, and south to Nyack, New York. By the time we would get to Nyack, Pap's boat would be ready, shipped in from Taiwan. He would hand over the center cockpit we were delivering.

Just before the little town of Waterford the rains came back.

Suddenly, along a very quiet and narrow stretch of the river, the diesel engine exploded with a pop and a bang. Pap slowed down, and we quickly tied up to the side. Thick, black smoke billowed out from down below. As he climbed into the bowels of the boat, everyone knew he'd do his magic and somehow make it right.

In the meantime, knowing that my little sister would appreciate a break, Mam and I went on a mission to find milk. We kept our foul weather gear on, as it was raining heavily. We climbed up the slippery, grassy incline near the boats and accessed a small bridge to a small dirt road.

We suddenly heard barking on the other side of the bushes on our right. I hurried forward to look around the bushes. Two black pit bulls with studded collars ran straight for us. I shot a glance at Mam and my sister. They had spotted the dogs and stood frozen, eyes wide with fear.

My heart sent out a quick call for help. I felt confident enough to face whatever was coming, even if I had to be mauled until help arrived. Somehow, I *knew* I would be fine.

I pushed my little sister behind me as I kept my eyes on those oncoming dogs. About ten feet away, they slowed down, lowered the front of their bodies as if to hug the ground, and then split, one on one side of us, the other on the opposite side. They growled softly, menacingly, baring their teeth, their raised noses crunched up and twitching with a quest for blood. Their solid muscular bodies twitched in anticipation of an attack. I sensed they were just about to jump.

Suddenly, this monstrous roar formed inside me. I bent over and belted out venom filled with the strength to kill. I lunged first at one and quickly at the other, growling like a lion. Startled, they bounced back and looked at each other. I whispered to Mam to take my sister and walk away, slowly and quietly. I cast a quick glance back to see them shuffling down the shoulder of the road.

Suddenly, teeth grabbed at my arm. My foul weather gear and sweaters underneath prevented them from puncturing my forearm too deeply. I kicked hard at the dog, while roaring and yanking my arm away. The dog squealed. I crouched down into a fighting stance, knees bent, arms out, hands ready to grab. When I sensed both of them gathering their resolve to attack again, I roared for the second time, and then lowered my chin. I growled quietly and menacingly.

The two dogs stared at me. Slowly, they backed away, then turned to run back to a house in the distance. My body was vibrating. Once I knew they weren't coming back, I straightened up but continued to watch them. My feet rooted victoriously into the ground until they finally disappeared behind the house.

It was only our second day.

On the third day, the late September skies darkened and the rain came down in buckets. We were just coming up to Schenectady when the Hudson started to rise alarmingly fast. By the time night fell, we couldn't see where the shore of the Hudson ended or where the highway that followed it began. If we got too close to the shoreline, we would do serious damage to the hull and keel of the boat.

Once night fell, I stood on the bow with a bright arc light, rocking and swinging the beam from one side to the other so Pap could get his bearings. He watched the depth sounder carefully to make sure we always had water under our keel. Suddenly, the river narrowed, and we were caught up in such a strong current that Pap had trouble controlling the boat. At one point, the current caught the stern of the boat. Completely helpless now, we raced sideways in the whitewater river. My arc light caught the stark profile of a bridge around a bend in the widened crazy water up ahead. We weren't staying in the center. We were going to hit the bridge abutment and the shoreline. Suddenly, out of the blackness, a massive downed tree came into view. Our hull scraped over its submerged branches. The wind roared, almost drowning out the groaning diesel engine. I couldn't hear anything Pap said from where he was bent over the wheel, so I moved closer and stood on the top of the main cabin, carefully grabbing at the rocking lifelines and teak handles along the side of the elongated cabin. I still couldn't hear him. The wind sucked the words right out of his mouth.

I couldn't tell what he was saying. His face was lit by the light of the depth sounder and it showed how the last couple of days had worn him down. Then I realized what he was saying. There were some rocks on the charts that would now be submerged under the higher waters. I was to stand right at the bow and aim the light slightly into the river to see if I could see them beneath the surface. We were still going sideways. I closed my eyes briefly. Boy, did I pray. I prayed we'd get that boat straightened out, and we would survive this ordeal without a scratch. Then I heard a new roar from the engine. I opened my eyes and saw that Pap was hard on the wheel. He had shifted into reverse and was now able to straighten out the bow.

Suddenly, an extra-large rolling wave bounced back from a rocky outcropping beside a boathouse that was almost completely under water. As the wave roared back on itself against the port side of our bow, it forced us toward the center of the bridge. With another crack and roar, I looked back and saw the small building let go and start floating behind us.

We raced past the submerged streets of Schenectady. Emergency vehicle lights flashed everywhere. It was a little easier to see what was going on around us because of the lights of the town and bridges, but it only showed us the danger of the storm. It was a major flash flood.

After a while, the rains subsided and the waters, still high and strong, became calmer as the river widened. Finally, we felt the mighty waters of Troy, and then we hung on as the river pushed us all the way to Albany. By that time, dawn was approaching and the waters deepened. By pointing our bow almost into the current, we were able to crawl sideways into the relative safety of the Albany Yacht Club, one of the oldest yacht clubs in the United States.

Naively, I thought the worst had come and gone.

But God wasn't finished with this boot camp yet...

• • •

Nyack, New York. A small town north of Manhattan. We docked at a large marina and handed over the boat. Then we unpacked the boat and dragged our things around to another wharf where Pap's new boat was tied up. We stayed for two weeks while we worked on getting the boat ready for the trip ahead. The aft cockpit was larger than the center cockpit of the model boat we'd delivered. We settled cozily into our surroundings. Each one of us finally unpacked our things and claimed our little territories within the floating world. Side bunk, drawers, and shelf for me on the port side. The bunks became couches to sit on during the day. My little sister slept in the forepeak cabin, while Pap and Mam slept in the main cabin.

Tiny, dead cockroaches lay in the crevices of the boat. We joked about them, saying we imported cockroaches straight from Taiwan. We removed the plywood sheets nailed into the beautiful teak decks, and we cleaned, organized, and stocked up. The masts and rigging went up, and we had time to teach my little sister some lessons. We also did a lot of fishing. We wandered into town, at times, and shopped and generally had a good rest.

Finally, the day came to untie the boat and head out again, motoring into the center of the great Hudson. We put up sails for the first time and we fell in with the sweet rhythmic song of the bow hitting the small waves of the great Hudson River.

Hours later, we sailed under the George Washington Bridge, and then, finally, with great anticipation saw the Statue of Liberty.

I looked as we slowly made our way through water traffic. It had been almost twenty years since seeing this gracious lady for the first time. At that time, we arrived as poor immigrants not knowing a word of English. Not knowing what life in the new world was going to throw at us. And here we were, on a beautiful boat heading down to the southern climes, waving at her for a second time.

• • •

After tying up at a club opposite Manhattan, I took a shuttle boat for a day's visit into Manhattan. Everywhere I walked, men whistled and made kissing sounds at me. One person looked at me and came over to tell me that a young, blonde pretty girl alone in New York was asking for trouble. I couldn't imagine anyone wanting to hurt me. Innocently I wandered everywhere my heart led me. Then when I reached Times Square, I understood the warning.

The sexual revolution, spawned by the likes of Hugh Hefner and *Playboy*, had taken a solid hold on New York City. There were strip clubs and more strip clubs. The streets were filthy. Everywhere I looked there were signs that read: *Burlesque, Gorgeous Girls and Nude Models, Mature Adults Only, 10$ Complete Nudity, Live Nude Girls 25 Cents, Erotic Joy of Letting Go, Topless Go-Go, Linda Lovelace Deep Throat, Hard Core XXX for Adults Only.* I felt very disturbed by what I saw. And the men who hung around these places all had an intense, dark look about them. They looked at me as if I stepped off the stages inside these places, and they undressed me with their eyes. They didn't see *me*.

The 1970's in New York was not a pretty time. I wondered if Hugh Hefner was proud of what he had done.

• • •

The next day, we allowed ourselves to have dinner at a seaside restaurant along the inner shore of one of New Jersey's smaller rivers. We were sitting in a restaurant with other boaters when something told me to look over. We sat at a large window overlooking boats at anchorage. I watched a particular boat. It sat as quietly as the rest of the boats, but then its anchor slipped and it started dragging its stern down river with the current. I rushed out of the restaurant while I yelled out that a boat was slipping. I hoped that the owners of the boat were in the restaurant to hear.

I clambered down to our inflatable, started the outboard motor, and screamed towards the helpless boat. It was heading straight out to the ocean. But there were about six boats in the way.

I managed to get to the boat. I searched for the key and ignition at the helm. It had an inboard diesel engine like Pap's, and, thank God, they had left the key. I turned the key, and the engine came to life. Quickly, I put it into gear in time to prevent hitting another boat. Slowly I went into reverse, then headed in another direction to take a wide curve around the other boats. I took it back upriver to its previous location. By that time, the owners of the boat caught up in their dinghy and took over the helm. I helped them drop anchor again and this time waited to make sure they had a solid grip.

We headed out to open sea again very early in the morning and headed straight to Cape May. There we would take the Delaware River up to the C&D Canal that connected the Delaware River to the beautiful Chesapeake.

However, about halfway there, with the boat hard on a starboard tack in strong winds, I was in the head when the windward shroud above my head, which was screwed into the deck, snapped and tore away like a bullet. The boat screamed, clanged, and knocked about. I could hear the swish wail of the end of the shroud as it shot through the air into the sky above the masthead.

Minutes before going down below to answer the call of nature, I was standing precisely at that spot. I held onto that metal shroud as I swung and dipped with the rocking boat and watched Atlantic City go by slowly in the distance. I would've been blinded or hurt quite badly. I sent up a surprised prayer of thanks.

Pap immediately put the nose of the boat into the heavy winds, so the pressure was off the mast. The sails had to come down instantly, but I was still down below. I struggled off the toilet and clambered out of the head as the boat heeled over. I scrambled over everything that poured out of the cupboards. My feet were almost on the side bulkheads and shelving as I fought my way out to help lower the sails.

Pap was able to right the boat. With the sea pounding our starboard side, we scurried toward Atlantic City with a wobbling main mast like a duck with a maimed wing.

● ● ●

It took a few days to fix the shroud before we finally left Atlantic City to continue our leg to Cape May. One of the prettiest places along the Eastern Seaboard. We tied up in the large public mooring.

At night, I was fast asleep when something gently woke me up.

Look out the porthole.

I got on my knees and focused my eyes on the lights on the shoreline.

When on a mooring, the boats sway, always following the wind. The wind naturally blows on the bow, and the boat is gently pushed away from their moorings or anchor. So, it wasn't abnormal to see the surrounding shoreline swing somewhat. Everything seemed fine.

Keep watching.

It took a few minutes, but suddenly the sound of the little waves against the hull changed. Then I saw that the shoreline did not swing back. Instead, it kept passing us by.

I scrambled into the cockpit and looked at both shorelines to get a bearing. I confirmed that we were indeed slipping. I looked behind us and saw that we were on a collision course with the next boat moored behind us. I banged the deck to wake my father up, and I stood by the stern railing gauging the power of the current. If it wasn't too strong, I could at least stick out a leg and push off from the other boats, but that wouldn't solve the problem. We would just keep on slipping. I couldn't leave the stern to get the key and start the engine because there wasn't enough time.

I called out to the other boat. As the stern came within reach of their bow, I stuck out my foot and pushed at the very point of their bow with my toes. I tried to maneuver the bow to the side under the pressure of my toes. Then I scrambled to my feet and grabbed their lifelines as I fended off our boat.

The people on board popped their heads out, immediately jumped into action, and helped keep both boats apart until Pap was able to get the engine roaring and pulled away.

We went back in the direction we had come from and picked up another mooring.

"How did you know we were slipping?" Pap asked.

"Something told me to wake up."

Pap looked at me blankly.

Once more, we went below to sleep. I lay in my bunk thinking back at the *Voice* as it *tells* me something. How do you explain something like that to your parent who says God is dead?

The next day, after breakfast, we loosened the mooring lines and headed for the bridge at the end of the harbor beyond which was the entrance into the Delaware River. We heard that a hurricane was ravaging Florida, Georgia, and the Carolinas. It was headed our direction, but Pap counted on getting to the relative safety of the narrow, manmade C&D Canal before it affected us.

I was at the helm when, suddenly, I knew something was wrong. "Pap, the steering's gone."

Pap lowered his binoculars and looked back. I rotated the wheel all the way to starboard and then to port, but it had no effect on the boat's direction. I slowed down the engine but kept it high enough so we wouldn't drift.

Pap jumped past me and tore the cover off the aft access to the housing for the steering mechanism. He took the wheel.

"You're smaller. Go in and see what you can find."

I quickly climbed in and crouched behind the pulleys and mechanism. I saw two jagged ends to the steering cable. I tried to connect them to see if it would be easy to connect by tape, anything. They only kept slipping the pulleys

"It's snapped, Pap, and I don't have the strength to pull the ends together."

Pap eyed the boats we were close to hitting. "Get out and let me get in. Take the wheel." By now we started drifting. There was no headway ahead of us to put on any speed. It would've been too dangerous. We were now going in the wrong direction.

I scrambled out of the cramped space, and he squeezed himself in. Then with his amazingly large and strong hands, he wrapped the jagged ends of the cables over each palm and settled further down on his tail bone. "Tell me how to steer. In degrees."

I nodded and looked ahead. We were on a collision course with a moored boat. "Pap, starboard eighty degrees."

"No. Can't do that. I can only do increments," he yelled.

Lordy. *How to do this so that we don't hit? We need to do a sharp turn.* I figured we'd have to take a chance and come dangerously close to a boat straight ahead of us. I yelled at the boat. "Help! We need your help. We have no steering!" Then I yelled down at Pap. "Twenty degrees port!"

The boat turned to port enough that it wouldn't be a direct hit with our bow.

Someone looked out of their open companionway just in time to clamber out and grab our bow. Without their help, we would have collided into their boat, perhaps scraped the entire length of their hull, and torn off their shroud by our forestay.

At the next boat, someone was already waiting on deck. He grabbed our bow and suggested we tie on. But the current was strong, the boat heavy, and he couldn't hold us. All he could do was walk our bow the length of his boat before finally pushing us free. Many people were now standing on their decks watching. Pap didn't see any of that as he sat blindly in the well.

"Ten degrees starboard!" I yelled. And so, we continued, blessed that there were always people on their boats ready to maneuver us away from their own within the tight confines of the moorings.

Finally, we were hooked onto a free mooring by floating over it and quickly wrapping the mooring line around a side deck cleat to stop the bulk of the boat. Slowly we came to a stop and rested. I took the mooring off the side cleat and walked it to the bow and whipped the loops over the bow cleat. We settled with the nose into the wind.

Oy, another prayer of thanks!

Everyone's nerves were frazzled. But after some coffee and a snack, Pap went back to jury-rigging the steering cable so that it would work until we got to Annapolis.

In the meantime, over the marine radio, we heard the hurricane would hit Delaware and Cape May after all.

When Mam understood what was going to happen, she said that it was a good thing we were tied to a mooring safely with so many other boats.

"No," Pap announced. He looked up from the chart he had picked up when he heard the update on the hurricane. "The winds are going to funnel right into this harbor. We can't stay here."

What ensued was another loud and embarrassing argument.

Mam screamed that she wanted to say where we were. She saw the other boats, the Coastguard Station on the shore. Saw the spit of land and wharf that separated the town of Cape May from the rest of the bad ocean. She felt safe.

"The winds are going to funnel right into this harbor," Pap yelled, "and with the steering cable the way it is, the pressure would more than likely break it again. No, we're moving on. I'm going to go right through to the mouth of the Delaware River. Then we'll race with the winds on our backs to the protection of the C&D Canal."

I looked at the chart. I saw the wisdom but it was way up the mouth of the river. We might not be able to outrun it.

"No, don't do it!" Mam started to spit with distress. Her face wrinkled even more. She turned gray, covered her mouth and moaned.

Pap got my attention. "This is what we're going to do. The waters are rising with the oncoming sea. We have to do this quickly and get under that bridge."

I looked at the chart some more and compared the route to the direction of the winds. "We'll have the winds on our backs. We may end up surfing, but we'll go fast as the dickens."

"Yup," he announced. "Pack up the sails so that they don't blow off the deck and let the mooring go immediately."

I ran to the bow. Just as I threw the mooring lines into the water, Pap had the engine going. I prayed the steering would hold. I was anxious but then felt pretty calm deep inside.

A hurricane.

Slowly we rocked and jimmied in the waters churning up from both currents coming in from the mouth of the river on the one side, and from the harbor with the moorings and the ocean behind us. I stood at the starboard shroud with my eyes glued to the pendant we had flapping at the top of the main mast. I looked back at Pap. Then back up at the oncoming bridge. It didn't look good.

"Pap," I said.

He slowed down the engine. Then he went a little in reverse to control the speed even more. We crawled forward.

I looked up in time to see the bottom of the high bridge begin to pass over us. Our foremast cleared easily, but it was the smaller of the two masts. My heart started to pound. I whispered a little prayer again. The rafters underneath hung lower than the rest of bridge. Then, since we had no choice but to keep moving, I saw the pendant and its holder at the top of the main mast bend under the first rafter. Then the next rafter. Then the next and final one.

We made it! We cleared! We were on our way into the Delaware River to out run that hurricane. Suddenly we heard a strange, explosive noise coming towards us.

Whoop, whoop, whoop, whoop.

We looked up at an oncoming Coast Guard helicopter, speeding straight for us. Then it hovered above our masts, its mighty blades churning up the waters around us, and whipping our hair. Someone leaned out with an electric megaphone.

"Marine vessel, turn back. Turn back. You are to stay within the mooring grounds. Repeat. Turn back. Hurricane is doing landfall. Repeat. Hurricane will hit Cape May. Go back and tie up. This is an order!"

We stood on the deck, our necks bent, faces craning upward. I looked over at Pap. Then we looked over at the white caps at the mouth of the Delaware River. We were so close.

Pap waved his arms. With a motion of turning around, he carefully did a U-turn. But as we headed back to the bridge, we could see that the water had risen substantially. It was lapping at the road along the shore off to the side of us.

"Pap, there's no height left."

"I know." He slowed down as much as he could without losing control. He looked at the retreating helicopter. Then he did a slight turn to port and eyeballed the bottom of the bridge again.

He increased the speed. "Nope. Can't. We're anchoring at the mouth of this canal."

I looked back at the white caps rolling into the mouth of the canal, but we had no choice.

Mam got upset. "I want to go back to the mooring with the other boats."

"Think, woman. We can't get under the bridge. We have to stay."

"I want to go back."

"Shut your mouth, woman. It's impossible."

Pap then ordered us to pull out three more anchors from their storage lockers along with all the anchor lines and chain we could find. By the time we dragged them out, the winds were already whipping to the point of very little visibility.

Then, with foul weather gear on, Pap and I worked together to put down the four anchors. First, we put one down in the middle of the canal. Then I stayed on board to make sure the anchor held as Pap went out in the inflatable dinghy to drop an anchor in the opposite directions. I put the boat into reverse so that the anchors would dig in deeply. We ended with two off the bow, stretching to both starboard and port, and two off the stern, spread as far apart as possible.

After that, all we could do was make sure they held. For the next 48 hours, we sat with our ears close to the marine radio. The boat was consistently flopping and fighting to free itself. The hull was pushed onto its side because the roaring, pounding wind kept it at an uncomfortable angle. We tried to sleep half on the bulkhead and half on the bunk, but it was impossible.

Mam cried when we heard that two boats were lost with all crew aboard. We listened to others calling *mayday, mayday* over the banging, smashing and other explosive sounds accompanying the curtains of pounding rain and spray. We heard the Coast Guard answer these calls. I prayed that not too many people were lost or hurt. We listened to rescues as they happened.

At one point, the eye of the hurricane passed over us. The skies above us had this large hole where we could see blue sky, but it lasted very briefly. Soon, when I climbed out to help Pap check that the anchors were still holding, the winds were so strong that they lifted me off the deck. My one hand, somehow, was strong enough to keep clutching the lifeline.

I will never forget the sound. It was as if I were a speck of dust in the largest pipe organ in the world. I thought of the mightiness of God, how much bigger and majestic He is. Then I thought of this lousy little hurricane on a tiny planet in our solar system. And yet, here it was, roaring like it was the end of the world.

I watched Mam with concern. She was frowning and wincing under the noise and movement. My little sister was a trooper and took it in stride. I tried on many occasions to look out the porthole or from the deck to see if I could see the shoreline but to no avail. Incredible. It wasn't that far away. But the wind and rain were so thick it felt like we were almost under water. The arc spotlight only shone on a white wall of rain and wind.

Slowly, as the second dawn approached, the boat righted itself and rocked a little less. Then, while it still rained, the dawn brought the promise of a new and different day. We opened the companionway and slowly climbed out. My little sister, who hadn't come out for two days, gladly scurried out in her life-jacket. She hung onto the straps and looked around wide-eyed.

So much turmoil. So much stress. Now a new calm.

But God still was not finished.

ELEVEN

Land of Milk and Honey and A Brothel's Madame in the Bathroom

"The wise leaders shall shine like the bright vault of the heaven;
and those who have guided the people in the true path,
shall be like the stars for ever and ever."

(Daniel 12:3, NEB)

I hung upside down by my hips off the main boom on Pap's boat while we were at anchor quietly resting, floating, turning in the quiet marshes of Virginia. My back had been bothering me ever since the car accident. By stretching my back off the boom, I could ease the pain somewhat.

I was mesmerized by the sparkling water, dancing, titilating my senses. Colors of bright green, deep blue, golden yellow all in sparkling shards, created a dancing, living stained-glass image. I thought of the church. The nuns.

All the near catastrophes on this trip, however bad they looked on the outside, were actually life-giving. I felt alive and functional. I felt closer to God. A filter had been taken away, and I felt Him more every single day. My heart burst with love for Him, and I felt so much more love in return. Almost unbearable love.

I let my tear-filled eyes wander over the changing upside-down landscape. The boat slowly turned and offered me a slightly different view of endless green fields edged by long marsh grasses. Crickets and frogs were singing and calling in the quiet hours of a lazy late afternoon.

"Hail, hail mighty Canadians!"

The call brought me back from my thoughts. I raised my head to look over toward the bow of our boat. In my upside-down world, I saw a man in a rowboat making his way toward our boat across the sparkling sky.

"Hail hail!"

I quickly straightened up, slipped off the boom, and walked along the teak deck to the bow. I clambered over the downed foresail and stood at the end of the bow spit.

"Hi there," I called in return.

The gentleman stopped rowing about forty feet away and, with his big bulk, stood up careful to keep the rowboat steady. He spread out his arms and raised his face to the sky. "Welcome to Virginia, the land of milk and honey! God's country!" he yelled out.

That brought Pap and Mam out from below.

Pap looked over at the gentleman and grinned. He made his way along the other teak deck and raised his hand in greeting. The man sat down and rowed closer to us. I noticed bushel baskets beside him in the bottom of the rowboat.

When he came alongside, he stood up and grabbed the toe rail of the boat.

"I thought you folks would like some Bluefish! Just caught this morning."

I looked over at the two bushels of shiny, dewy Bluefish. I thought of the baskets of fish Jesus blessed during the Sermon on the Mount. Pap took his tow line and helped steady the boat as the gentleman bent over to pick up the bushel baskets. He handed them up to Pap before grunting as he climbed aboard. He had a happy glow about him. His cheeks looked like the milk and honey he talked about. His conversation was warm, welcoming, and friendly.

"Y'all know that there is piracy in these here waters," he asked, concerned.

Pap motioned to the cabin. "That's why I have a shotgun next to my head where I sleep."

The man nodded. He pointed out over the marshes towards the ocean. "Well, I heard that a young man, who was sailing alone on his little boat, decided to take a straight route right down to the Bahamas. You know, they found his little boat, but he wasn't on it."

I saw Mam's beautiful face pale.

"We'll be okay," offered Pap. "But boy, we had quite a time coming down."

"Oh yeah?" asked the farmer/fisherman, "Do tell."

And Pap did, with Mam and I jumping in with our own additional and excited comments.

Our friend, the farmer/fisherman nodded and offered his own recollections of storms.

"It comes with the territory of living on the ocean. God has really blessed us though. Our farm has never really seen damage except for some erosion. After thirty years of living here, I have yet to come home with nothing after a morning of fishing. This is God's country, you know."

I looked over at Pap. He took pride in thinking that he knew *better*. He always felt superior to those who professed a faith. He liked to discuss religion and had pet arguments about why one shouldn't waste their time. He was about to dig into it when my little sister suddenly piped up.

"We had lots of things happen. Mam was scared."

Our guest leaned in, eyes twinkling. "Oh yes, little lady?"

"Ooooh, yeah."

He looked at Mam and his eye twinkled some more. I noticed he had the bluest, clearest eyes I had ever seen. "Well, if I may say, I think your mother is quite lovely." He leaned in towards Mam. "Now, you shouldn't worry your pretty little head over anythin'." He motioned to Pap. "It seems you are in good hands."

Mam loved compliments. She smiled so broadly that her dimples showed. I silently thanked him for calming her so beautifully. My attention snapped back to what Pap was saying.

"Yah, that hurricane was something. It hit us on the nose in Cape May. We got stuck on the Delaware River side, but we survived."

"You are blessed, mah friend. I heard that many of the boats let go at their moorings. They went like dominoes, all pushed in through the harbor and stacked against the shore like a deck of cards."

I looked at Pap. "If we hadn't gone under that bridge to try and leave the area, we would have been in the mooring and also lost the boat, Pap."

I saw God's hand in this. I started to feel overwhelmed with emotion and gratitude.

"We never even got close to losing the boat. Ha!" he said, pointing to Mam, "And you wanted to stay!"

I looked over at Mam who was standing in the companionway now. Her glow from the kindly gentleman's compliment waned, and her face wrinkled in embarrassment. Pap had a way of embarrassing Mam. Now she was wilting in front of the kind gentleman who thought so highly of her. I could see she felt ashamed. There was going to be another argument tonight.

I jumped in with whatever came to mind to prevent her from sliding into that terrible hole she sunk into because of Pap's jibes and taunts. "Mam, that was really something, wasn't it?"

Her brows knitted even tighter. "Yah, dat was terrible. Terrible."

Our guest could read the fear and weariness. Pap spoke up again.

"Ah, in the end it was nothing. Just a bit of wind and noise. If you covered your ears and closed your eyes, you wouldn't even know it was a hurricane." He turned to our guest. "You have to understand my wife is so afraid all the time because she doesn't see it for what it is. She doesn't have the ability to look at it from a logical point of view. Most women can't."

"Pap," I said, quietly. I looked over at our guest. He shifted his weight, and then cleared his throat again. He slapped his knees.

"Well, that was quite a storm you lived through. There were lives lost you know. Someone was praying for you real strong like," our guest said.

Mam suddenly disappeared from the companionway which caught my attention. I sunk lower into the cockpit to look through the companionway and watch Mam at the gimballed stove. She pretended to make more coffee.

I started thinking. Anyone who hated sailing as much as she did, almost lose her home, couldn't swim, and was afraid of everything you can think of under the sun deserved a chest covered in medals. Being so conditioned to be a hard-headed Viking, I barely understood her. I hadn't yet experienced the maturity and humility of life. I adored and worshipped my father, and, unfortunately, saw my mother as he did—weak. But something slightly shifted in me.

This upside-down world of intense adventures was rounding off my sharp edges. I was becoming more empathetic towards my mother.

I turned to the conversation in the cockpit.

"Oh, I have cows 'n a horse. I grow wheat, too."

"And you fish. It must all keep you busy, man," Pap said, laughing.

Our guest laughed, too. "Oh, I don't have any idle time but I am blessed. I have good land, lots of good, clean water. A nice river runs through it, and the cows go down to drink under the willow trees. I am blessed. It's good land."

"Well, I know nothing about farming. Ha, we come from the city in the homeland. I was very young when I started working for my father in the garage. I had coveralls when I was four already."

"Sounds like a tough upbringing."

I piped up. "Well, you can imagine. Pap can do anything, right Pap?"

"My daughter, she thinks I am God. Please, I'm not that perfect."

"Pap, you fixed that steering cable while we were motoring!" I turned to our guest. "He literally held the frazzled steel ends in his hands and steered manually. And Pap," I turned to him, "when we're stuck in situations, I know that everything will be fine when you're in control."

Our guest turned to Pap. "Sounds like your daughter really looks up to you."

Pap grinned and shrugged. "That's her problem," and he chuckled.

• • •

The next morning, I slid the top of the companionway open and poked my head out. I primed the gimbaled stove and put the kettle on. Pap was out on the bow sanding a spot on the toe rail. He always found something to sand at 6:00 in the morning. It always woke Mam up.

I liked slipping the anchor so early in the morning. A mug of hot chocolate for Pap, mist off the water, sunrise, sitting with him in the cockpit. Dunking the bucket into the water to rinse the pungent marsh mud off the anchor and chain and then rinsing off the teak decks. Checking the charts so that I had an idea about what we were going to do and anticipate what the day entailed.

This morning, for some reason, I looked at my watch the moment I locked in the rinsed anchor and Pap started up the engine.

"Pap, we'll drop anchor at exactly at 4:35 this afternoon," I said.

Pap stood at the wheel and made a face. He looked around the mist-covered marsh.

"Don't be silly," he said, "How can you possibly know?"

"I don't know," I said. I didn't.

But later that day, I had another insight. I had a notion that something big and wonderful was about to happen that would put all the upheaval of the trip into perspective. Things were shifting. That feeling stuck with me all day.

Pap stayed at the helm for a bit. Mam hung the wash over the life lines. My little sister sat huddled on the bow going over her lessons. I went down below to use the head. Then, as I passed my bunk, I looked over and spotted my well-used, ratty Bible leaning against the other books. I reached over and let the Bible fall open. Deuteronomy 8:7 jumped out at me.

"For the Lord thy God bringeth thee into a good land,
A land of brooks of water, of fountains and depths
That spring out of valleys and hills
A land of wheat and barley, and vines, and fig trees,
A land of olives, oil and honey."

A good land. I remembered our guest. *A land of milk and honey.*

I felt a chill for a second at the realization that I was starting to get it. God was right here. With me. It was an ongoing conversation. He was there in the cockpit listening. The Bible verse almost perfectly mirrored what our guest had said about his land.

God was teaching me how to have an ongoing conversation.

Quietly, I started to cry. I straightened up and took my Bible with me. I wanted to *converse* some more. I climbed out through the companionway.

"Oh, heh, heh. There she is, with the Bible again."

I straightened up in the cockpit and looked at my Bible. "I like reading it, Pap."

"It's only for people who need crutches. You're stronger than that."

I ignored that as I always did. "You want me to take over?" I asked.

"Yah, I'll go and do some sanding."

I looked over and knew why. Mam just hung up some wet wash. Great way of ruining the wash. He just couldn't help himself.

I took the helm and heard him start to sand something.

Then I heard Mam yell.

There they went again.

Later that day, we dropped anchor and Pap turned off the engine. I looked at my watch.

"Pap, 4:35," I said. I raised my wrist and showed my watch. He looked at his.

"How'd you do that?"

I smiled. "I'm not sure." But I was getting it.

• • •

After a peaceful evening and another dinner of Bluefish, we slept well, again finding ourselves in the marshes. I looked over onto the shore early in the morning. I had heard animal noises and rustling in the undergrowth. We were very close this time, close enough for tree branches to hang over our side. We were tied up to an old jetty, so there was very little rocking and swaying, but there were sure a lot of scratching noises against the hull. Mysterious noises.

Pap and I had pushed away from the jetty and let the boat slowly drift out into the channel through the marsh. The depth finder showed a lot of water under us, enough for the six-foot draft of the keel. As I coiled the dock lines for storing over the lifeline stanchion I quickly looked at my watch. 6:10 a.m. Pap turned on the engine and we put-putted a little further into Roanoke Sound. We were now in North Carolina.

"Pap, we're going to tie to a dock at exactly 5:13 this afternoon."

"Why do you do that?"

"It's fun."

Pap made a face. "It's impossible to know that." He looked down at the chart. "I didn't tell your mother but this is Alligator River. Apparently, it's full of alligators."

I looked at him. "Really?" I saw it was called Alligator River, but thought it was just a name. I had never seen an alligator in my life.

"I think I heard them in the night," I said. I don't think he heard me. He looked up ahead of the boat and then down at the chart again. I finished tying the rope to the lifelines and turned to face the breeze. *Alligators. Ha!*

For some reason, suddenly, I knew again something special was going to happen that day.

A couple of hours away from tying up at Morehead City, I found myself entirely alone at the helm. Everyone was doing something down below.

Then I felt *Him*. So clearly. I froze and reveled in the connection, the comfort and the love.

Look to the right.

I looked to the right.

My heart stopped. There was an endless field of daisies ringed by brush. Daisies. *In October?* I remembered the endless fields of daisies I sunk into behind that Dairy Queen when I was young. And the little shed in the middle. As if it were built just for me. To be alone with Him.

Look ahead.

Right before my eyes, a perfect rainbow appeared over the trees. I stared at it. I knew the science behind it, but I also knew this was not a coincidence. Time stood still. I didn't hear any bugs, it was almost as if I tuned out. I didn't hear the sound of the engine. There wasn't a sound down below. It was like I was absolutely alone on the boat isolated from the rest of the world by this magical marsh world. Daisies, Rainbows.

I went around a bend. Slowly I became aware of a true presence beside me, different from the feeling I got from conversing with God. It was a smaller form.

I watched the bow of the boat move toward the center of the end of the rainbow.

But that was impossible, I thought.

Don't think impossible.

I lowered the speed of the boat and put it into neutral. The boat drifted forward right through the rainbow. It was as if the bands of color caressed the boat. Over the bow, across the teak deck, over the cabin, and then it enveloped me. I couldn't breathe. A curtain of moisture covered and caressed me. As the boat continued to drift, we left the rainbow behind. I turned and watched the rainbow recede. As I steered the boat around another bend, it disappeared from my sight.

I took a moment to collect myself and then increased the speed. The engine roared as I returned to five knots, a comfortable pace. My heart pounded, almost jumping out of my chest. I felt as if I were floating, and somehow, part of me expanded.

Later, we tied up to the wharf in Morehead City, North Carolina, at exactly 5:13 p.m.

Mam wanted to go shopping, and she took my little sister along. Pap stayed on board to putter around, and I took the opportunity to go to the public showers and stand under some hot water for as long as my conscience would allow.

I walked into the ladies' bathroom with a towel roll and shampoo under my arm. I was surprised to see a woman bent over brushing her long, black hair from the nape of her neck. Suddenly, she flipped her hair back up and started to brush and whip the hair in sections around her forefinger.

"Oh, don't mind me," she said. "This is how I was taught to do curls. I don't have any way of curling my hair but this works perfectly fine."

"You have beautiful hair," I said, which was true. I started to unroll my towel and looked around at the stalls.

"Thank you. Oh, now it used to be more beautiful than this. I used to be a Madame of a brothel, you know. I was quite an impressive woman at one point."

I was taken aback and giggled a little. She continued to chat. She talked about giving up the brothel, correcting her way of life, travelling around, and living in her car. Then she started to talk about rainbows and Daisies.

My heart stopped and my feelers went out. The top of my head tingled as did the bottom of my feet.

She then spoke about subjects that were close to my heart. She spoke about astronomy and about what I learned about Black Holes.

Then she took my breath away.

"I'm talking about all these things to show you that what I am about to tell you is real. God always confirms things so that you know the message is real, not just your imagination."

I looked at her. "Okay," I said, remembering my red-headed co-worker on the Go Train.

"Jesus taught me how to curl my hair. I know it may seem such a trivial thing for Jesus to care about but that's how He loves me. The smallest things that please me can make the angels sing. It's the love that is the connection. Everlasting love that is there for the big and powerful reasons and it's there even in the smallest of gestures. Now, I know that you know how sweet Jesus really is."

I had tears in my eyes, quite overwhelmed. "Yes, I've been *feeling* things. *Real* things."

"Oh, I know. That's why I'm here to talk to you. You've been wondering about the scriptures, how it can make a woman look like she's evil and worthless. I'm here to tell you that's absolutely not true." She chuckled and smiled. "And that's coming from a former Madame who loved her girls. Ironic, isn't it?"

I smiled. What could I say?

"Also, I am supposed to tell you that there are other forms of Bibles. You have the King James version."

By this time, I no longer was surprised.

"There are a number of translations. It's important to get acquainted with all of them. For instance, you've never heard of the New English Bible with the Apochryphal books. That one you should have."

"The Apochryphal books?"

"Yes, they're left out of your King James Bible."

"New English Bible."

"Yes. Don't worry about finding it. I will send one to you."

I was confused. "We're on a boat. I don't have an address for the next nine months or so."

"Not to worry. You'll be home long before that."

I looked at her, lost for words.

"You write the address down. You will receive it just after you return." She handed me a piece of paper and a pen from her bag.

I shakily wrote down my name and address and handed it back to her with her pen. She folded the piece of paper and put it into the side pocket of her purse.

"Now, God wants you to know you are not alone. In fact, I believe He is going to do something very special with you. That's why I'm here to talk to you today."

"Thank you," I said meekly. My legs were trembling.

She gathered her things together, swung her purse over her shoulder, and then lifted her bag of toiletries and towel. I noticed that her hair was drying in beautiful ringlets. As she passed, I reached out and hugged her. I fought tears.

"Thank you very much."

She returned the hug. "Don't forget. You read that Bible when you receive it."

I nodded mutely and then watched her leave. I stood there for a very long time.

$$\bullet \quad \bullet \quad \bullet$$

It rained and stormed all night. At 5:30 a.m. Pap and I went above decks wearing our foul weather gear. Slowly I pulled at the mooring and then unhooked the ends from the bow cleat. I threw it as far as I could from the boat to clear the prop. Pap turned on the engine, and we quietly putted from the public moorings. I looked back at Morehead City in the rain and thought back at that woman in the bathroom. I wondered what was next along this adventure of mine.

Eventually, everyone woke. My mother decided to make a pancake breakfast—pancakes with cheese melted on top and then rolled. They were easy to eat by hand. The billowing warmth coming up from the galley was laced with smells *amplified* by the fresh air and rain.

About an hour before sunset, we coasted into position in Waccamaw River near Murrells Inlet, and I threw out the anchor. I stood in the rain holding onto the forestay at the bow and looked around the gray marshes as Pap put the boat in reverse to hook the anchor into that slimy muck bottom. I stayed there until I felt the familiar jog in the movement of the boat.

Pap wiped his hands and smacked his lips. "Now for a nice cup of coffee. You coming?"

Stay.

"No, I'll stay for a while."

"You're soaked. You should get warm and dry."

I shook my head. "I'll be right down."

He disappeared down below. I heard the companionway slide shut against the rain.

I took a deep breath. It was so very quiet. The only sounds were of the rain pelting the river surface and the clang and bang of pots along with chatter down below.

Suddenly, my eyes caught a movement in the marshes to the right. The edge was about a hundred feet away. I wiped at my eyes and focused harder.

Why did you want me to stay? I asked.

A tiny little stick figure moved along the marshes and then disappeared. It appeared again a little further from the marshes until the rippling effect of the waters hid it. Again, it came into sight, this time a little closer towards the boat. I moved to mid-ships, and held onto the shroud, and bent over the edge of the boat to see as well as possible through the rain.

I stood back surprised. It was the head of a snake with its little tongue popping out. I saw that it was well over eight feet long, maybe longer, as some of it was submerged. But it kept slithering and coiling through the waves.

It was coming directly to where I was standing.

"Pap," I called. Clatter. Chatter from below.

About ten feet away, it stopped and looked right at me. Its tongue flicked while its brown mottled body rocked up and down, this way and that with the wind-driven waves.

"Pap!"

It lowered its head and came right below me, flicking its tongue against the hull of the boat.

Suddenly, it was as if I could read its mind. It was looking for a way up. Out of the water. Out of the rain. I knew that it would follow the hull looking for a point of access even before it started following the hull. I walked along the deck and followed it around once. Then I saw it head back toward the anchor rode.

It looked up towards the bow.

"Pap! Come and see!" I yelled loudly.

I heard a bang, and the companionway slid open with another bang.

"What!?" Pap's head was sticking up through the companionway. He was chewing.

I pointed down in a jerking motion at the anchor rode. He climbed out and made his way over the wet deck. He reached me just in time to see the snake curve once around the rope and slowly slide upwards. Quickly, he jumped to the cabin and pulled out the boat hook. He lumbered back, bent down and slapped at the snake.

I felt the shock. It pulled back and looked at us. The tongue flicked. It moved more slowly, more intentionally, and deliberately wrapped more and more around the rope.

Whack! This time it didn't stop, it only dodged its head. It slunk higher and higher. The head was almost at the opening to the deck.

Whack. Whack.

"Now, yah!" yelled Pap. He twisted the hook around the snake's head, yanked, and loosened its bulky body off the rope with all his might. Then, with boat hook bending under the weight, he flung the snake as far out into the water as he could.

We both stood in the rain rooted to the bow. We could see it's long, massive body floating as if dead. But I knew better. It was only stunned.

"Yah! It's dead!" Pap announced.

"No, Pap. He's still alive."

"No, look for yourself. It's not moving." With that, he turned, lumbered along the deck again and went down below. Bang went the companionway.

I stood swaying with the boat. Watching the creature float, waltz, float, disappear, float.

Watch.

Why?

Just watch.

Suddenly, the head shot up and looked straight at me. Then I saw the body come to life again, and it headed for the boat.

My insides turned to water. *Holy crap.*

"Pap, it's still alive!"

"Give it over," I heard mumbled from below.

The snake went straight to the anchor rode.

This excited me to no end. I felt it. It was angry. It wanted to get back at us. *It wanted to show who was boss.*

"Pap!"

Bang. Bang. The companionway opened again. Pap came straight toward me at the bow, picking up the boat hook along the way. He hovered over the climbing snake once again. King Kong ready to fight the dragon from the depths. He held up the boat hook. The snake stopped.

I stood back mesmerized.

It wasn't frightened of me, but it sure was of Pap. Pap roared as he swiped at it again. The snake dodged this way and that. Finally, it stopped crawling and hung back, flicking its tongue.

Pap motioned to it, "Go away!"

The snake was thinking. I could feel it. Slowly it loosened its hold on the rope and slid down the slant of the rope back into the water.

Slowly it turned slightly and slithered away from the boat, stopping to look back at us, its tongue flicking. It did this every few feet. Slither, stop, look back and flick. Finally, it disappeared into the marshes of Murrell's Inlet.

After Pap went down below, I stuffed the two anchor rode holes with whatever I could find to prevent it, or any other snake, from coming on board.

What were you wanting to teach me with this, God? I did not sleep that night.

• • •

The next day, the symbolism of the snake in the Bible clung to my mind.

The day was clear with sunny skies. We stopped at Charleston for the day, and then at Hilton Head to buy some famous Blue Crab. Going through Georgia, we crossed the border into Florida and passed the massive steel cross along the Intracoastal Waterway into St. Augustine. Suddenly, there were white sand bottoms and aqua waters.

It was as if we had arrived in paradise.

We stopped for a few days and went to the Alligator Farm. I asked the ranger, who was doing a show with snakes, about the one we had seen. I described its triangular head, the brown mottling, and its actions. His eyes opened wide.

"That was one of the few truly poisonous snakes in the States, a Cottonmouth."

I laughed. The name sounded so benign.

He shook his curly, sweaty head. "Don't laugh. The Cottonmouth is about the only snake that takes revenge." He stepped closer to me. "It takes *revenge.* You were very lucky."

I told Pap later that afternoon.

"Oh, give over. It was just a little snake," he said as he coiled some rope. I smiled and said a prayer of thanks.

• • •

Later, at Palm Beach, I hung over the side like a little kid to watch the clear bottom strewn with conch and clam shells swinging this way and that. I felt like I had died and gone to heaven.

I looked up in time to see a massive monster navy ship slowly appear in the gap, the engines shaking our bulkheads. The rumble brought everyone out from down below. We stood in awe.

American Navy. It was thrilling to see.

Eventually the mammoth floating engineering wonder moved across the gap and out into the ocean. All along the top deck, sailors gathered and waved at us. We could hear them whooping and hollering in the distance. Mam, my little sister, and I enthusiastically waved back.

The next day, we continued on our trip and stopped in Fort Lauderdale for two weeks for a rest and for restocking supplies. And finally, from Hollywood Beach, we headed off to Bimini Island, the first tiny island in the Caribbean on our way past all the cays to Nassau, Bahamas.

The waters of the Gulf Stream were of a deeper, richer blue color. We rocked like a hobbyhorse all the way. I sat at the end of the bow spit getting dunked up to my waist in the ocean waves. Then I would swing up way into the sky and then down again. But after about eight hours of motoring, Pap realized he hadn't factored in the strong northward Gulf Stream current. We were drifting north of where we had to go. Finally, we had to head almost due South on the black ocean.

It took another ten hours to see the tiny light at the gap of the little island. By that time, the heavy batteries were overheating, and the plastic housing was bubbling in the heat. Pap had no choice but to keep going. Otherwise, we would've been swept up the Gulf Stream towards New England.

When we finally approached the little navigation light, I put on the arc light to make our entrance easier. Below me, in the shallowing waters, I was startled to see a great shark go by.

Finally, we dropped anchor in the relatively shallow bay of Bimini Island and went to bed for a well-deserved rest.

The next day, elated at our surroundings of palm trees and puddle jumper planes floating at anchorage around us, I jumped in for a swim with snorkel and fins. As I searched the ocean floor for conch, I saw the entire sea floor rise under me. I flew out of the water back onto the deck.

It was my first experience with a giant manta ray. It must have been about eight feet wide.

Later, we walked along the shoreline of Bimini Island. We discovered ancient rock paving stones and parts of what looked like a Roman column under a foot or two of water. We joked it had to be part of the fabled Atlantis but was more likely from an old 18th century plantation house.

We were sorry to leave the incredibly charming island. But, we had to keep moving.

We raised anchor and sailed to Chubb Key. From there, we motored over the shallow Flats through the Bermuda Triangle.

The Flats were mysterious. We motored a full day and then anchored for the night. The entire Flats were just six feet deep and flat with a bottom of soft, crystal-white sand. Very little grew in that sand, and we didn't see any fish. However, one night, we accidentally left two fishing lines hanging over the side. When we awoke, we discovered the lines had snapped. Something large had taken the bait hanging off those hooks.

That next day, again, was nothing but motoring over the beautiful Flats with the crystal white sandy bottom.

Finally, we entered deeper waters and headed to Cat's Key for diesel. There we saw great sharks and massive tunas hanging from tall poles, the fishermen standing beside them for photos. Just like the ones Pappa Hemmingway had taken with his catches.

Finally, we headed for Nassau.

Our arrival to Nassau had a touch of magic. I saw it as another little love note to me from Heaven because the first boat we saw coming into Nassau Harbor was a trimaran called,

Teo. When I was twelve years old, I had spent the summer with a family of seven children who lived in a rough little cottage on the sand spit separating Lake Ontario and Frenchman's Bay. In our bathing suits, we crawled around the bare wooden bones of Teo and did the fiber glassing of the hulls and bulkheads, just for the pleasure of doing it.

And here it was, taking charters from people all over the world, ten years later. It was a lovely reunion with the skipper, who was a real playboy when we were children. He had a number of beautiful women come to visit and stay with him at his cottage as we looked on, scratching at a combination of fiber glass dust and sweat on our exposed skin. Needless to say, it was a different woman now in the role of the second mate, his most recent lady friend having left the year before.

A week or so later, we celebrated Christmas by stringing lights up the forestay as we lay at anchorage near the new Paradise Island Bridge.

Boxing Day morning, we got up at 4:00 to join in the celebration called, Junkanoo, a Christian tradition brought over from the U.S.A. with slaves belonging to Loyalists during the American Revolution. We spent hours following a parade of people in massive headdresses shuffling and bouncing to the tune and beats of whistles and drums.

The waters in the Bahamas were clear as glass. I swam in waters so clear that I swore I was floating in the sky. If I swam under the boat, I imagined the boat above me was in mid-air. I snorkeled at Rose Island, not far from Nassau. There I came face-to-face with a large Barracuda, its mouth opening and shutting showing off its fangs for teeth.

At night, especially during a full moon, our dinghy appeared to fly through the sky leaving a wake of iridescence, like a flying-star, shooting through the night skies with a trail of sparkles.

We went deep sea fishing and caught a massive Walleye Tuna. But, when we cranked it in, the large glistening head with frantic looking plates for eyes had been bitten off behind the gills. A massive shark had devoured the rest of the body in one bite.

One day, I sat on the edge of the cabin, gazed over the aqua waters of Nassau Harbor, and came to a conclusion. If I only had one life to live, I would do exactly what I wanted to do. I would become a professional actor for a while. Then I would give it up and dedicate my life to God.

And the only way I knew to do that was to become a nun.

But then Buddy flew down with a diamond ring and proposed.

TWELVE

What Do You Mean
I Can't be a Nun?

"Obey with a will ..."

(Isaiah 1:19, NEB)

1978

I said yes.

What else could I say? On one hand, we had an intimate relationship, so I owed it to him to complete the circle of commitment. On the other hand, I know God wanted to end the relationship. I wanted to be a nun!

Oh, I was so weak. I could not say a simple 'no' to a man.

I was too weak to follow through on an uncomfortable piece of Divine Guidance. Then I persuaded myself that marrying was what the rules and regulations set by society was and a Christian Bible demanded. I believed that perhaps by my example, Buddy would also become a Christian. Then we would not be *unevenly yoked*.

So, with a claim on me and a promise to wed, my fiancé whisked me away from the warmth and beauty of the Bahamas and brought me back to our wintry Toronto home.

It looked like the *nun* option was no longer available, so I returned to the modeling agency and signed up as model and actor.

• • •

Immediately, I landed a lead role in a Canadian film production of *Bad Company*. It wasn't until after I won the part I realized there was nudity involved. I told the producer and director I couldn't do it. They rewrote the script to include a second female, who was then given the nude scene.

Those were the days when movie scripts had roles for a dozen men and only one female role which included a nude scene. Women were treated terribly. I became aware of the crude term *T&A* (tits and ass) and spoke freely against any sexism.

One day I went for a photo shoot with the *Toronto Sun* newspaper. By then I was an unofficial queen of a popular swim-suit line, so wasn't surprised when I was hired to do another company's swimsuit shoot. I arrived at the newspaper offices and was directed to the studio. I was given a couple of swimsuits, did my hair and makeup. While I was posing, the big, hairy pho-tographer said, "Pull the straps down."

I looked sideways at the straps. I didn't think the designer would want the straps down. "Are you sure? It would start look-ing a bit too sexy. We won't be focusing on the suit itself."

"That's what I want. I want you to stand straighter and …. Well, here."

He walked over, lowered his camera on its strap, and with both hands positioned my body so that my breasts were sticking out, my back was curved, and my bum was prominent. He didn't even ask if he could touch me.

"No," I simply said and stood in a pose instead. A natural, sporty pose.

"You are here to pose for me. This is what I want." He was getting testy.

"I'm sorry. I'm not here to do a sexy pose. It's demeaning."

"Well, if you're not going to do it, there are thousands of other girls who would. Don't you want to be a Sunshine Girl?"

"A Sunshine Girl?"

"Yeah, our *Playmate*, so to speak."

I started to panic. "Really? Your *Playmate*?" I stepped away from under the lights and backdrop and hurried to the dressing room. I suddenly felt naked. A moment ago, I felt sporty, dignified, healthy. I still wore the same outfit but now I felt like I had been pawed and undressed in this guy's imagination. I took off the bathing suit, got dressed, and pulled back the curtain.

"I'm sorry, but I can't do this."

He was leaning on a stool, half sitting on it, looking disgusted. As I walked away, he said, "Fill your boots. You had your chance."

You had your chance.

I was up for another job as a model for a wrestling show. Again, it was a skimpy outfit, a tiny bikini top, and an almost G-string bottom with spike heels. I turned that down. I was up against another blonde in the movie, "Meatballs" with Bill Murray for a role called the *Love Goddess*. When I read the script during the final audition, I realized the camera would primarily zoom in on my breasts. Still torn about whether or not I should do it, I walked past the long line of extras signing up for background and was just about to go through the door when I intuitively knew I would get the role.

What of your sons? One day they will see this.

I stopped. I looked at the doors. I didn't doubt what I *heard.* But *sons* ...?

No, if I had sons, I couldn't imagine them one day seeing their mother in a skimpy bathing suit, and the camera zoomed in on her breasts.

I turned around and walked away.

I read then Hugh Hefner had become a hero in Hollywood by spearheading a fundraiser[10] to restore the Hollywood sign overlooking what had become a den of iniquity, drugs, orgies, the center of the Sexual Revolution and murder[11].

Soon, however, I got into a rhythm I did like. I auditioned for a famous runway commentator, Norma Wildgoose. She

---

[10] Hugh Hefner hosted a fundraiser at the Playboy Mansion and raised $27,000 which covered 1/9th of the cost of restoration.

[11] The Manson Murders had set an ominous tone in Hollywood.

accepted me as an ongoing model for all her fashion shows. Some were at Yorkdale Shopping Mall. Others were in smaller malls all over the city. Through the end of September, she booked me in up to three shows a day at the relatively newly-built Eaton's Center in Toronto.

I took modern dance and as many acting and voice lessons as possible. Ultimately, I wanted to do theater, but my looks kept garnishing me auditions for TV, film, commercials, and print. I made upwards of $650 an hour for print and $1,200 for a day of runway work. I was truly blessed.

But my relationship with my fiancé still felt wrong. I talked myself into thinking marrying him was what I was supposed to do. But I would consistently get the scripture verse,

> *"Be ye not unequally yoked together with unbelievers:*
> *…Wherefore come out from among them,*
> *and be ye separate …"*

2 Corinthians 6: 14-17

I spoke to my fiancé about this conundrum. But he was a self-professed atheist. Until now, it hadn't been an issue but after the boot camp of a trip, I had changed and there was no going back. I saw what God was saying, but I did not want to break a heart if I could help it.

Regardless, I still believed I should commit my entire life to God. And the only way I knew how to do that was to become a nun. So, I thought, *To the nunnery!*

I walked down to St. Basil church for midday mass whenever I could or to meditate and pray in the church on my own. Once in a while, a couple of young people and I would hang back and talk and chat with the priest. I asked about applying to be a nun and pondered on it.

Out of the blue, my agent suggested I teach self-improvement and motivational classes in the evenings. She called it a good source of *bread and butter*, which was a bit tongue-in cheek as

I was making very good money, but teaching was something I wanted to do. So, I said yes.

I thrived on it. The women generally started off shy, tentative, and sometimes awkward. But, no matter which program they enrolled in—the longer or shorter one—they eventually transformed into beautiful, confident women. They learned hygiene, hair, and makeup as well as dressing and body movement. The courses helped correct the false notion they had to look like sex goddesses to be sexy and desirable. They became dignified in the way they carried themselves. They unshackled the now common notion they must look like a Playmate in *Playboy* to look and be perfect.

I emphasized positive thinking and taught them to break through the boundaries set by their upbringing, their culture, advertising, and fashion. In other words, I taught them to believe in themselves.

One day, a large package arrived in the mail with no return address. When I opened it, it was a copy of the New England Bible. My friend, the brothel lady in Morehead City, had kept her promise. I sent her a little prayer.

I devoured that Bible. Later, when I told the priest about this translation of the scriptures, he replied, "Oh, the Apocrypha is not in the King James Bible because it's of little importance."

"But it has so much more about women. Wouldn't it still be the Word of God?"

"You doubt the Holy Spirit's guidance of how these scriptures were translated?" He had squinty, bright blue eyes and white hair and loved drawing people into conversations.

"But without them, few positive remarks are left about women. The rest are fairly negative. It would be nice to think that the Catholic Church would recognize the scriptures in the Apocrypha." I didn't mean to be contentious. I was very sensitive about the traditional belief of women's less desirable position. At least, the way I was taught.

He looked up at me from the stone steps of the church, took a drag off his cigarette and chuckled.

"Well, first of all," he flicked his ashes to the side, and I watched a bit of ash blow up to the sky by the gust of wind between the steps and the wall of the church. "The charismatic end of the Catholic Church does have a broader perspective on the scriptures in general, but I'm not into all that guitar playing and liberal way of thinking. They're even starting to talk about the Pope officially allowing birth control. They're also talking about recognizing and accepting homosexuality. It all goes against the original precepts of the church." He shifted his weight, leaned back on his elbows, and stretched out his lanky legs over the other stone steps. "But you are a daughter of Eve. It was Eve who transgressed and involved Adam. Why should the Holy Ghost not keep that in perspective? Why suddenly show women as faultless as a whitewashed bedsheet? Neither are men, you must remember. You can't change the scriptures."

I thought back to the cottonmouth snake in Murrell's Inlet. Eve's fault.

I didn't know what to say. In spite of having become *born again* at the age of 15, I still looked to the Roman Catholic Church for answers.

I was walking home pondering what he said when, suddenly, somebody thrust a brochure under my nose when I stopped at the crosswalk at Yonge and Bloor. I glanced at the title quickly. *P.S.I. Offers Courses on Memory and Meditation.*

I took the flyer home and read it in more detail. I felt that familiar *nudge*. I was to take the course. It was scheduled over three evenings and a weekend at a hotel west of Toronto.

My fiancé was already mumbling about me not being home evenings, but I told him I really needed to take it. The next day, I called and signed up.

That following Friday evening, I drove to the hotel early to register and pay and waited while about 40 people sauntered in. As I watched, I sensed a different mindset amongst the organizers of the course, but I couldn't put my finger on what it was. They seemed to be acutely mindful of everyone. When it finally started, each of the four organizers pointed at the audience and rhymed off each attendee's full name.

It was very impressive. They could only have matched name with a face when a person signed in. The attendees were strangers to them until the moment they walked in to register.

They proceeded to teach us a memory exercise which they guaranteed would enable us to remember 100 random words in fifteen minutes. And they were right. There was not one person in the audience who could not complete the tasks. The ability to memorize such details became extremely handy in many areas of my own life. Especially when it came to quickly memorizing lines for auditions or performances.

When we returned early the next morning, the course focused on meditation. Our class went late into the night. We were warned that Sunday would be focused on remote healing and would also last into the night.

When I returned home late Saturday, I shared with my fiancé what had happened and then proceeded to tell him what was on the agenda for the next day, Sunday. I had heard about remote healing being connected to the U.S. and Russian military, so I was quite intrigued.

I was surprised when he suggested I had been duped by a cult. Apparently, he had taken the brochure to his friends at the Waldorf where we routinely went for a few drinks. They had nothing good to say about the organization.

"A cult? I'm only learning a memory trick, some meditation techniques, and a stab at something even you have heard about."

"It's a cult." He stubbornly repeated. He set his chin a little higher than normal. He was about two heads taller than me, so this movement made him appear even loftier. He held up the brochure and read some of the text out loud. "*You may not arrive having smoked, or, having drunk alcohol within twenty-four hours of the sessions. We will be able to detect if you had and you will be turned back at the door.* What the hell do smoking and drinking have to do with it?"

"I think they want people to have as little toxins in their system as possible. Maybe it helps with focusing? Besides, they also said they would reimburse the fee if they did."

"Ok, but that's not the point", he said, as he tossed the brochure onto our square white coffee table. "I'm asking you not to go."

"You forbid me to go?" I looked around the small one-bedroom apartment. I knew I owed him a tremendous amount. He never asked for money toward the rent, or food, or entertainment. He spoiled me. and I owed him to at least work with him to maintain the relationship, right?

But goodness. How could I tell him I was supposed to go?

I sat down on the blue sectional couch we had and looked down at my hands. "I'm sorry. I have to go." I looked back up. His freckles and red hair grew brighter against his pale skin. He was a jovial person, always laughing, except for spurts of temper during races at the club when things didn't go well. But I overlooked those entirely. Now, I could see that he was getting just as upset. He lit a cigarette, took a drag, and leaned back on the couch. He pointed at me with the hand holding the cigarette.

"You go, and I'll call your father. He'll have a lot to say about this."

"Pap? Since when would he care?"

"Since I spoke to him last night while you were with those idiots. He told me your nose was always in that damn Bible. You're brainwashing yourself even more by going to this circus."

I stared at him for a moment, speechless. I got up and wordlessly went to the bedroom. How could he and Pap possibly understand the beautiful love I felt? They thought I was crazy.

Am I crazy? I asked.

No. Unevenly yoked.

Silently, I got ready for bed and climbed in without saying goodnight. I heard the TV in the living room go on, but I fell asleep long before he came to bed.

• • •

"Close your eyes. You may leave your palms resting on your knees. Slowly take in a deep breath."

I could hear everyone take in a deep breath.

"Now, slowly let it out."

I was sitting in the second row on a chair in the darkened meeting room. There were about twenty-five of us. A few from the night before did not return.

I learned about the chakras and envisioned myself going down, down, down to the count of ten. I had already visualized a place to go that I could use as a starting point for meditating. My vision started at a park and entered something akin to a phone booth. But inside there were stairs going down into the ground. Ten steps down the staircase. I counted backwards: ten, nine, eight—each time I exhaled, inhaled, and imagined going deeper and deeper. Once I arrived at one, I opened a door into a black, marble lobby with gold trim. To the left, I had created a shower which I stepped into and turned on. Pure, white light poured through the top of my head and with every inhale, I was filled with white light. It went as deep as it could until it reached a blockage. The light loosened the blockage and as that disintegrated, it loosened the name of what caused the blockage in the first place. Then I exhaled it out before inhaling another cleansing breath of light. I continued until I felt totally cleansed of negative energy. Illusions that distracted me from finding my *center*. The first blockage was my *fiancé* and being *unevenly yoked*. Exhale. It's gone. Inhale. Something else dislodged. It had the priest's name on it. Exhale. Gone. Inhale. Dislodge the *photographer* at the *Toronto Sun* newspaper. Exhale. Gone.

Before I knew it, I was totally filled with light. All the unnecessary negative items had been washed away. I felt amazing.

Finally, I left the shower and walked to an elevator further down the hall.

I pressed the elevator button. It opened instantly. I stepped in, and went down, down, down into a netherworld. When I stepped out of the elevator, I was in an open lobby of black marble again. But this time, it was drenched in sunlight pouring through a wall of glass thirty-feet tall. Through it, no matter where I stood, I could see majestic mountains. Distant eagles soared on the updraft from the valleys below. This place was in a cliff face.

I stepped down two steps, and to the right was what looked like a tanning bed. I lay on the tanning bed and turned it on. Slowly, the colored lights of the chakras filled me. I was humming with white light and, as I lay there glowing, I was filled thoroughly with red light energy. I felt the bottom of my tailbone tingle. The red energy filled that chakra and then overflowed into the rest of my body. Soon I felt baptized in passion, energy, ambition, sexual, and sensual energy. I felt an inner strength, a fierceness of certitude and truth. I felt the heat.

Each chakra came alive. Orange: solar plexus for talent, contentment, empathy, compassion. Yellow: health, happiness, and sunshine. Positive and excited. Green: truth and peace. Mature and wise. Blue: true blood, royalty, the power to speak the truth. Purple: spiritual energy, connection to God, intuitiveness, meditative. Then finally that point of white light above my head.

I was ready. I got out of the suntan bed and went to my lab by the large glass wall. I looked out, overwhelmed with the grandeur of the sight. I felt so small. Yet so strong. I went to work.

In my lab were challenges and issues that needed attending to—whether by prayer, meditation, or analyzation and strategy. Here I connected to the flow. God energy.

I finished that Saturday an entirely, different person. The intuitive insights I had had on the boot camp trip were forerunners of a heightened sense of intuition I now felt. The knowing about when we were to drop anchor a full twelve hours later, after sailing through winds and currents, motoring, and slowing down for lift bridges. There were so many factors that played into when we would drop anchor, but I always knew to the minute. Or the times I woke up moments before the boat was about to slip anchor.

My Catholic-self was tempted to not understand the connection between meditation and prayer. But, the side being taught directly by the Holy Spirit understood they were a pair.

I realized that God was re-programming my brain so that I was more open to His guidance.

As we left that night, we were reminded not to smoke or drink before coming back the next morning.

My fiancé was asleep by the time I arrived home. I gently crawled into bed beside him and applied one of the things I had learned that day. Of sharing love from my own self.

I put out my feelers to sense his state of mind. I saw only gray. I also sensed the edges of his mind were burdened by his concerns about me. He saw the beginning of the unravelling of us, threatened by my faith in God and things of the spiritual world. I took a deep breath and filled him with an intense white light filled with love.

He groaned and smiled in his sleep.

Then I fell asleep, happy as well. Somehow, I lifted him up, even if it was only in his sleep.

• • •

"Sorry, you can't come in."

"What!?" One of our students stood with his mouth open. He stared wide-eyed at the young woman by the door. "Why?" He wore a Fu Manchu and had shoulder-length black hair. I remembered him as the reporter from some publication.

A young man, who was one of the instructors, stepped over and stood beside her.

"You had alcohol last night, and you smoked."

Our reporter stepped back in surprise. "How on earth can you tell that?"

"You miss the whole point. We're sorry. It's important you're not tainted by these toxins."

"But I paid for the whole course!" He turned to the rest of us and raised his shoulders. "What the hell is this?"

I looked on. They were explicit the night before. No alcohol or cigarettes. It remained in the system for days, they had warned. And these things in our systems affect how effective we could be during the exercises. Especially those we were to learn of Remote Healing.

"We'll give you your money back," offered the young girl.

"Shit! I don't care about the money! I care about missing today's lessons!"

"Sorry." The young man gently put his hand on the reporter's back. "Come, let's get you your money back." With that, he led the reporter out the door. That was the last we saw of him.

And boy, did he miss a lesson!

• • •

I sat with my eyes closed. I had gone through all the steps of cleansing and refilling myself with all the energies of the chakras. Having completed one person's remote healing session, I was preparing myself for the next. I opened my eyes and looked at the 3 x 5 card in front of me. There was the first name of a man and an age.

I closed my eyes again.

Slowly I began to see the man. I looked at him for a bit, getting my bearings. I waited until I was satisfied I had finished checking his emotional health. If anything, he had a jovial demeanor.

I took a deep slow breath and saw him only in his skin. Nothing. I checked his blood circulation and general health. I saw a slightly high level of blood pressure. I also saw that he was about fifty pounds overweight. I could see there were markers of something wrong with an organ.

I took another deep breath and slowly exhaled. Now the muscles. I saw he had large calf muscles, so he either walked or stood a tremendous amount of time. He also had strong buttock muscles. He must sit tensely on a chair for some of the time. He had a hernia in one of his stomach muscles. His forearms were strong. So, I knew he had a job that required sitting, he felt stress, and he used his arms a lot. Suddenly, I knew he was a ticket master in the Frankfurt Train Station.

Under the muscles. I saw a danger marker on his liver. He drank, and he was diabetic. He didn't seem to be aware of it, but I could tell that he worried he might acquire it. His father was a diabetic and lost a limb. He was terrified of losing a limb.

I went further into the skeleton and ligaments. Save for a sore foot (wrong shoes), his skeletal system seemed fine. Wait a minute. No. The ligament on his right hip was stretched, and there was a bit of wear on the bone. The same leg as the sore foot. He often walked to work. With his bulk, he'd do better losing that weight.

I took another deep breath. Exhaled slowly. I went to work imagining fixing the hernia, levelling out the blood pressure, and then patting fine warm oils on the stretched ligament. As I massaged it some life returned, and then, finally, the memory of a healthy ligament flowed through the body's natural healing properties. Basically, he was healthy in every other way. He ate well, drank well (sometimes too well), but he'd live another 30 years, if not more.

I sat up, woke up a bit, and wrote my notes on the 3 x 5 card. I put it to the side. Then I picked up the last of the three I had to do that evening.

A girl's name. It sounded like a younger generation name. Yes, she was 17.

I slowly got ready for this young, bright teenager.

She was upset. Depressed. Suicidal. Oops. I sensed she was concerned about a boyfriend and she wanted to tell something to her mother. But it was hard, frighteningly hard. Her mother was a single parent. No father around. Always very little money. I saw the boyfriend in a leather jacket. Not the right kind, but she was worried about losing him.

I sat back. I sensed I had to go through the chakras of my own body again. This was a subtle and special case.

Then I sat back and focused.

Outside, pretty. Skin, good. Some acne. Arteries, vessels, everything seemed fine. Except she was slightly sick. There was something foreign in her blood.

Muscles, fine. Nervous system, fine but frazzled nerves. Organs. Nausea. Stomach …

Suddenly I was hit by the brightest light I had ever *seen.* My body jolted back against the chair. My breathing stopped. My heart jumped. And I was in awe … wow, wow, wow.

She was pregnant.

I wanted to cry.

I saw holiness.

I saw a life in the making.

I was overwhelmed and momentarily relished the sight and presence of something so sacred. I knew I had to keep moving forward so I went on to give her courage, wisdom to find the right words for her mother, wisdom to find the right words to get rid of the father who was not right and would be a destructive force in the child's life. I filled her with hope and strength and resilience and determination to bring this child, this new spirit, this new life from God, into this world. I prayed for the child's benefit that God would bless it greatly. That He would bless them with a happy life, and an amazing future.

Then I sat back and cried.

• • •

"Your father agrees with me. You have to stop."

I looked at my fiancé. "I did stop. It was only for the weekend."

We clung to the boat, rocking and swayed to the rhythm of the waves. He stood at the helm with one hand on the stick and the other on a life line. I leaned into the wind in the cockpit beside him. Just the two of us. We used to have more crew for racing, but for a sweet guy, his temper had done its damage. Up until then, it was never directed at me. But one-by-one, over the last year, they dropped out.

If someone made a mistake on the boat which cost us a race, he became enraged and went after them with a winch handle. He was a big guy. And he was intimidating when he erupted. I didn't really blame them for giving up. It never occurred to me to reproach him about his temper. Besides, it wasn't anything I wasn't already used to growing up with.

It was the first long-distance race of the year. The icy-cold spring winds bit into our faces, our hair was wild and greasy, our noses froze and ran, and our eyes stung so bad it was hard to see. We were on a starboard tack on our way to Whitby from Frenchman's Bay. There was a second leg straight to Niagara-on-the-Lake after rounding a flag marker. That night, there was a party planned with boats rafted on to each other. We would head back to the finish line in Frenchman's Bay the next day. Lake Ontario was rough and choppy, and I felt the lack of the usual four to six crew members. But I also felt I could probably handle anything so long as he was at the helm.

The winds shifted, and it looked like it was a good run, so I went down below to dig up the spinnaker. We were second in line which was good considering it was just the two of us. I fed the spinnaker through the fore hatchway onto the foredeck so I could hurry on deck and prepare it for hoisting. I did everything right, holding one hand onto the forestay to keep from falling overboard while the other hand hooked up the halyard snap shackle into the hole at the top of the sail. I tied both port and starboard sheets, or lines, onto the lower holes on each side and fed them to the cockpit. I looked back at the competition. One crew beat us in getting the spinnaker up.

"Hurry!" my fiancé yelled at me excitedly. I rushed back to the mast and started to winch up the spinnaker. It went up and up and up when suddenly, the halyard snap shackle let go at the top. Our poor spinnaker suddenly dropped like a lead weight and was scooped down into the chop. The current of the water going passed our hull pulled it under. This cost us our second-in-line lead. As I was about to yank and pull at the spinnaker to get it on board for a second attempt, my fiancé threw the winch handle from the cockpit toward me. It just missed my head and it clanged onto the deck, then slid and stuck against the metal toe rail near the bow. I looked at a chip in the fiberglass deck caused by the throw. Then I looked back at the winch handle, rocking with the bucking of the boat. I was surprised we hadn't lost it over board.

"F---! F---! F---!"

I turned around just in time to see a six-foot-three four-year-old stamp his feet and cry. He banged the helm so fiercely I thought it was going to snap. Then he pummeled the compass, then the companionway trim. He sputtered and spit and cried and then finally fled down below. Then he slammed the companionway closed and threw in the slats to close it entirely. The boat was left to flounder with the main sail slapping and slacking in the chop and wind.

I had no choice but to secure the loose spinnaker and then take over the helm. There was no sense continuing on with the race. A few other boats had already overtaken us, and one or two even witnessed the tantrum. It was hard to miss. Even in a storm, noise travelled.

I slowly sailed back to Frenchman's Bay. It took almost three hours, because I was tacking into the wind, but that whole time, my fiancé never came up from the cabin below.

• • •

It was obvious to both of us that things were not right. A boat builder friend of ours was sailing a new model to Denmark and asked my fiancé if he was interested in crewing. He felt he should accept the invitation. He said it would be a good opportunity to think. Give us a break. A few days later, he left for the three-week trip. I said good-bye and then was alone with God.

I went back to the priest and told him that I wanted to apply to be a nun. He looked at me with an amused expression.

"Are you sure you want to do this?" We were sitting outside, this time on a bench further down the lawn towards the Avenue Road.

"Yes, I'm sure. All I know is that I want to live for God. My life is His. I don't want to do anything else." I fiddled with the hem of my spring coat.

"Look at you. You are an actress, a model. You can be on the cover of *Playboy*."

Is that what he thought? Have I, without even realizing it, bought into this degradation?

"You live with someone in sin," he continued. "How do these things match?" He looked at me as if I were pretty naïve. Perhaps I was. Perhaps I was pretty stupid.

"Please. I'm correcting things. I'm going to move out of my fiancé's apartment. I started looking for an apartment this morning." I was about to cry but held back the tears. "Let me make an appointment for an interview."

He closed his eyes. "Dearie, you walk around looking like a lady of the night."

I stared at him. "How can that be? I make a point of just looking *nice*."

The priest looked at me as if I was a walking billboard asking for sex. More precisely, asking to be a sex toy. Just like *Playboy: Entertainment for Men*.

I thought I had been so careful not to fall into that. I turned some work away precisely with that in mind. Had our culture become such that a woman only fell into one category? Eve, the fallen sex?

I then thought of the times I was accosted on the street. It was a consistent, daily inconvenience. I thought of the four youths who followed me for about three blocks after I had stepped off a bus near China Town. The only way I got rid of them was to turn and roar like I did with those two pit bulls in New York State. Then I thought of that man who came up to me when I was sitting in a public resting place outside of Union Station. He loudly yelled that now that the pill was out, all the young women were ready for sex. "Was I ready for sex?" he demanded loudly as he grabbed my arm. I threw off his arm and, as others watched, ran frightened-to-death into Union

Station. I felt dirty, humiliated. I thought of the time I modeled Marilyn Munroe's *Happy Birthday, Mr. President* dress for Edith Head, the famous Hollywood Fashion Designer. While I waited, someone offered me money to go off with them to a room.

Perhaps he was right. I didn't see the difference anymore. I couldn't believe the only option was to dress like a Mennonite. And then I realized, perhaps that was one of the aspects of being a nun I liked. You didn't wear make-up or fancy clothes to fit in with society. You weren't really part of it anymore as a nun. Was that also something that attracted me? Did I want to be safe?

I thought of one of Mam's aunts in the homeland. Raped three times, she gave up and became a nun.

But it came back to this: regardless of my level of comfort and emotional need, I knew I needed to give my life entirely to God.

And the only way I knew how was to be a nun. I became more determined.

"No, it's what I have to do. I want to be a nun. I believe it's what God wants."

He made a quick jerk of a nod. He made an appointment for the following week.

The next day, I found a little one-bedroom apartment. It needed some work, but I felt confident I could fix it up. I signed a year's lease and could move in anytime. But I had no idea how to get ahold of my fiancé to let him know. So, I planned to leave a note with a copy of the key and my engagement ring so when he returned, he didn't feel totally abandoned. Perhaps we could still remain friends. However, I did keep a beautiful gold watch he gave me the year before. I thought perhaps I could. I loved it so.

I hoped God wouldn't mind.

In the meantime, auditions and modeling go-sees kept me busy, as well as work. A go-see was a type of modeling audition where you meet a photographer or potential employer and show yourself and your portfolio. There was a lot of convention work which, unfortunately, consisted of wearing skimpy uniforms and handing out brochures. But it was good money.

Trying to think of the work as theatrical, I stood handing out brochures for the restaurant equipment supplier who hired me and another girl. We wore tiny blue togas and high-heeled sandals with straps wrapped around our calves. As usual, many of the salesmen and people coming to the shows hung around to talk. Some were polite, some were outright obvious about what they had in mind, but I learned to be diplomatic. I made a point of learning about the product I represented then steered the conversations to talk about the services and merits of the products. Then I would direct them to the guys who worked the floor for the company.

The second day, a frail-looking gentleman came by. Freckle-faced and pale with hazel eyes. He was polite and discovered I liked seafood. Several times a day for the rest of the show he came by with seafood samples.

Afterward, I forgot about him, as I did all the men who approached me. In the meantime, I had been accepted for an extravaganza musical fashion show that was to depict a hundred years of fashion in Canada. It was part of the birthday celebrations for the Canadian National Exhibition. Rehearsals started immediately after the convention. Somewhere in that tight schedule I still had to teach at night and move to the new apartment.

My interview with the priest and a Mother Superior was the following week. I figured I could squeeze in a quick modeling go-see in the morning. I selected a little summer dress, curled my long blonde hair, so that it was wavy, and bounced as I walked. I put on see-through plastic high-heeled sandals. I wore a pale nail polish and fairly little make-up.

After the go-see I hurried to my interview still carrying my portfolio. It was at a different building than I'd ever been to, just off Queen's Park. I walked through the stately stone portico and rang the doorbell. Eventually, the heavy, darkened-oak door opened, and a nun stood there. She studied me as I explained I had an appointment. She bowed with a smile on her face and let me in. She led me to a waiting room and showed me where to sit.

Thanking her, I sat on a cracked red leather seat. I looked out a large plate glass window with an upper stained-glass insert. It reminded me of the one I looked at during a thunderstorm while sitting on Nonna's lap so many years before. She taught me to see the beauty in a flash of lightening, while Mam cowered under the blankets in her bed.

Suddenly, the same nun returned and interrupted my thoughts. She motioned me to follow her through the main hallway toward the back of the building. She ushered me into a large office with heavy bookshelves. Ancient looking geranium plants rested on the ample window sills. Sun streamed in from behind the desk, highlighting streaks and smudges on the glass.

Shortly the priest came in and settled into his rocking, desk chair. I smiled nervously while we waited for Mother Superior to arrive. We hardly spoke, but he eyed my summer dress and hair. I didn't know what to think as I fretted and wrung my hands. Eventually, there was a light knock on the door. Mother Superior came in along with another nun. I stood and went to shake hands, but they both kept their hands in their tunics. I sat down as lady-like as possible.

Father sat back down and leaned back in his chair. "So, why don't you explain to Mother Superior and Sister Maria why you feel you have a calling to take a vow as a nun." He settled as far back as the chair would let him and nodded at me to speak.

Overwhelmed with emotion, I became teary-eyed while I tried to find the right words. I faltered at first but then found my voice. "I ache while I go through the days. I realize I look like I may not feel so, but all I want to do is live for God in whatever capacity He wants of me. The only way I know how is to become a nun. Please, it's what I believe I'm supposed to do." Tears streamed down my face. I quickly wiped them away with Kleenex the priest gave me.

When I finished, I continued twisting the wet Kleenex and waited for someone to respond.

Mother Superior and Sister Maria did not say a single word. They both looked from me to the priest and remained quiet. I looked at the priest.

He sighed and rocked anew in his chair. He interlaced his long fingers and looked down at the edge of his desk. "Well, I can see that you feel strongly about living a life you believe God may have in store for you. I think all three of us can see how sincere you are with your desire to take up vows. But I think I can speak on behalf of Mother Superior and Sister Maria that ..." he leaned forward, and his chair squeaked.

I couldn't breathe.

"Well, that, perhaps the confines of the Church will not meet with your personality." He motioned toward me as if to show I probably dressed too promiscuously or suggestively.

I somehow left the building and made it to our apartment building. I prayed and cried all the way. "Please show me what you want of me." I felt I was suddenly at a dead end.

When I made it into the apartment, it felt like God told me to go up to the roof and sit by the pool. So, I did. I sat on a lounge chair and overlooked the city from there. The warm sun and the sparkling reflection of the turquoise waters of the pool calmed me down.

Go back to the apartment and turn on the TV.

TV? I felt that was a cop-out. I prayed for it to be clearer.

Go to the apartment and turn on the TV.

Like a shot, I ran one floor down back to the apartment. I quickly turned on the TV.

The black and white TV showed a blonde woman talking to someone. Then, as I settled down, I saw her name coming across the bottom of the screen. It was exactly as mine.

The woman turned to the camera. "I am an artist. I think you are, too. I have never been on TV before, but I know that I am here because you need to hear what I have to say. Pick up that phone and call the number on your screen. Jesus loves you and wants you to come home."

I scrambled to get a pen and paper and wrote down the number.

I turned off the TV and dialed the number.

"100 Huntley Street, may I help you?"

I paused. I lived at 77 Huntley Street. "That's funny. You're on the same street as I am."

"Well, Praise the Lord. Can I help you?"

I explained what happened at the interview. "I know this may sound crazy to you, but I believe God is telling me to call you. I don't know what else to do!"

The young woman didn't think I was crazy. In fact, she told me the words I needed to hear. She quoted the same scripture God gave me earlier about being unevenly yoked. Then she said, "If you live right across the street, why don't you come and see if you can sit in the audience?"

"Okay, I'd love to. What's the name of your company?" I asked.

"100 Huntley Street," she answered politely.

"No, I mean the company. I know the address," I persisted.

"No. That is the name of our show. 100 Huntley Street. It's a charismatic Christian show."

I was stunned. All this time, right across the road, there was a Christian TV show. Every day. I had seen the big sign out front every time I came home or left for an appointment. It was right under my nose, literally. But I always thought it was simply a very large civic street address.

My voice cracked when I finally said, "Ok. I'll be right over."

I ran out of that apartment, went down the elevator, and ran out the front doors of my building across the road to the stone steps leading up to the front doors of 100 Huntley Street. My heart pounded as I opened the heavy glass door and walked in. There was a young woman at a desk close to the doors, and I went to her.

She smiled. "Can I help you?"

"Yes, I just got off the phone with one of your counselors. She suggested I come across the street—because that's where I live by coincidence—and see if there is room in the audience today."

She looked at a big book and said, "I'm sorry, we're booked solid, but there's an opening in October."

It was the beginning of July. That didn't help me one bit. I thanked her, turned, and left.

I went down the stone steps and prayed to God. I was at another dead end. Then, suddenly I heard my nickname being called. I looked up toward a parked car just up from where I stood. The sun glared off the windshield so I couldn't see who the form was that stood beside the car.

I squinted against the glare. "I'm sorry, who is that? Can't see because of the glare."

Then that freckled, frail-looking young man came closer and stepped into my sight. He raised his hand toward the building behind me. "What are you doing here?" he asked, surprised.

Standing there in the shade of the large trees on the street I explained what happened with the interview with the priest and nuns. How I cried. How I didn't know what else to do. I took the chance and spoke honestly about God telling me to watch TV. I told him I wasn't crazy, that I had a strong faith and I felt all I wanted to do was live for Him. I explained I had been inside to see if I could be in the audience, but it was packed full until October. I didn't know what to do.

"Oh, that's no problem. I've been volunteering here for two years and know everyone. Let me take you in and introduce you to everyone."

He took my arm and gently led me back inside. We walked past the young girl after he gave her a big bear hug. Then he took me further into the great hall, and I saw a little lady with white hair and bowed legs coming toward us.

He called out and said, "Regina, let me introduce you to someone I know. This is …"

Regina did not let him finish. She closed her eyes and held her hand up toward the ceiling. "Wait. I have a prophecy for you.

God is saying not to hide your light under a bushel basket, but to let it shine from the mountain top for the world to see." She opened her eyes and grinned.

I didn't know what to say. But I saw this as confirmation that I was not to be a nun at all.

Wow.

I thanked her. She had no way of knowing what I was going through that day.

Regina and the man talked and laughed and then she had to go. With a wave, she left.

"Come, let me introduce you to David Mainse and his wife, Norma Jean." And so, he did. I must have met twenty people. I met David Mainse, Norma Jean, Norma Jean's brothers, and many more people who all seemed wonderful, lovely people.

He showed me the studio and the audience area and then the offices, meeting rooms and the cafeteria. Then he turned to me and said, "Let's have a coffee. There's a little coffee shop around the corner I go to. If we stay here, too many people will interrupt us."

We went to the coffee shop on the first floor of my apartment building. I had never been in there. And for the first time in my life, I spoke to someone who totally, openly admitted to *hearing* a Voice, also getting messages through scripture, and yes, TV. He even added the radio. "God uses whatever works to get the message across," he said. "Even a newspaper, a magazine, or someone walking by and you happen to hear them say something that means something to you."

We sat with our coffees. He smoked cigarettes from a black package. Holding one up, he said, "I know. I'm going to stop. I'll be without cigarettes in two months."

I nodded. It had been a very emotional day. Still was. He pointed around the coffee shop. "Even here, what do you see?"

I looked around. There were straw crucifixes all over the walls. Different sizes and colors. "People may not even notice them, but those who get something out of them do. Like us."

I was drained. I thanked him for his time and the coffee.

"Well, can we keep in touch? It seems to me that God has you on a path that perhaps you may need to speak to someone about, share things with. Can you give me your phone number?"

I didn't want to give him my phone number. Besides I was moving. So, I told him, "I haven't moved into my new apartment yet, and won't have my new phone until after I move in."

"Oh, okay," he said politely. I bade him goodbye and I thanked him.

I went back upstairs to the apartment and got down on my knees to pray. I was so drained that I had no words. I just knelt there feeling close to Him. He could read my heart, I thought. I fell asleep in the kneeling position with my head on the edge of the bed.

I had absolutely no inkling of the great and painful adventure He had planned for me.

THIRTEEN

A Different Kind of Nun

"...They are one flesh.
What God has joined together, man must not separate."

(Matthew 19:6, NEB)

I had spruced up the little apartment and it felt quite comfortable and homey. I was setting my hair in rollers and getting ready for a runway rehearsal when my newly installed phone rang. I looked at the ugly green thing on the wall and wondered who it could be. I didn't think I had given it to anyone as yet, not even my agent. I answered it.

"Hello?"

"Hi, it's me. God told me to drive to the corner of Charles and Parliament to come and see you. I'm not sure where you are from here."

"Where's here?" I asked, stunned.

"I'm in a phone booth on the southwest corner."

"How'd you get this number?"

"From the phone company."

"But how'd you get it so fast? I just got it installed."

"I got it once I got into this phone booth."

I was quiet for a moment, my thoughts racing.

"Where are you?"

"Just a minute." I let the phone receiver dangle against the kitchen wall while I looked out the kitchen window. There, to the left, was a phone booth I had never noticed. Inside was a man wearing a camel-haired coat. It was the freckled one. I dropped my head. I didn't want to be interrupted as I had very little time to get ready.

I went back to the phone. "Believe it or not, you're right outside my window."

"Praise the Lord. Thank you, Jesus."

I took a deep breath.

"May I come in?"

"Well, I'm just getting ready for a rehearsal …"

"It won't take long."

"Oh, okay. I'll let you in." I walked out into the hallway of the building and opened the front doors. I looked out and over to the far-right corner of the building. I saw him lean out of the phone booth. I waved. He hung up the phone. I waited for him to get to the doors, and then I led him the two doors further to my apartment. "Come on in. I don't have much time, though, as you can see." I pointed to my curlers. "I have a rehearsal and have to leave in about twenty minutes."

"Can I give you a ride?" he offered.

"Oh no, I'm going by subway. Can I make you a quick cup of tea?"

"No, not if you're in a hurry. Would you mind if I bring a friend over on Saturday? I would like you to meet him. He recently accepted Jesus into his life."

"Sure, come for lunch. I'll make sandwiches."

He left after a few minutes but I was unsettled, and a little frustrated. I was waiting for God's direction and I found this persistent man distracting. I left for my rehearsal.

At noon, Saturday, he arrived with a man who was a midget. "This is my roommate." I shook his roommate's hand and then asked them to sit down on my sparse furnishings. I made the sandwiches and hot, sweet tea. They both ate as if they hadn't eaten in days.

The freckled one sat back at one point and looked around the apartment. "You're going to move soon."

I looked at him, startled. "I just moved in and have a year's lease."

"God is telling me you'll be out by the end of next month."

"Impossible," I said.

Then he changed the subject. "Would you help my sister with something?" he asked. "She, her husband, and two kids moved back from California to live in Guelph. She has a lady's problem, but no one to talk to. It has to be another Christian woman."

"Oh, what's the problem?"

"I don't know. Can you come tomorrow?"

I was completely unaware of the shock waiting for me the next day.

• • •

West of Toronto on our way to Guelph, he suddenly pulled over and turned off the car. He turned to me and said, "God told me I should ask you to marry me."

I choked. I quickly thought about my response, a resounding but polite no of course.

"You know what? That's lovely of you to ask. However, having just been turned down by the church, I don't think I have any plans to marry. Thank you, but no."

"Are you sure?"

I must have frowned. "Yes, I'm sure."

He started the engine, and we got back on the highway. A few kilometers later, he pulled over and stopped again.

"No, God is telling me that you and I are to be married. As a matter of fact, God is saying we should get married on September 21."

I smiled, relieved. "Well, He knows I'm already booked that whole day. Besides, I think He should tell me Himself what He wants me to do."

"Well, that's what I know," he said, pleasantly.

We finally made it to his sister's house. I walked into a small, post-war home and met a lovely family. His sister was sweet, her husband delightful and humble, and their two little children well behaved and gentle. A little later, his sister led me to the backyard where we sat down on patio chairs.

"What is the problem?" I asked. Perhaps it was something I could teach her.

"Well, I'm in a quandary. I don't know if it's Christian for a woman to shave her legs or not. Mine are so hairy, and I want so much to go barelegged in the summertime."

I looked down at her dewy legs and smiled. "I'm sure God wouldn't mind you shaving your legs. If they were hairy men would look at them more than if they were not hairy. Also, if it pleases you to shave and it doesn't hurt a soul, wouldn't Jesus want you to feel good about yourself?"

Apparently, that did the trick.

In the meantime, my ex-fiancé would be back shortly. I still hadn't done anything to break up with him. God nudged me to write a note to call it off, but I chickened out. I was about to learn that if you don't do it, God will, and His mighty Hand could be frightening to watch.

One day, my freckled friend called and told me that God told him to come to my place to sleep in my bed. Not to be *with* me, but to lie on top of the covers while I slept.

That sounded like a come-on.

"I'm not trying to pick you up or anything. It's important I'm there tonight."

I prayed about it. God said, *trust me.*

So, that night he showed up at my apartment. I slipped into bed fully dressed; he stayed on top of the covers. "What else did God tell you?" I asked, nervously.

"Nothing, He said to do nothing. Just lie here."

"Oh, okay." We lay exactly as he said, and I turned the light out. Not ten minutes later, I heard a key in the door.

My eyes widened in the dark. I saw my ex-fiancé come in the dark doorway. He called. I didn't say a word. I saw his hand try to find a light switch on the wall, but couldn't find it. In the light of the street lights outside my window, he began to walk over to my bed. He gently sat on the edge against the legs of the freckled one, and then put his hand on the freckled one's leg.

I stared at his hand. My heart almost jumped out of my throat.

"Hi," I said.

"Listen, you don't need to move away. I ..." His hand slipped off the leg, and then he felt mine. He felt four legs. He shot up to his feet, yelped, ran out and slammed the door shut.

That's what I mean about God doing the very thing you drag your feet on doing. He does it in a very expedient and frightening manner.

• • •

"I told you. God wants us to marry."

We had gone over this already. I made tea. We were both still in our clothes. I was shaken. By this humiliating experience. "That was awful. Now he thinks I've cheated on him, and I would never do that." I felt sick to my stomach. "He must be hurting so badly right now."

"Well, that may be true, but God wanted you to break it off. So, He had to do it."

"Yeah, but like *that?*"

"God told me we should go to City Hall tomorrow and book the wedding."

I wanted to scream at this man. Then I challenged God.

"He has to tell me in such a way that it's obvious only to me. I have to pray about this. Please, let me have some privacy." I looked at him beseechingly. "You must understand this is difficult. I mean, I don't really care for you. And you say we should marry. I'm so sorry. It really has to be between God and only me."

He finally left. I settled down and talked to God about this. "God, I am not going to do something that I hate to do. If it's something You really want me to do, then I will do it. I've given you my life. Totally. But I have to hear it from you. Not someone else." I took my Bible and sat on my loveseat. I focused on His presence and let the book open where it would. I read:

"Therefore, a man shall leave his father and his mother and hold fast to his wife, and they shall become one flesh."

Ephesians 5:31

I lowered my head and prayed, "Dear Father, my parents are still on the trip and will be here at the end of September. I was about to be a nun. I don't know this man, and I don't even like him. But even with all this working against me, I will do as you ask of me. Definitely. You know I would. It just has to be so obvious to me there is absolutely no room for doubt. It has to be a 2x4 between the eyes. And I thank you, Lord. Amen."

It was in His hands now. I trusted it would be very clear. If not, I wouldn't do a thing about marrying anyone. I went to bed and slept soundly for the first time in a long time.

• • •

Several dancers and I sat out in the sun, drenched in sweat, after a grueling five hours rehearsal for the 100th Anniversary of Fashion for the Canadian National Exhibition. It was a musical, with great dance numbers and singing. There were constant costume changes showing the 100 years of fashion in Canada. The grounds were deserted except for a group of soldiers training in the distance. I had an Orange Julius from a little stand nearby.

I thought hard about this challenge I put to God. The freckled one still said we were to go to Old City Hall to make an appointment for September 21st. I hadn't told him I was booked six months earlier for three shows at Eaton Centre that day. So, in my book, that made it a nonstarter. But I agreed to go to City Hall just to humor him.

In a couple of hours, he would pick me up to drive the half hour to Old City Hall before they closed. I sighed loudly, downed the remainder of the juice, and groaned as I got up to go back into the theater. The other girls were chatting, rearranging messy pony tails, and pulling at their bodysuits at the neck to let a breeze flow down their chests.

I heard marching and looked over. The soldiers, as a group, were marching toward us.

I groaned inwardly. Just what we needed. Here were six young women in tight-fitting latex bodysuits out on the steps, and forty testosterone-filled young men marching right by us.

I walked up the stairs but wasn't in the building before all the whistles and catcalls started. I heard the other girls giggle and laugh.

I looked back. Sexuality. Rampant sexuality. If I was in a different mindset, I would've been giggling along with the others.

But I wasn't in that mindset anymore.

• • •

As we entered the registry, I noticed the doorway was right across the street from one of the exits at Eaton Centre. I stopped and looked over as it looked oddly familiar. I started to walk to the mall's entrance.

"Where are you going?" the freckled one asked.

"I'm checking something. This will just take a second." I ran across the laneway and walked through the entrance into the mall. I looked around. This was where the runway would be for the fashion show. Curious. I turned and looked out the glass door to where the freckled one was standing. Forty feet away. Then I pushed the door open and ran over.

"What were you looking at?"

"Nothing. Something caught my attention."

He motioned for us to go in. They would close in ten minutes. We entered a cold marble hallway and headed for an old doorway with a large frosted glass window. Painted on the glass in gold letters was, *Old City Hall Marriage Registry*. We both walked to the door, waited for a couple exiting, then entered.

We walked to a counter where a tired looking woman stood with a very large ledger.

"Hi, can I help you?"

"Yes," said the freckled one, "We'd like to get married on September 21."

"Oh," she said, "I'm sorry. We're booked solid until the end of October."

I was relieved. "Thank you very much," I said, with a big smile to her.

"You're welcome," she mumbled.

The freckled one and I turned to leave. Just as we were squeezing through the door side-by-side, I heard her voice call out.

"Oh, sorry. Actually, we had a cancellation today for September 21 at 12:30. Would that do?"

Turning back toward her, I felt my body shake with the beat of my pounding heart. Slowly I nodded.

My fashion shows were booked for 10:30, 2:30, and 4:30 immediately across the lane from the Registry. And this fashion show had been booked for six months

Wham, bang! A 2x4 right between the eyes!

BOOK THREE:

The Holy Years

"So instead of perfume you will have the stench of decay,
and rope instead of a girdle, baldness instead of hair
elegantly coiled,
a loin-cloth of sacking instead of a mantle,
and branding instead of beauty."

(Isaiah 3:24, NEB)

FOURTEEN

The Prophet and His Jezebel

1978

"In the name of Jesus, I command you to move."

The car in front of us turned on its signal and moved into the next lane. It was Saturday. The freckled one dropped by my place earlier to chat, but I was on my way to do a fashion show at Yorkdale. He held me up enough that I would be late. The subways didn't run as frequently as on workdays, and I hated to be late.

"I'll take you there," he said. But even by car, I wouldn't be on time. He looked at his watch. "Nope, we'll arrive there three minutes before they open the doors."

Even though it was 7:30 in the morning, traffic was heavy all the way up to Eglinton. Then he said God told him to drive over to the Allen Expressway and go up that way instead of up to the 401 and over.

I watched the clock on his dash and felt queasy. When we finally made it to the Allen Expressway, my heart sank at the bumper-to-bumper traffic.

He pointed at the cars directly in front of us and prayed over each one. They got out of the way. When he dropped me off at the side entrance to Yorkdale, he pointed to the dash clock.

"See, three minutes to go. The doors aren't even open yet." I looked out and saw the other girls waiting, laden down with their bags of curlers, shoes, and everything else needed for a fashion show. "We even have time to talk," he joked.

"I used to do that, too," I said. "While sailing, something would always tell me what time we were going to finish tying up the boat, or when we would drop the anchor."

"That's God," he said.

I looked at this strange fellow and nodded. What kind of an adventure was I getting into?

• • •

My blonde uncle discovered I was marrying a complete stranger and called to say he knew what it was like to see the face of God. He almost drowned in the sea as a child and saw a bright light. When he was rescued, he knew he had gone to another place and was touched by God Himself.

"Then you understand that I believe God is telling me to marry this man." I told him of my challenge to God, and how He made it clear this was what I was supposed to do.

"I am going to tell your father what you are planning to do. This will be very upsetting for them both. You know they'll be back on the 29th. You can't even wait until after they're back?"

Oh, that tugged at my heart. I would never, ever go against my parents in anything. But I knew if I waited they would talk me out of it. God knew that very well.

"No, I'm sorry. I believe this is what I'm supposed to do. I know I'm stepping out on faith. But I have to do this."

"Then I disinherit you as my niece," he said, and he hung up.

I stood with the phone in my hand, shocked and heartbroken. Standing in my kitchen, I prayed, "Oh God, this is hard. So hard. But if this is what you want, I will do it. Please give me the strength to pursue this. And please show me again this is precisely what you want of me."

During this time, the Canadian National Exhibition opened, and the freckled one came with me for the six performances. Packed crowds watched each show. We went from the early 1800s of Canada with our long dresses and head pieces right through to the present day, concluding with top hats and canes singing and dancing *Chorus Line*. By that time, we dressed in the newest body-hugging latex leotards in bright red satin. It did not leave a lot to the imagination.

"Who is that young man in the audience staring at you?" asked the girl beside me at the make-up mirror.

I was too embarrassed to say I was about to marry him. The truth was, I still didn't like him very much, though I respected his strong faith and closeness to God. After all, the confirmations from God of my last year's lessons came directly from him. Other than the woman in the showers in Morehead City, I did not know anyone else who walked so closely with Him. Not even the priest, Mother Superior, or the nun.

He and I spoke the same language, and faced and followed the same God, and Savior, Jesus. And, on top of that, we saw we were on the right track through daily mini-miracles.

I lied and said, "Oh, he's my brother."

"A brother looking at you like that?" She made a face. "Weird brother."

It didn't occur to me that he may be seeing me as a woman as well as a sister in Christ. That made me feel very nervous and frightened.

We must have lost another ten pounds off our already skinny frames. It was difficult and hard work in a theater without air conditioning. And even though it paid the same for an entire month of rehearsals and performances as I received for a single day in a fashion show, it was theater, and I thrived on it. I loved performing for a live audience. The ham was still there.

As I packed up my curlers and other things after the closing performance, I noticed my watch was missing. The beautiful, gold watch from my ex-fiancé. I looked around. There were so many strangers coming backstage—friends, and relatives of the other dancers—that it was quite possible one of them stole it. I was sure none of the other dancers would.

It was God's way of cutting all ties to my ex-fiancé.

It occurred to me the freckled one only had one set of clothing for during the day. One or two old shirts, a ratty tie, and a blazer and pants that did not match very well. I took him to a men's shop and had him outfitted in a brand-new three-piece suit, three new shirts, a couple of pairs of pants, a sweater, a few ties, socks, and new shoes.

I didn't buy a dress specifically for the wedding. I chose a lovely, long two-piece silk dress I bought in Montreal a while before and planned to wear the same see-through little sandals on my feet I wore for the interview.

In the middle of September, I moved out of the apartment and put the few things I had in storage in a shed he knew about. Then for the last week before getting married, we stayed at the Seahorse Motel along the lakeshore.

We remained celibate and sifted through what was left to do before the wedding day. We also dropped by 100 Huntley Street. While there, a friend of his offered the use of their cottage for a week after our wedding. A retreat for a honeymoon during which we were going to hike, fish, and contemplate and meditate on God's Word.

"God is telling me we should live in an apartment up in Downsview," he told me after one of these visits. "He's saying we should drive out there right now."

"Do you know where?"

"I remember a woman in Downsview who knew my parents. I think God is telling me they'll have something to rent." And so, we dropped everything and drove up to Downsview. Driving along a street of postwar houses, we parked in front of a large bungalow on a corner lot. He rang the doorbell, and a short, heavy-set woman opened the door. She smiled.

"Oh, hello! How are you!?"

The freckled one said he was fine and his parents were fine. Then he said, "We are getting married. I thought we'd drop by to see if you know of any apartment that might be available."

She was taken aback. "Why yes," she said, disappearing for a moment. "You won't believe this. I just wrote out this little card to put on the bulletin board at the grocery store. We renovated the basement, and I was going to rent it out."

I looked at the card. I mutely followed the freckled one into the house where we sat and signed a slapped-together lease on a piece of writing paper. We had an apartment we could move into any time for $50 a week.

Early, on the day of the wedding, the freckled one took me to his parents' house. I met them first when he introduced me as the woman he was going to marry. His parents were devout Anglicans, very British, and seemed supportive and almost relieved for him. They gave us their blessings and offered to have a lovely party at their place after the wedding. It would be a small wedding. His brother would be Best Man, and his sister would be my Maid of Honor.

Before the 12:30 wedding ceremony, I had a fashion show at 10:30, so he drove me to the Eaton Center around 9:00 in the morning. While I pranced along the runway, his family, even those I had not even met, gathered immediately across the lane in Old City Hall Registry's lobby.

After my morning show, I changed into my wedding outfit, redid my hair and make-up, and strode across the lane. The Justice of the Peace pronounced us husband and wife. Then everyone trailed behind us as we returned across the laneway to the runway. They rested on benches while the models and I got ready for the next two shows. My new family stayed, watched, and grinned during the 2:30 show. Then they all went to my new in-laws' home to get ready for the dinner. I did the 4:30 show and by 5:30 I was at my new in-laws' home eating and doing the proverbial kiss together to the tune of forks against crystal glasses. Our first kisses.

My mother-in-law baked a beautiful wedding cake. Photos were taken of us cutting the cake. After a long evening with delightful people and children, we headed off to the Haliburton's for a one-week honeymoon and our time to meditate and pray.

There were no relatives or friends from my side at the wedding.

My parents were to arrive after being gone for a whole year the day after our return from the cottage. How on earth was I going to explain what I had done?

My whole world had gone topsy-turvy since the last time I saw them in the Bahamas.

And they weren't able to do a single thing to stop me.

• • •

The week at the cabin was idyllic. We brought all our Bibles and found there was enough firewood for heating and cooking. We laughed, slept, prayed, and hiked along a gorge. It was cool, so I wore a sweater, knitted while on the boat, and my favorite jeans that were more like farmer's overalls.

I swept, cleaned, and cooked while my new husband brought in the firewood and chopped more. We tried our hand at fishing and caught a couple of rock bass that I filleted and fried over the wood cook stove. We slept like babies in the cold fresh air under a pile of quilts. That week was over too soon. Now I had to face some very difficult hurdles.

Namely, Pap and Mam.

• • •

I got out of my husband's car and stood for a moment looking over Frenchman's Bay. The club was decked out with colorful flags flapping in the stiff breeze while the halyards zinged from masts along the packed docks. White, blue, and pink balloons were grouped everywhere, fighting with the wind. Harry Belafonte sang to bongo drums over the speakers screwed to the corners of the clubhouse. The bounce added to the celebratory feeling of the day. The sun was bright and hot for late September. So different from the day when we left Toronto exactly one year before.

"Shake, shake, shake Signora,
Shake your body line,

Shake, shake, shake, Signora,
Shake it all the time...[12]

I looked over at my new husband. It was a strange environment for him. Wearing a sweater, shirt, and pants I bought him, he stood smiling and watching some young boys clambering over a small sailboat which had tipped. They laughed and screamed while they tried to right the boat. No one paid attention to them. They were well-trained. It was all fun.

The boats along the docks and tied to moorings danced and rocked seemingly to the beat of the blaring music.

I searched the parking lot for my ex-fiancé's car and found it near the main dock. I knew he was probably inside at the bar doing the elbow exercises he joked about.

Everyone waited for the arrival of my parents and little sister. No doubt, as Commodore, he would do a speech and presentation to them later on.

I had had enough. "I'd like to go now."

"Why? Look. There they are."

Pap and Mam's boat was entering the gap separating the bay from Lake Ontario. There were hundreds of people pressing towards the main dock to welcome them back. Newspaper reporters were ready with cameras to capture the moment of their return. In those days, it was still very unusual for someone to sail down to the Caribbean and back.

I was proud of my family. But I didn't want to draw any attention to myself from friends of mine at the club. In their eyes, I was a two-timer. I cheated on their friend and their Commodore of the club. I was happy to stay at the far end of the parking lot, in the shade of the bushes.

"We should really go closer to the docks," my new husband repeated.

---

[12] Jump In The Line, Harry Belafonte, composed by Lord Kitchener, 1952, RCA Victor.

I shook my head. "No, I'd rather stay here. If I don't speak to them today, at least they know we came. I can talk to them tomorrow, or once they settle in at home."

I sensed he had no idea about my emotional turmoil. But he respected my wishes. Suddenly the crowd cheered. I looked out and saw Mam at the bow searching the crowds. Probably for me. I saw the concerned dark scowl on her deeply-tanned face. Pap was at the helm his dark hair streaked blonde from consistent sun. A head taller, my little sister had matured and was standing at the port shroud mid-ship ready to throw a coiled dock line.

Finally, as the boat rocked into place dockside and Pap reversed quickly against the following wind, my little sister beautifully timed herself, throwing the line to someone ready to catch it. Pap threw a stern line to someone else close by, and I saw Mam simply bend through the bow spit and gently hand her line to another smiling person.

I let out a deep sigh and climbed back into the car.

"You want to go?"

I nodded. "I'll see them once they're settled in."

● ● ●

"What were you thinking, marrying a complete stranger? And not having the decency to wait until we came back. Is this some loser manipulating you? Are you crazy!?"

I closed my eyes. I called their house from our basement apartment in Downsview.

I spoke as gently and clearly as possible. "Pap, I told you. I understand you don't believe in any of this, but God told me. I prayed and prayed about this. I wouldn't just marry a stranger. I didn't even want to be married."

"Including your fiancé?"

"Pap. I wanted to be a nun. Just live for God."

"And the church turned you down."

"Yes, I told you."

"Of course, they turned you down. You know why? Because they saw you weren't in your right mind. You have a screw loose. Come now, you're smarter than this."

I sat on my little love seat and looked up at the high window of the basement apartment. I saw a white dove fly by.

You're okay. You're in the right spot.

Pap hung up, disgusted with me. I didn't expect him to understand.

I felt myself sinking into that familiar abyss of depression.

Turn on the radio.

Carrying my pain and aching heart, I slowly got up and went to the little portable radio I had near the window ledge. I turned it on. A piano intro ...

"You are so beautiful to me,"

I dropped my head. Tears welled up.

"You are so beautiful to me."

I started crying. I didn't understand why God was so good to me. Why He would go out of His way to even send me this message. I was such a total dunce all the time.

"Can't you see?
You're everything I hoped for...[13]

• • •

Days later, I sat on the green couch in my parents' living room. The ugly box house Pap bought a few years before now had an extension that reached into the small backyard. This room was somewhat of a great room. It contrasted strangely with the rest

---

[13]   You Are So Beautiful To Me, Joe Cocker, 1974, written by Billy Preston and Bruce Fisher.

of the box-like house, but it added dignity and space. It was a space Mam loved.

The room dropped down by a couple of carpeted steps with a cathedral-type ceiling with a large plate glass window at the very end. There were narrow strips of yellow glass along the top of the wall. When the sun shone, the entire room was bathed in golden light.

I looked at my new husband's profile. He sat on the top step that led into the living room. Pap was in a trim-looking La-Z-Boy. Dressed in a sparkling black top and matching velour pants, Mam sat in the armchair closest to a new fireplace. A gentle fire snapped and crackled. My little sister sat in the other armchair playing with a Sesame Street hand puppet.

Who is this stranger God had me marry? I wondered. He was an enigma to me. I knew practically nothing about him. I loved his family. I loved the communion and prayer. I loved that we were both very sensitive to what we believed God wanted us to do.

"Hey man, have another drink," Pap offered. "And tell me more about yourself. I wanna check you out to make sure you treat my daughter right."

I laughed nervously. Pap was searching out all the pitfalls, warts and secrets in this young man's personality so that he could show me later that I made a stupid mistake. For me to leave the man. Get some counseling and straighten out. Be a normal person.

Like him.

Like my uncles.

There was very little my husband could say in response to Pap's question. He worked for an immigrant entrepreneur selling posters, flags, and velvet paintings on the side of the road. I didn't know this until recently. He used to work in a jewelry factory, monitoring and managing the acid baths the jewelry were dipped into before they were cast in gold. After years of this work, the fumes burned the sensitive tissues in his nasal cavity. It bothered him quite a bit.

I trimmed his hair the night before. He wore the three-piece suit I bought him. His freckles looked almost fragile on his porcelain skin. He was gentle and kind and poured attention on my little sister and Mam. I felt the tension in the room lower slightly after the first few minutes. But now Pap raised it alarmingly.

"What are your future plans, man? You can't be a husband if you don't have any. I don't know if you plan to have kids ...?" He motioned to me. I groaned inside.

"Yes, we would like children," said my husband. We hadn't spoken about that yet. I was going with the Holy flow.

Pap raised his shoulders and his palms. "So, don't you think you should do better than sell velvet paintings of Elvis Presley on street corners?" He darted a look at me.

I squirmed, wanting to leave. I looked into my cup of coffee. I thought I 'd control the conversation somewhat.

"He's thinking of starting a line of personalized mirrors," I offered. "I would help him." I threw the ball at my husband.

The freckled one took the ball and ran with it. He talked about plastic adhesive sheeting, mirrors, acid baths, photographs, and putting together the framing.

"Let me know when you're ready. I can help you, man. Set you up."

I looked at Pap. It was another trap. How well would this young man accomplish something if given the chance? Did he have it in him? Pap wanted to make it clear to me that he was willing to invest and lose money just to show me what a loser the freckled one was. Then he said something I could've taken as sarcastic or sincere.

"Well, I guess if you believe in God there's got to be some good, right? At least you'll treat my daughter well."

The freckled one looked over his shoulder at me and smiled. I smiled back.

• • •

"God wants you to stop working."

I looked up from where I sat doing my make-up. We were just about to leave for an evening fashion show downtown.

I looked around the basement apartment. My parents gave us their old furniture and the old standup piano. I made the apartment look cozy. We still slept on my three-quarter bed.

He wasn't making any money and what we had was from my work. I didn't mind that. If God wanted it this way, that was fine with me.

"Remember when we were driving back from your parents and you agreed that if God wanted to test us to live on faith alone, you would do it?"

I remembered that conversation well. I started feeling a bit queasy.

"Yes."

"Well, it's time we did exactly that."

I looked down at my nails. Another challenge. Not working. I groaned inside because I knew what Pap would say and think. That he was lazy. Crazy. But didn't I have total faith this was His path for me?

Of course, if God wanted it, then that's what we did.

I broke my contract with my agency. They were upset and warned I was making a big mistake. I was doing well and had a long, lucrative career ahead of me.

The freckled one also told me I was to stop wearing make-up and what he called suggestive clothing. He looked through my clothes and threw away what he thought was not becoming. He also went through my books and threw away any books that showed nudity. That meant, of course, everything to do with art: Leonardo da Vinci, Michelangelo, Rubens, Picasso …

Then he announced that God wanted me to stop taking the pill.

By then I felt a little disoriented. We were both going through a major fast. At night, we watched *100 Huntley Street*, *PTL Club*, and *700 Club*. Anything to do with *born-again* Christianity. We read the Bible together. He came home with books written by *born-again* authors. We learned a tremendous amount about living on faith and the mysterious way God moved.

We ate simple bread and had the occasional peanut butter. We drank pure fruit juices but refrained from everything else as was traditional with fasting. My head was starting to buzz.

But recently, an odd little thing happened that surprised me. I walked up the hallway toward the open door of the bathroom. The freckled one was at the mirror shaving. The bones in my foot snapped just as I got to the door. Suddenly he jumped out with his face half covered in shaving cream, and a fist raised ready to punch me in the nose.

Then one day we were talking about someone we both knew at one of the churches we had visited recently. The freckled one sat at the table with the November sun pouring through the basement window highlighting the red in his dark blonde hair. Suddenly, he began to spit out a few vicious words. It was so sudden, that I blinked and wondered if it was my imagination.

"That f---ing bastard deserves a kick in his ass."

He continued to spew more vulgar terms and said terrible things about the man. It was such a shock compared to the always gentle demeanor he had that, without realizing it, I slapped him. I wanted him to stop.

He *woke* up. He touched his cheek, and said, "Oh, sorry, I have no idea where that came from."

That was the first and last time he acknowledged this behavior as strange. The gentleman in him had left the room.

● ● ●

"God says we are to conceive a baby."

I was reading one of the Christian books he brought home. I now wore used clothing we found at a Goodwill that showed less leg, arm, and neck. A baby? I never really thought about actually going ahead and planning for one.

That's what we did. I felt the exact moment a new life began. The *exact* moment. It was as if I was visited by someone.

Someone gently stepped into my life. And I knew his name was Joel.

Three months later, Pap gave us a belated wedding gift of $4,000 in cash. We curled up all the bills and placed them in a little multi-shelf toolbox I had. We lived on that until it ran out.

In the meantime, the freckled one began to claim I was to be *taught* some lessons. I still had the *Jezebel* in me. By this time, we became so tuned in to each other that we could clearly read each other's minds. Not so much the actual words, but the thoughts and emotions. When he said I was to be taught lessons because there was a Jezebel in me, I felt appalled and insulted.

He felt that.

He grabbed me by the front of my dress and pulled me closer. His face was right into mine, he was truly angry. "You are nothing but a whore, a f---- whore." He slapped my face and dropped me on the couch. Shocked, I held my cheek while tears welled up in my eyes. He pointed his finger at me. He came in close again and started jabbing me in the face with that finger. "I know what you're thinking. You're blind to how evil you are!"

Tearfully, I defended myself. "How can you say that? We're both living for God, and I've done everything you asked."

"But He knows you don't want to do this. I know you wish you still had the clothes that showed off your f---ing body, your t-ts, your legs up to here!" He did a chopping motion to his neck. "What's the matter? You miss showing your p---y?" He grabbed my ankle and roughly spread my legs.

I quickly pushed my dress down between my legs. I kicked him away which was a bad move because he then grabbed my hair, pulled me up, and dragged me out the living room, down the shared hallway that led to the landlord's laundry room, and into the little bathroom we used. He threw me in front of the sink and pulled my face up by the hair.

"See that!?"

I saw my face and his in the mirror. My hair was crunched up in his fist. He was glaring at me, his hazel eyes looking pure black. He shook my head.

"See that!?" He squeezed his fist of hair so that it felt like it was being pulled out of my scalp. I screamed.

"Yes! I see!" I burst into sobs.

"Well, that is the face of a whore. A f---ing whore!"

He let me go and stomped off, leaving me leaning over the sink in front of the mirror. I stayed there for a long, long time crying and praying to God. What had I done?

• • •

1979

Mam had given me beautiful material for Christmas, so I sewed all my own maternity outfits. I also wore a scarf over my head as I did when I was a young hippie. I had become housebound because I was now not allowed to leave the house unless I was with the freckled one.

One day, in May, we didn't have gas in the car, but we needed food. We had just a bit of money left. So, it was a toss-up. Gas or food. I was forced to fast consistently and was becoming quite anemic. So the freckled one said that God told him to take me for a walk to get some sun and to pick up liver for me. By that time, I hadn't been out of the house for four months.

It felt strange walking out in the street in shoes that didn't fit anymore. They were flats from Goodwill. When we first bought them they fit, but now I was six months pregnant, and my feet had spread a little. All my beautiful sandals and heels were thrown away. Not given away, because they were evil. They were thrown away with the garbage.

The sun was bright. As we walked along, a young man came toward us. I glanced up at him as he walked by. He looked at me, and I was ashamed. I was pale, no make-up, six months pregnant walking immediately and dutifully behind my husband, and I must have looked frightened. Suddenly I felt the freckled one in my head. His feelers were out. He didn't even have to look back at me, I knew that he knew I had looked up and met this young man's eyes.

An hour later, as soon as we walked through the door to our little living room with milk and liver in hand, he closed the door and pushed me from behind. My head snapped back as I fell forward. I reached out to keep from falling on my stomach and somehow maneuvered myself to land on my side. I could feel the baby jerk. I slowly got up, crying as quietly as possible, because crying made him more upset.

I had learned if I pled for mercy, he became angrier. If I tried to reason, I got the same results. If I stayed mute, he would be angry and pull words out of me under physical threat and then get upset at what I said. There was no way around his episodes.

At times, when he saw he cut or bruised me, or if my face swelled after an episode, he stopped and stared at me for a moment. Then he would fall on his knees and cry, begging for forgiveness.

I would sit there, on the couch, or floor, or bed, bedraggled and drained. I learned the best thing to do was nod and whisper "I forgive you." Then he would grab me with hugs and kisses and tell me what a wonderful woman I was. How blessed he was to have me as his wife and what a wonderful mother I was going to be.

He never did these things in front of the rest of the world. Never.

• • •

"You can visit your Mam this weekend."

I looked up from my needlepoint. I was making baby shifts for Joel out of red gingham and I was doing a cross-stitch along the top to create little creases. I had learned to think carefully before I spoke. I was also very careful to control my thoughts.

By this time, Pap and Mam had sold the box house because Pap was rebuilding a marina for the family business. For the time being, they lived on the boat in the summer at the marina but during the school year, Mam stayed in a penthouse apartment in Ajax while my sister went to a local school. Eventually, the plan was to build a home for Mam and Pap. But first the docks had to be built, and the business developed.

The only times the freckled one would allow me to see them was when he decided to hit Pap for money. He had a pet saying every time Pap would say, "How are you doing?"

The freckled one would joke, "Nothing a million bucks won't fix."

Then Pap would ask, "Do you guys need money?"

And I'd hear the freckled one chuckle and say, "Oh, it wouldn't hurt."

"How much?" Pap would ask.

"Two hundred would do for now."

It took me a while to catch on. I pretended not to hear. I was so ashamed.

I knew that the freckled one only wanted to go and ask for money again but I wanted to see them one more time before I gave birth. I was almost due, and I knew also I'd be cooped up in the house for a long while afterward. First, however, we needed a tank of gas for the trip as it was almost two hours' drive one way. The freckled one said that God told him to go to the mall. He came back an hour later with $50 in his pocket.

"Another miracle today. God told me to go to the far end of Yorkdale and I bumped into that guy from the Episcopalian church downtown. God told me to say that God had told me to ask him for fifty bucks. You know what he said?"

I tried to be pleasant. Always. "No, what did he say?"

"*Well, isn't that funny, I just came back from the bank machine with sixty bucks. I spent ten, and that was all I really needed. God must've wanted you to have that fifty dollars.* Thank you, Jesus."

"Praise the Lord," I said. I was grateful that money trickled in now and again. Going on welfare was not an option for two reasons: according to the freckled one it wasn't living on faith anymore; and, second, I would rather die first than go on welfare while we were both capable of working. But work was no longer an option for me. I was a prisoner.

We drove up the following Saturday for the day. We never stayed overnight. The freckled one said God didn't want us to because Pap and Mam were evil people, and the less time exposed to them the better.

It was a hot day, and we spent the afternoon sitting in the cockpit of Pap's boat. Pap would go on land to deal with work, or pick up the garbage barrels with the front-end loader, or deal with one of the few clients he had.

As Pap was away, Mam started making an early supper, so I decided to go on shore and wade into the water. It was dreadfully hot, and I didn't feel very well. I was suffering from Toxemia and had gone from 117 pounds to 185 pounds. Food would not stay down and many times I had blood-shot eyes from the intensity of being sick.

The freckled one followed as I was never to be out of his sight. As I waded in, I had to lift my dress, which hung to below my knees, to about mid-thigh so that I could go into the cool water as far as I could. It helped relieve the discomfort. I felt much better.

Later on, we went on board to eat supper. Pap was talking about some of his clients.

"One is a teacher who is a pretty good guy. He likes to take your sister and her friends onto the boat for a ride. It gives your sister something to do."

Something about that disturbed me inside.

My little sister, who by now was thirteen, piped up. "Yeah, but I think he's a creep. He takes us out on the water, and then he tells us to lie down on the bunks. I go on the higher one, but I had to pretend to be asleep when he got too close. I think he was touching my friend." She was looking over the edge of her glasses that had fallen down along her sweaty nose.

I looked at her shocked. "What did you say?" I asked.

"Oh, come now. He wouldn't do that," Pap interrupted.

"Yes, he did!" I could tell she was traumatized by this.

"Why would he do such a thing and be found out by me?" Pap kept eating unconcerned.

"I don't know," my sister mumbled, deflated.

I dropped my fork. "Pap, that's not right."

"Oh, come now. Don't make a big deal out of it."

"Big deal?" I thought I would vomit. "This man is a pedophile!"

"Listen, he's a customer, and he likes to take them out for a ride on his boat. They don't have to go if they don't want to. What's the big deal?"

"How did he get you on the boat?" I asked my sister.

She pushed her glasses up her nose and sat up a little straighter. "Well, he said he had all sorts of snacks for us and he promised to take us to the drive-in movie after that."

"Did he?" I asked, knowing the answer.

"Nope. And I was looking forward to it. It was *The Jerk*."

I looked at Pap. "Pap, you can't let this guy get away this."

"Come on. Give it over. What is he getting away with?" Pap wanted to brush it aside.

Perhaps it was because of all the stress I had been living with, or more importantly the fact that no one was there to protect me from my teacher when I was so young, I wasn't going to let this go. I got a little heated. "Pap, this guy is sick. How can you let this happen? This kind of stuff needs to stop!"

My little sister got up and sat beside me. I put my arm around her and squeezed her. "Stay away from this guy."

She squeezed me back. "He didn't hurt me. If he did, I would've kicked him in the balls."

I laughed through my tears. "Good for you," I blubbered. "Good for you!"

On our way home, the freckled one was very quiet. I wasn't sure if it was about me getting upset with Pap or something I wasn't aware of entirely. It was dark driving back, and I didn't want to rock the boat by saying anything. I just sat and stared out the window.

As soon as we came in the door, that's when it happened. He was ahead of me. Suddenly, he turned and bent down to put his face into mine. "You f---ing, sleazy whore."

My mind raced. What did I do? Was it what I told Pap?

He pushed my left shoulder. I stumbled a bit and stepped back. I lowered my gaze. He put his finger into my cheek and pushed hard. His face took on a disgusted look. I stumbled back again and tried to pull my face away from his finger.

I couldn't take it. "What?" I cried.

He grabbed the hem of my dress and pulled it up, almost exposing my belly. "What's this, huh?! Showing your legs off to all the sailors, huh!?" He grabbed my breast. "You want to show this, too?"

I slapped his hand away. "Don't!"

"Oh, you don't like it!?" He slammed me against the doorframe.

"Don't. Please, the baby!" I cried, allowing myself to slip down the doorframe and on the floor. I cried hard. Was there no dignity? Carrying a child. Was it not morally wrong to treat me like this? If it was just me, that was one thing. But with a precious child?

I let myself slip into an abyss as he continued to curse and swear at me. The most soul-destroying language.

"You're nothing but a f---ing sperm receptacle."

My heart screamed for God to come to my rescue, but I felt nothing. As I pressed my hot face to the coolness of the vinyl flooring, I asked God what was it that I did that was so wrong. Was I so evil that he needed to punish me? I silently apologized.

I sensed him lunging towards me again and knew he could hear what I was thinking. He nudged my prostate body with his foot. I almost screamed because I was afraid he was going to kick the baby. "You think God is listening to you? Drama queen? Why do you think I do this to you? It's not me. It's God punishing you. This is God's wrath for being the evil whore you are."

God's wrath.

I started to believe he was right.

During tearful prayer, I received the scripture Hebrews 12: 5-10:

"My son, despise not thou the chastening of the Lord, nor faint when thou art rebuked of Him. For whom the Lord loveth he chasteneth, and scourgeth every son whom He receiveth. If ye endure chastening, God dealeth with you as with sons, for what son is he whom the father chasteneth not? But if ye be without chastisement, whereof all re partakers, then are ye bastards, and not sons. Furthermore, we have had fathers of our flesh which corrected us, and we gave them reverence; Shall we not much rather be in subjection unto the Father of Spirits, and live? For they verily for a few days chastened us after their own pleasures, but He for our profit that we might be partakers of His Holiness."

For His Holiness, I was to endure. So, endure I did.

• • •

I woke 2:30 in the morning. At first, I simply thought it was the usual bad backache that I suffered as a result of the car accident eight years before. Then as time went on, the back spasms were rhythmic. They also started to feel very urgent. I gently woke the freckled one.

"I think it started," I whispered.

"Thank you, Jesus," he announced sleepily.

We called the hospital, were told to wait a couple of hours, and to time the contractions. When they quickened at 4:30 a.m., we headed for the hospital. Soon after that, my water broke.

By 9:00 a.m., the contractions were about ten minutes apart. Hours later, by midnight they were about three minutes apart. By this time, the pain of back contractions was too much to bear, and I was given an epidural. By 4:00 a.m. the contractions were still three minutes apart. I could not move my legs, but an amazingly uncomfortable and agonizing syndrome set it which I could not alleviate on my own. Restless legs came on in full force. My legs had to be manually moved in circles to alleviate the pain that wasn't touched by the epidural.

By this time, we discovered that because I was more than two weeks over-due, my own doctor was on vacation, so another doctor stepped in. Around 8:00 that night, he came by holding my file, and sat down to explain a few things.

We knew that Joel was quite a large baby. Also, by this time, I hadn't had anything to eat or drink for almost two days, so I felt quite weak, and he was concerned. My heart skipped at times, and they wanted to keep an eye on that. They were continually checking to ensure that Joel was not in too much distress. Then my ears perked up.

"I also see here apparently your birth canal is smaller than normal. Combine that with the size of your baby I'm not surprised that you are experiencing a longer than normal period of labor. You are simply not dilating enough. How are you feeling?"

"Weak," I said, truthfully. "And thirsty."

"Well, we can't let you eat or drink anything. But you can suck on a wet cloth or an ice cube. I'll come by in another hour or so."

The wet cloth and ice cubes kept me going. The nurses coached and coaxed me, and checked to see how much I had dilated. But the doctor did not come until closer to 10:30 p.m.

"You haven't dilated enough, but I see the baby has lowered further into the birth canal. That could be a little problem if we decide to do a caesarian."

By 12:30 a.m., I started pushing. At one point, the freckled one looked between my legs and said, "Thank you, Jesus. Praise the Lord. It's coming!"

The nurses both looked at him queerly. I knew what that look meant. We had a problem here, and this guy did not understand the seriousness of the situation.

By 1:30 a.m. they were getting me ready for a caesarian. Just before they were to operate, they checked the baby's heartbeat.

He was in distress. Immediately, because he was halfway down the birth canal, they opted to pull from the head. They snipped me completely open and went in with forceps.

The doctor yanked and tugged at Joel's head. I was worried he would cause some serious damage. He was in a hurry to save both Joel and me but it was as if he was pulling me inside out. I wanted to push his hands away, so someone came over to my head and pinned my hands down.

After a lifetime, my ten and a half pound Joel was born.

When we were finally face to face—me under a warmed blanket and he in a plastic warm crib twenty-two hours of labor later—he turned and searched for me the moment I called his name.

We were buds.

• • •

1980

I stacked all the boxes against the far wall of the little living room. The freckled one told me that God said we were to get ready to move. Where, we didn't know as yet. As usual, we had no money.

The freckled one went out to drive with what little gas was in the car. It was an old car Pap had given us. The last one, the station wagon that the freckled one drove when I first met him, gave up the ghost. It was never serviced, and it sat making dents in the paved driveway of the house we lived in. The landlady complained, rightfully so, that we could not have two cars in the driveway if one of them was simply abandoned.

The freckled one got upset with her over that. Not to her face but afterward. I had to deal with the violent outburst.

I tried to reason with him that she was right. I made a massive mistake trying to reason with him while holding Joel. It didn't stop him from shoving and pushing me around. He slammed my body against the wall while I struggled to keep my hold on Joel.

It was as if in his anger he was blind to everything except for his hatred for me.

By this time, I believed everything he said. Yes, I was willful. Yes, I was vain. Yes, I was stubbornly stuck to things I had learned through the Catholic Church. I became more obedient. However, I still did the occasional thing wrong without meaning to.

At one point, the cloth diapers I used for Joel could not dry quickly enough for me to reuse them. Though I wasn't allowed out, I naively surmised that he would make an exception if I hung them outside to dry, so long as I ran out and back as quickly as possible.

I was very wrong.

He saw the diapers hanging on the clothesline when he returned. He came in through the door with his nostrils flaring, and his eyes black and wild but he started off quietly.

"How did those diapers get on that clothesline?"

My heart sank. I looked over at Joel in his white crib Mam had bought him. I moved away from it as I tried to think of what to say. I felt him pinning my thoughts against the wall.

"I had to hang them outside because they weren't drying fast enough." I squealed when he suddenly grabbed a handful of material on my right shoulder. I automatically raised my hands towards my face. *Not my face again please.*

He heard that and grabbed my face with his other hand and squeezed my cheeks together. I tried to pull my head away, but he kept his tight grip on me. Then he dragged me backward and threw me on the couch. As I lay there half on and half off, he started to pummel me over my head and shoulders while he cursed and swore.

He stopped, and I curled up and cried.

Suddenly I heard him yelp. He fell to his knees and tried to pry my fingers away from my face. He saw the red welts and groaned and held me tightly. He rocked me while he cried.

He then begged me for forgiveness.

This was the seesaw of my marriage.

• • •

Pap gave the freckled one money to start a business to do the mirrors on a larger scale. There was enough for six months of rent in a unit and for supplies for making his sulfuric acid photo mirrors. I asked Pap not to, as I would be so ashamed if it went nowhere.

Every time he spoke with someone, he did their mirrors for free. We made no money, and once Pap's money ran out, we had to back out of the lease and walk away.

At the same time, we were evicted at home. On the morning when the sheriff was to come and physically remove us, I called Nonna to see if she had the downstairs apartment available. She did, and we moved in, having just enough gas to complete the task.

I was pregnant with a second child and I knew him to be Ethan.

• • •

I prayed a great deal. Hidden away in a corner while he slept.

Now at Nonna's house, it was harder to hide the dysfunction within our marriage. I was so tired of the aggression, the violence, the poverty, and the stress. It was demeaning to have to move into Nonna's house because of being kicked out of our apartment. I was dying inside.

My pride, the vanity that the freckled one warned me about, took another major hit.

One day, I thought I would be able to take advantage of a mellow moment in the freckled one. He had met the neighbor's wife and seemed to get along with her. In fact, he was outright flirting with her. If anything, I was relieved that the attention was taken off Joel and me.

I was now close to delivering Ethan and was concerned that we couldn't do what we should for the children. I needed to go out for a walk to clear my head.

I still thought that a pride in work was of tantamount importance. But it was just another thing in me that had to be burned away. Not that love and pride in work was sinful. It was a hindrance when it came before God's guidance. A very subtle but pronounced difference.

So, I told the freckled one I was going out to think, and he could hit me if he wanted when I came back but that's what I needed to do. Miraculously, he didn't stop me.

I put Joel in the stroller, and we walked out of the subdivision into a little playground. I put him in a baby swing and pushed him gently for about a half hour, talking with God. I asked permission to somehow make money—enough to pay off the freckled one's credit card debt which resulted in constant credit collector calls.

I put Joel in the stroller again and walked further looking for cans and bottles for deposit. Suddenly, I saw an empty Mountain Dew bottle and excitedly ran over.

Someone had stuck it straight up in a very large mound of dog doo.

I stood there staring at it. I saw that bottle as the lowest point in my life to date. And it asked me: *how desperate are you for money?*

I lost all pride. I went over and picked it up. I cleaned it thoroughly by wiping it in the grass. One young woman walked by and averted her eyes. I averted mine from her.

Another part of the old me died.

• • •

My youngest uncle still lived upstairs in the same room he had locked himself in with a shotgun all those many years ago. Generally, he was not quite as depressed these days. He was enthralled having a little child in the house. Often, he would come down to watch me feed or bathe Joel.

The freckled one did not appreciate this. Every night, he would tell me that my family was evil, and he called them vulgar names. It hurt me deeply, but in the back of my head, I saw a pattern forming. Not that I appreciated the way it worked, but I was starting to see what God was doing.

Everything that was dear to me—pride in my work, pride in my home, pride in my family, pride of my roots in the Catholic Church, pride in making money, my adoration of Pap, my pride in my looks—was being burned away.

Because they also represented fears of mine.

Fear of being poor and not making money, fear of being homeless, fear of disappointing my family, losing my looks, fear that ultimately, I would go to Hell, and fear of losing what little love I felt I received from Pap.

By understanding this, I analyzed the freckled one. There was no doubt, however misdirected, that he had an immovable faith in God. There was no doubt that he had an uncanny, intuitive awareness of God's guidance. He also had this uncanny immovable belief that things would fall into place, whereas I continuously thought it was the end of the world.

I was unlearning bad habits and learning good ones.

However, the process was almost unbearable.

I needed to understand my husband, so the few times I was exposed to his sisters, I started to ask questions.

• • •

My parents-in-law were very young when they conceived the freckled one out of wedlock. They married, had three daughters in quick succession, and then immigrated to Canada. They initially lived in a small cabin along a highway. A little later on, his youngest brother was born.

There may have been problems right from the beginning. He constantly irritated his father and was slapped across the head quite often.

For years, the family lived in a rented house on a farm next to a farmhouse.

They were fairly close to the farmer and his wife who were very good to them. My father-in-law became a traveling salesman for a food company. He was gone for long stretches of time, leaving my mother-in-law to raise the five children, so they were grateful for the extra support.

In his teens, the freckled one was caught stealing and joyriding cars. He spent a brief time in the small town's jail.

When he finally left home, he did uncommon things such as live in an apartment, leave it when he decided he didn't like it, then sign a new lease for another apartment right across the street, leaving the other to go into arrears.

He suffered from chronic fatigue which I misinterpreted as laziness.

Once, he picked up a few hitchhikers and they offered him LSD. He complained that he didn't feel anything after one pill and asked for more. Hours later, as per their minister's instructions, his sister put him in a dark, locked room as he was overdosing. He attacked her when she checked on him. She barely escaped before being badly hurt. Everyone believed that the overdose caused some brain damage which may have caused one of his eyes to never close.

He fell in with the wrong crowd. He was hired once to kill a man. He was given a gun, bullets and instructions about who, when, and where he should do the *hit*. Apparently, this was through a Chinese underground gang which was known for killing anyone who did not fulfill their objectives. He drove to the man's place of work and stayed in the car till after dark to surprise and kill the man. But he couldn't do it.

He lived in terror for many months expecting to be killed himself. It explained his reaction that day I inadvertently surprised him in the bathroom while he was shaving.

He moved in with his parents briefly. They asked him to leave after he went after his mother with a broom.

Then he moved into a basement apartment in a house belonging to a woman who was crippled by arthritis. She was ornery, demanding. Part of the lease conditions was that he help her get ready to sleep at night. It meant carrying her out of her wheelchair, running a bath, and making sure she had everything she needed. After she covered herself, he would put her into bed. A nurse always came in the morning, and she had help for the rest of the day.

He hated doing these things, but he said it was God's way of making him learn to be empathetic.

Once he told me he hung around a bar wanting to seduce the barmaid. She would not go out with anyone. She was a decent human being trying to make a living. But he challenged himself and did everything possible. He was nice to her, brought her flowers, wooed her. It took months, he said, but finally, she took him home. He seduced her and then got dressed. He said he had left her saying something like he finally bedded her and thanks for the memory.

He admitted feeling bad about that. He said he was not a nice guy before God took over.

Quite often I went over those days leading up to our marriage to see if Pap was right. Perhaps I was duped by a very clever and manipulative man. But I still came to the same conclusion: it was God's will. The manner in which He made it clear to me cemented my conviction. You can't get more precise than being hit between the eyes as He did me.

• • •

On a dark, cold, moonless night, back contractions woke me. It was a repeat of the last pregnancy. This time my doctor said the second baby would be much easier.

The violence was increasingly abusive during this second pregnancy, and I was frightened for the child within me. It took almost just as long to bring Ethan into the world as it did Joel, but he was only six pounds.

Things became extreme for me. Now I had two little children, one who never stopped crying because of colic, and another who needed just as much attention from me. My poor children knew nothing but upheaval and fear.

I slept very little between nursing and walking precious little Ethan who suffered so much.

One day, I was down in the living room where I used to listen to Chuck Mangioni and The Moody Blues back in university days. I still had a little black and white TV. Something told me to turn it on. There was my Paul, playing a baby grand piano and singing a gospel tune on his own.

I stared at that beautiful face and listened to his soothing voice singing praises to God. It was a poignant moment. I briefly wondered if my walk with God had gone astray and couldn't help but wish I was with Paul instead. But then I couldn't truly believe that. These two children, two amazing gifts from God, were supposed to be born into this world through my union with the freckled one. For, no matter how faulty or misdirected I thought their father was, his internal brilliance and light could not be ignored. It was why he initially charmed so many people.

He believed he was a prophet of God. He said so to me in as many words. By then, I was thoroughly brain-washed into being an obedient wife and mother, quietly suffering the evictions, constant worry, and prayers about money. But one thing I could not fully accept: a life imprisoned in a house—though unhealthy for an adult—was even more so for children.

And just as I never heard the term wife abuse, I rarely heard the terms schizophrenia, bi-polar, and narcissistic personality disorders. If I knew he had these conditions, perhaps I may have helped him find help. Instead, I only feared him.

His credit card debt bothered me. I felt duty bound to pay that off. It was over $2,000 and I figured out a way of doing it. I approached the freckled one and said I wanted to borrow money from Mam to sell Mary Kay. I felt it was right up my alley and I just needed $500 to start.

Perhaps because it was his debt that I wanted to clear, or he was still in a mellow mood, he said yes. So, I called Mam and asked if she wouldn't mind lending me the money. She agreed. I found some material in one of my boxes and made a two-piece suit. Though I looked pretty sad compared to what I used to look like, I was still able to pull it off.

Months later, I paid off the credit card debt and Mam but from that point on, almost like clockwork, he would show up at the parties, with both children in his arms screaming.

It was embarrassing and unfair to the ladies, but it was also unbearable for me to see the children so upset. But what upset them so much? Why not before I was able to pay off the debt? Or was it God telling me that it was time to get back to my lessons? I don't know. I quit selling Mary Kay and went back to being imprisoned.

Then a friend of his decided he believed in him so much that he mortgaged his home for $100,000 and gave the money to the freckled one to start another business.

Again, it involved acid washing mirrors. But this time it included small promotional brooches with a pin glued on the back. His younger brother, who worked for Disney, agreed to be the salesman. He managed to get a massive order for the broaches from K-Mart.

It was an auspicious beginning. He hired many people to assemble these broaches, but they all ridiculed the freckled one. Each morning he made them stand in a prayer circle. Then he unnecessarily criticized them while he wasted the whole day doing nothing. Without quality control, the shipment contained badly-traced images with glue smeared front and back. The mirrors were scratched having been dumped carelessly into each box.

In less than a year, that $100,000 was gone and we were even more in debt.

Then he came home and said we were to start packing. God told him where we were moving further north of the city. While he didn't have an *exact* location, he said it was imminent.

I was relieved to be quite honest. I didn't want Nonna exposed to my world any longer.

We moved to an old farmhouse on a 200-acre campground that belonged to the Boy Scouts of Canada. We lived there for almost two years.

During that entire stay, we paid four months' rent.

FIFTEEN

The Children, The Children, The Children

"For a man's anger cannot promote the justice of God."

(James 1:20, NEB)

"Please, you can't do that," I pleaded. "These fences are like a hundred years old."

"They will burn all the better then."

The freckled one came in from the snow with an armload of long pieces of dried wood. These formed the crisscrossed fencing along one of the neighboring farms.

We used up the firewood stored in the old barn for the wood stove. We had no oil for the furnace. And we owed the oil company money. I used the wood stove for cooking as well. The electric stove had broken down, but we didn't dare complain to the landlords.

The wood stove was enough to warm up the entire house so long as we kept it fed. The house was old and the walls were over three feet thick. It was quite comfortable most of the time.

Set back from the country road, a long narrow lane led from the road to the side of the house. I loved it there. Surrounded by fields and flowers, bees and birds, it was beautiful. But this was winter, the worst season for the freckled one.

The more frightened I was about not having food for the children, or even toothpaste for our teeth, the more I doubted his leadership. I prayed about these things, but, of course he heard what I thought and corrected me. By chastising me. Pushing me around. If it was really bad, he used extra force and objects. But inevitably after he went through his litany of vulgar terms and assaults, he would end by crying and begging for forgiveness.

An agonizingly torturous challenge arose—he expected me to love him. Caress him. Touch his hand. Kiss him. I didn't love him and his abusive treatment made it difficult to see the good. There wasn't a single thing I did or didn't do which was right. I continually drew his wrath and disappointment. How could I love him? Ultimately, of course, I was there only for God.

I know Scripture teaches that the woman gives in to the man, but scripture also says that the man must treat his wife with respect and love her as someone worthy of love.

It didn't matter. He didn't see his treatment of me as a reason for not obeying God. I didn't love him and that was becoming my worst failing in his eyes.

The freckled one graduated to threatening to kill my children if I so much whispered a word about how he treated me.

One night, Ethan, who continually had problems with Colic, needed comforting. I was so exhausted I thought I would collapse. I hadn't slept well for more than a year. I begged him to take Ethan, who now was almost a year and a half old, and comfort him. I just needed a tiny bit more rest before I started breastfeeding again.

That was a mistake.

He grabbed my hair and raised a thick brass curtain rod in the air. It was his new weapon for me when he didn't like something I said. "I'll f---ing kill you, evil b----. You know what you are? A f---ing, spoiled whore. Everybody sees it. Everybody hates you. They only tolerate you because of me. Everyone wonders what I saw in you. You're nothing but a goddamn sperm receptacle. I see you when we're out. I see you looking at men wanting to f--- them. You whore!"

Just because I asked if I could sleep a little more.

Joel was asleep and woke up with a start. When he saw what his father was doing, he started to cry in terror. I looked over and reached out to him over Ethan, also crying. My poor children, both crying, and I felt so helpless. I tried to soothe them.

Suddenly, he pulled my body up by the arm. I tried to cover both children.

He slapped me across the back of my head. "See what you're doing?! You're upsetting them. Give him your breast!"

I covered my head with my hand and blubbered, "You're getting both of them more upset."

That was the wrong thing to say. He leaned over, grabbed my nightgown, and yanked it open, ripping off a button.

I quickly put Ethan to my breast. He hiccupped and sniffled still as he nursed but eventually calmed down. I pulled Joel closer and caressed his blonde hair and forehead. I looked straight into his eyes with a look of love, comfort, and the feeling that all would be well.

Later, in the early morning hours, I sat on the bedroom's deep windowsill while the freckled one slept. I couldn't leave the room for very long, because he could sense it whenever I did. Even if I went to use the bathroom, he would be standing outside the door once I finished. So, I stayed nearby, but I hid behind the curtains so he couldn't see me crying.

I looked up at the winter moon and prayed that someone would come to take the children and me away. Then I closed my eyes and prayed. I told God I was sorry for whatever it was I had done in my life to deserve this. I didn't know there was any other way of looking at it.

Then I opened my eyes and looked over the endless frozen cornfields. I looked in all directions. There was no house close enough for the children and me to run to before he'd wake up and notice I was gone. And running through frozen farmers' fields was almost impossible.

It was a prison. And this time it wasn't just for me. Now it included my two sons.

"Lord," I prayed, "Please show me what to do. What is it you want from me. Is this really your wrath coming through him?"

The top of my head tingled.

James 1:20. Your Bible.

I sniffed and wiped my nose with the sleeve of my night-gown. I looked back through the curtains into the bedroom. Though his eye seemed to be looking at me, he was asleep.

I got off the ledge quietly, tiptoed over the cold creaking boards, and gently took my Bible from the night stand. I went back to the windowsill, where the moonlight was bright enough to read. I turned to James 1:20.

"For the wrath of man worketh not the righteousness of God."

I covered my mouth with my hand. I took a deep breath and let it out slowly as quiet tears of relief ran down my cheeks.

It was the very first indication that perhaps God did not want all this wrath directed at me.

"Thank you, Jesus," I whispered. This revelation gave me the strength to survive a little longer.

But as time went on, the incidents became more dangerous. He pushed a little more, pressed my face against the wall a little harder, threw me a little farther each time. Instead of slapping, he used his fist on my back as I cowered.

I had deeper conversations with God. I saw that some of the things burned out of me were meant to be burned away but I was beginning to doubt everything he claimed I was. I sensed God spoke to me now just as much as the freckled one. Then God said to me that only *He* should talk to me directly. That I was no longer to listen to the freckled one.

I tested this out.

On a warm early spring day, we went for a little walk through the grounds with the children. I saw one of the camp outhouses up ahead.

"See that outhouse?"

He wheezed as he carried Ethan whose little legs were tired. I continued to walk with Joel. He looked ahead at the outhouse. "Yes, what of it?"

"I think I should start listening to God directly instead of through you. I believe He is teaching me how to listen to his Voice."

I saw his struggle.

"Don't you agree?" I pretended not to care too much about it. I looked around the beautiful property. I looked down at beautiful Joel and smiled at him as he looked up at me. He smiled and squinted against the sun behind my head.

"So, what is He saying now?" He shifted Ethan in his arms. Ethan, beautiful Ethan.

I stopped. "Well, let's try something. I know this isn't very important in the long run. But if I ask God something and you ask, we can see if it's the same answer."

He thought a little longer. "Okay."

"I'm going to ask God if there is any toilet paper in that outhouse. What do you think?"

"Yeah, okay. He says there isn't any."

I stopped and looked at him. *God, I know this is a silly and perhaps demeaning thing to ask, but please bear with me. Is there toilet paper there?*

Yes.

"He's telling me that there is toilet paper there."

We walked to the outhouse and looked inside. There was a beat-up roll of toilet paper hanging on a rod and wire.

Taken aback, he was quiet from then on. I knew enough not to talk or even think about it anymore. I had gone too far already. But I saw a chink in his armor. And that gave me hope.

● ● ●

By this time, we had no phone, so there was no way the Boy Scouts of Canada could reach us. One day, the freckled one said that God was telling him to go down to Toronto. First, he was to contact an old friend of his from the church. He was to ask for gas money.

Just after he left, there was a knock on the door.

It frightened the children. The freckled one taught Joel that strangers were likely to steal him and cut him up into tiny pieces. Joel was well brainwashed and conditioned to fear even a random knock on the door.

I prayed for strength. I knew I looked like a very poor woman—faded kerchief on my head, barefoot, an old shift over my skinny frame. I mustered my courage, walked through the cold mudroom, and opened the back door.

A short man with red hair and freckles stood there. Surprised, he looked at my dress and my bare feet.

I smiled. "May I help you?"

"Yes," he said, looking uncomfortable. "Is your husband home?"

"No, I'm sorry. You just missed him."

I knew he was a debt collector.

"I'm from the board of the Boy Scouts of Canada. I'm here to deal with the overdue rent."

I turned beet-red. "Yes, I'm so sorry. I don't know what to say." I looked into the mudroom toward the kitchen where Joel stood wide-eyed. Ethan suddenly came into sight. He was walking in his bare feet as well. They both looked so pale and thin. "Would you like to come in?" I asked.

"When is your husband coming back?" he asked.

"I don't know. He doesn't go out often, but he went to Toronto, so he may be late."

He lifted a gloved hand. "No, that's okay. Tell him to contact us." He pulled out a business card from his upper coat pocket and handed it to me.

I looked down at the card. The Boy Scouts of Canada. I wondered if he would notice that we used up all the firewood and that almost all of the fencing was missing. "Again, I'm so sorry. It's not like me to not pay the rent." *Yes, it is. Have been for a while.*

He looked over to his left. I thought he saw the missing fencing. When he pointed to the side, he said "I see you're tapping the Maple trees. Are they running well?"

"Yes, I already have a small jar of Maple syrup. Please! Just a moment!"

I ran in through the cold mudroom again, my bare feet freezing. I ran into the kitchen and reached up over the barely-functioning stove the freckled one bought with Pap's money. I grabbed the little jar of syrup. It was probably all I'd be able to make, but I thought it was a small token toward all that rent we owed. I ran back to the back door with the jar.

I held it out to the gentleman. "Here is my home-made Maple syrup." I smiled as broadly and apologetically as possible.

He took it and looked at it. I could see he was very uncomfortable. He nodded. "Okay. Thank you very much. Please tell your husband to call."

"I will. Thank you." I closed the door and rushed to the side of the house facing the lane. I leaned into the window well to watch him drive away. I waved goodbye. He didn't see.

• • •

"Boy Scouts came today looking for rent."

The freckled one was taking off his over-boots. His pants, the pair I bought him before we were married, looked threadbare. I had pressed them so many times they looked like thin paper. I helped him with his heavy coat. It was dark out, and we could see our breath in the mudroom under the single bulb hanging from the ceiling.

"What did you say?"

I shrugged, frightened. "What could I say?"

He stopped and looked at me, reading my mind. He flopped his arms in exasperation. "How many times do I have to tell you this is what you signed up for. You wanted to live on faith alone."

I walked into the kitchen and sat down at the table. My back hurt quite a bit these days and there seemed no way around the pain. Every day, I asked him to stand on my back to loosen it.

"I know, but the Bible says what belongs to Caesar, goes to Caesar."

THE KINGDOM OF GOD AND PLAYBOYS

He stood hunched over at the kitchen looking at me. I saw the eyes start to turn black and his face harden. "Where are the children?"

"In bed. Did you get any food?"

"No."

"What did God want you to do today?"

"I did exactly what He told me. I went into town, bumped into my friend, and I asked him to lend me $40."

My spirits brightened. Gas, milk, eggs. I made my own bread, so milk and eggs would be wonderful. "Can we get milk and eggs tomorrow? The children need some protein."

"No, we can't."

I looked at him while my heart sank. I tucked my bare legs under my skirt onto the kitchen chair. I traced some crumbs I had missed on the table. "Why not?"

"Because I don't have any money left." He still stood there looking at me. I could feel it.

"What did you do, then?" I ventured a look at his face.

"God told me to go to the movies. Then I went for a drink."

"A drink?" Now I didn't care if he could read my mind. *How could he do this when he knew we needed things here in the house? The children!*

The children!

The children!

He stomped into the corner to the curtain rod against the wall. He never buttoned his sleeves at the wrists, so they hung low, flapping. The sight reminded me of a gorilla in a shirt who never learned how to do buttons.

I put up my hands. I felt myself go pale, suddenly wanting to throw up.

He threw back his hand holding the curtain rod, and I squealed as I tried to cover my head. He didn't have to do very much anymore for me to break down.

He threw the curtain rod at me and stomped into the living room. I continued to cry as I heard him turn on the little black and white TV to full volume. He knew the children were asleep upstairs. I unfolded my sore body and quickly ran upstairs to the children to make sure they were fine while his rage passed.

I listened in the dark while he continued to swear to himself. I heard him throw something across the living room at one of the walls. Then I heard him in the kitchen slamming cupboard doors. Then I heard him open the fridge.

"We have no goddamn food in the house!" he yelled.

• • •

I was pregnant a third time. I found out the same day we were officially served eviction papers.

I couldn't bring another special angel into the world to be fathered by the likes of the freckled one. What if he ever did go through on his threat to kill me and the children? He would be killing three precious ones, not two.

As was his habit, the freckled one was gone when things had to be packed but I was used to this by now. I wasn't going to be careful and made an effort to push hard, perhaps lose the child. I had learned to keep the boxes we used to move handy and reused them: kitchen stuff into the box labelled kitchen, toys to the box labelled toys.

I moved the furniture and gathered the rugs together, piling them into the kitchen.

While carrying a heavy dresser down the stairs by balancing it on my back, it slipped and almost flipped over the railing to the floor below. The physical exertion it took to keep it on my back caused a sudden jab in my gut.

As time went, I experienced what felt like back contractions. Shortly after that, I sat by the toilet with blood through my clothes. I had miscarried. Though I was full of remorse, I was also relieved.

I asked the baby for forgiveness. I explained it was not a good time to come. That it would only be met with suffering, tears, fear, and maybe even death in this miserable life.

A week before we had to be out, the freckled one found a townhome for rent in Toronto. We were going back to the big evil city of *Sodom and Gomorrah.*

• • •

I sat watching my children play with two cheap toys we somehow scrounged money for. We went to a *Giant Tiger* and found a large plastic red car and a plastic yellow and red fire engine. It was Ethan's birthday, and Joel could not understand the concept of birthday presents, so I encouraged both of them to open a gift.

They both looked so pale. We had been living in the townhome three months now and were two months behind with the rent already. By now, I knew not to mention it.

I wanted to get the children outside for fresh air and a bit of play. But, according to the freckled one, we were in the *big city* now where people would kidnap and butcher us.

I had no winter clothing for the boys. They never played outside in the snow, and I thought it was time. I prayed to God about this when suddenly, I received an inspiration.

I had learned how to talk to him. I knew not to make it look like I myself wanted something. I was the enemy of the freckled one. The evil one who was not to be spoiled even with the most basic things. So I learned to point out the benefits of things as they may be related to the children, especially Ethan.

An hour later, while eating supper, I said, "I noticed today how pale Joel and Ethan are." I kept my eyes away from his. We were having the usual dinner: a cheap cut of pork roast, potatoes, carrots and onions. I was spooning some homemade apple sauce into Ethan's mouth.

I looked at both children while I waited for an answer. For toddlers, they had very deep, dark circles under their eyes. The intense fear caused by their father's continual eruptions left them drained.

"Yeah, they do look a little pale," he said as he continued to eat. I looked over at him. He was looking down at his plate. When he looked down, the eye that could not close remained open.

"I was thinking. The backyard has a tall fence, and if I could get some second-hand snow outfits, I could stay out with them. Maybe teach them how to do snow angels."

"I'll go to the Salvation Army, and see if I can find some suits for them."

All I said was, "Thank you. That would be nice."

I never really knew where he kept disappearing to during the day. I wasn't to ask because then I was a *'f---ing nag.'* Now, it was a blessing when he did go. I had time to do happy things with the boys. Teach them to read, sing songs, look out the window at the world going by, and tell stories about anything that caught their attention. One day, he arrived earlier than usual. He had somehow gotten money and came with a cardboard box full of wilted vegetables and some cereal. He also had two faded, stained snow outfits for the children. One was pink and the other a faded purple, but they fit.

I thanked him very politely.

The next day, before he left, I said I was going to take them out into the backyard once the sun reached past the neighboring buildings.

He put his coat on and his over-boots and went out into the yard. I watched him from the kitchen window. He squinted at the neighboring buildings. He checked the fence and then went to the side to check that the gate was closed. He stuck a stick he found next to the gate into the lock mechanism so that it wasn't easy for anyone to get in.

He came back in.

"People can see you in the backyard."

My heart sank. I looked out the window again. "Really?" I said, trying to think of what to say so he would allow us to go out. I thought of something that might work. "What about the far corner next to the big oak tree where the fence is highest? If I run with them to that corner and stick to that area, I could make sure we are out of sight from these other buildings.

"Won't work," he said, starting to look irritable

"Could you please check? I'm concerned that if they don't get some sun, they will get very sick. It's flu season coming up. And you don't know what kind of people you are exposed to." I tried not to look frightened. My left eyelid was twitching.

He looked down at the children who were in the hallway playing with the red car and yellow and red fire engine. Without a word, he went back out.

I watched. My heart skipped beats. I was desperate to get my little boys out into that fresh air. He stood in the corner, looked around the oak tree. Then he bent down to the boys' level and stood up. He came back to the back door.

I tried not to look too anxious, but he answered before he came back into the kitchen.

"Okay, but you run there and you run back. And only for fifteen minutes."

So, in this manner, my two boys in used girls' snow outfits were allowed to go out with me into the icy cold air and bright sunshine. There wasn't very much snow in the corner, but it was a start. They finally got their little noses runny and their cheeks red. I, too, shivered in delight. I was careful to crouch down low enough not to be seen by anyone, but that was fine. I thought we'd only been there for about five minutes when he called that we were done.

"Time to go back in," he said. He looked at all the windows in the surrounding buildings and homes as if shooting glares at anyone who would deign to look out onto us. He motioned to me to hurry into the house with the children.

I held onto them for dear life as we hustled back in.

A week later, I tried again. This time I asked for permission for something else.

"May we go to the little playground at the end of the street?"

"No."

"Have you seen the little playground? You can see it from the living room window if you look way to the left."

"Woman, you want them to be kidnapped and killed?"

I left it alone for a bit. Then one day, I sensed he was a little more lucid. He was talking about meeting someone who was interested in starting a business with him. It was going to be great, and he was going to make a million dollars. As he was getting himself ready, I mentioned that perhaps it was time for the children to have some air again.

"May I take them about five houses over to the little playground? We will only walk on this side of the road and cross over on the other side to the park. I promise we'll only be there to swing and do the seesaw a bit and then we will cross the street and walk back on this side again?" I had to be very specific.

He went over to the living room window and carefully opened a tiny hole between the sheer curtains to look out. The sun came out that moment and brightened the world outside.

He came back. "Yeah, okay," he put on a coat he'd found at Salvation Army. "But if anything happens to the children, I will kill you."

I nodded.

I waited with my heart racing as he pulled out of the driveway, I continued to wave until he was completely out of sight.

"You want to go to a park?!" I excitedly asked the children. They looked up from the carpet. They still looked so pale and undernourished. The image squeezed my heart. "You wanna go to a swing?"

Ethan looked at me blankly. He'd never seen one before.

"Remember a swing, Joel? Once at Nanna's and Grandad's and I pushed you on a swing?"

He brightened up and sprung to his feet.

I hustled them to the back door and put on their snowsuits. Then I put on my running shoes and the heaviest coat I had. Before I touched the doorknob, I realized I had no key to get back into the house.

Oh, my God. If I left without locking the door and something happened to the house, he would kill me. My body started shaking.

No, I thought. *This is more important, so please, God, protect the house while we are out.*

My hand felt numb when I turned that doorknob. I let the children out and carefully checked that the door wouldn't lock behind me. Then I walked along the sunny back wall holding both children's hands. I looked around the tall buildings and hoped that no one was looking at us.

Then, I faced the driveway. I was pushing this particular envelope for myself as much as I was for the boys. I was afraid to say boo to anyone. I never went out shopping with the freckled one now. He didn't trust me to keep my eyes averted. So, except for the occasional visit to his family and even more rarely, my own, I was not exposed to anyone else. I had become chronically paranoid.

Slowly, we walked along the sidewalk on our side of the road. I looked around constantly to see who was around us. No one. I went a little further, and finally, right across the street from the playground, I held both of their hands tightly.

"Now," I said, bending down to their ears. "Every time we cross the street, we first look right and then left to make sure there are no cars coming. Okay?"

We looked right, and then I pointed to left. "See anything?"

They both shook their heads. I was about to step off the curb when Ethan pulled back on my hand and cried.

"No, it's okay. There are no cars, Ethan. See?" I lifted him up and pressed my head against his. "See, nothing there or there," I turned the other way, "See? It's okay now."

I held Joel's hand and led him across the road. Then, at the swings, I put Ethan into a baby swing while I sat on the regular swing with Joel on my lap. Gently I swung Joel as I held onto the baby swing. Slowly they started to relax.

Then my heart sank. A young woman was coming toward us with a little boy. I looked the other way. My first thought was to get up and leave. Then I thought it was exactly what I shouldn't do, especially if I wanted to push myself against this unhealthy fear of people. I stayed on the swing, and both children remained quiet while she played with her son on the seesaw.

I was relieved when she finally moved on. We didn't exchange a look or a word.

I felt faint but also victorious. We were outside that prison!

• • •

"That's quite a garden," I said, speaking to my sister's father-in-law. "You must have freezers full of vegetables!"

The frail and bent man stood looking over his snow-covered garden. I had asked about it because I loved gardening—I had a large one at the Boy Scout house one summer. I also wanted to be pleasant to this sweet man. We chatted about the style of tomato he preferred, and how he grew his own cauliflower. I was thrilled to be outside while the party was going on inside.

It had been over a year since the children and I were allowed to take part in something like this. The children, timid at first, played with other children inside. Joel acted out a bit, hiding his face in my skirt while pushing his cousin away. I looked at my sister to see if she caught that. But she was busy laughing and joking with someone else. Eventually, he settled down. I saw the freckled one chatting with someone. I felt almost elated. It allowed me a bit of freedom to enjoy myself. So, I went outside.

Alone. With a man.

It was the wrong thing to do. Even though the man was eighty years old and sweet as can be. When we left and driving along the highway, he began to pull at the top of my dress.

"So, you s---ed his d---?! You whore!" He pushed me against the window. Then he grabbed me by the neck, and pulled me forward, pushing me against my door. I craned back to look at the children, concerned. They both started to scream and cry. "I should kill you now, b----!" He yelled.

I glanced out quickly to see if other drivers and passengers saw. There were two who craned their necks.

"Stop! People are watching!" I cried.

"You ashamed they'll know what a Jezebel you are? Do you know that God is disgusted with you? You'll never change, whore!"

I let him continue slapping, pulling, and pushing. I didn't know what else to do. I just covered and protected myself as much as I could.

SIXTEEN

Pap, Don't Give Any More Money

"How blest you are, when you suffer insults and persecution and every kind of calumny for my sake."

Matthew 5:11

1982

I knelt on the carpet, devouring a newspaper the freckled one brought home and left behind by accident. I was shaking with delight.

On the front of the Life Section, was a long article about husbands who abused their wives. I had never read about this or heard that term before though I recognized it as something that had happened in my own extended family. But then, I started feeling sick to my stomach as I realized I perfectly fit the profile.

Stunned, I sat back. God was allowing me to look through a window at my life. I looked over at the boys playing in the partially empty living room.

Now I knew for certain that God recognized the misery of my situation. He was holding up a mirror for me to see the truth. I intuitively felt a door opening in my heart. A door I could now go through.

The boys would enjoy books.

Books. I didn't have money to buy books. How would I get books for the boys?

The library.

The library! The library was a few blocks away. Perhaps he would allow me to take the boys there.

Waiting for the freckled one to return, I burned the newspaper in the corner of the backyard and flushed away the larger burned pieces.

"I think God is telling me to teach the boys how to read," I told him as he watched TV.

"That's a good idea," he said, looking away from the *PTL Club.*

"There is a library not far from here. I can walk there and back. It would be good for them to go out again for some fresh air. They're still so pale."

He was quiet, laughing at something on the TV and muttered, "Thank you, Jesus. Praise the Lord."

I stood by the door into the living room. The boys were playing with some of the toys in the corner. Joel yelped as Ethan grabbed a toy away from him and he yanked back. Ethan screamed.

"Mine! Mine!"

"Shut the f--- up!" he yelled at Ethan.

My heart hurt when he spoke like that to the children. I bent over and gently took the toy away from Ethan and gave it back to Joel. As Ethan started to cry, I swept him up and took him to the kitchen to distract him. When he settled down, I took Ethan back to the living room and directed him to another toy.

"Ethan is very bright. He would find books as a great outlet." I waited.

"Where is the library?" he said, not looking away from the TV.

"Just about three blocks."

"Okay, but only when I'm home. That way I can time you."

"Tomorrow?"

"Yeah, tomorrow. In the morning. You'll have fifteen minutes."

"Can I have a bit more? Joel walks slower than I do."

"Twenty."

The next morning, the children and I walked to the library. I hurried as fast as I could, even lifting Joel onto my hip to move more quickly.

My heart raced, and I prayed for strength. "Thank you, Jesus. Please watch over us."

While waiting at the traffic light as the cars sped by, I was overwhelmed by the noise, the sights, and the feel of the slush against my shins. I wore running shoes because I didn't have boots. My shoes were soaked, but we only a bit more to go.

When the light turned green, I hurried across and through the doors of the library.

I forgot we needed a library card.

"You can't check out a book without a temporary one. I'll write you one, and we will mail you a permanent one."

I put Joel down to fill out the form. When I looked at the clock above her head, I realized we had no time to look for books. Oh, well. At least I had a temporary card for the next day. As I signed my name to the form, I looked down where Joel stood but he wasn't there. I looked around me. No Joel.

I panicked, shocking the woman behind the counter.

"Joel!" I called out. *Oh my gosh, he's going to kill me. What if he's been kidnapped?*

"Joel!"

I looked between the aisles, pushing Ethan in the stroller in front of me.

Joel came around the corner lugging a heavy book. "Mommy, I want this book!" he said.

I took it from him and read—*How to Get a Divorce in Canada.*

• • •

The freckled one approached me about selling the cottage lot I owned on the Magnettewan River near Parry Sound. He wanted the money to buy socks as he still thought this business would make him a millionaire.

After reading the article and the library book Joel randomly picked up, I felt strengthened. Perhaps my exercise with the freckled one was coming to an end? I had fulfilled my task with him.

No.

I said, "No."

He didn't hit me or threaten me. He simply nodded, walked into the kitchen and picked up the phone. I heard him talking, and then my ears perked up. He was talking to Pap. A few minutes later, he said Pap wanted to talk to me.

"Tell him we really need the money. I asked him for a thousand dollars. You talk."

I went to the kitchen, surprised he didn't follow me. Usually, he hung around to check every word I said.

"Hello?"

"Hi. How is everything?"

"Oh fine," I said, trying to sound light and cheery.

"You always say that. I need to know because I don't think everything is fine. Why don't you just tell me what's going on?"

I didn't want to tell him what was going on because I believed the freckled one when he said he would kill me or the children if I told anyone.

"Nope, everything is fine." Then something reminded me that God was now leading me into a different direction. Perhaps I could open up a little. Lowering my voice, I tiptoed as far as the phone coil would go and saw that the freckled one was still sitting on the couch watching TV. I went the other way down the hallway into the bathroom and closed the door. I had about a minute. "He wanted me to sell the cottage lot so that he could buy a thousand pair of socks. He thinks he can make a million dollars going door-to-door selling them."

"What did you tell him?"

"I said no, Pap. So please, don't give him any money. I don't know what he told you he needed it for but he wants to use it to buy socks."

There was a long silence on the other end. "So, you're telling me not to give money?"

"That's right. Please, don't give him anything. Pap, all he needs to do is work. And he won't let me work, otherwise I would."

"He won't let you?"

I said too much. "Pap, thank you for thinking of me all the time, but please don't give him any more money. He's lying if he says it's for something else."

I pushed the door open and tiptoed back to the kitchen. Then I raised my voice. "Thank you anyway, Pap. Love you!"

"Let me know when you need anything, anytime."

"Thank you, Pap. I will. Lots of kisses." And I hung up.

I went into the living room.

"So, is he going to give us the money?"

"Pap said they're tight at the moment, but as soon as he can, he'll let us know."

He wasn't happy with that but didn't push it any further. No arguments. No punishment.

• • •

We were being evicted again. And for the first time, the word *con artist* came to mind describing my husband.

Was he aware of what he was doing? Sweet talking all those people who lost so much money on rent while allowing us to move in without damage deposits, to use their phones and keeping utilities under their own names. How he so easily charmed them in trusting him. Did he calculate we had three, maybe four, months before a landlord caught on?

Or was he so sick he couldn't see it?

This time he said God told him I could choose where I wanted to live.

Family.

"Near family," I said quietly. "For the boys' sake."

"Not your family," he said.

"Okay, then your family," I said, hoping against hope that would be possible.

The next day, I started packing again. This last time I hadn't even opened them all.

A few days later, the freckled one said his sister had a neighbor who was moving and needed to rent her townhouse. She wanted to rent to someone she could trust. His other sister and family, father and mother, and younger brother also lived nearby. It was perfect.

We arranged to meet the woman and her children. She was delightful, a single mother. I felt that I could take good care of her house. She listened to the freckled one and agreed to leave her phone, power, and oil under her own name. She gave all the information, and the freckled one promised we would take care of everything.

She was greatly relieved.

We signed a thrown-together lease which didn't demand a damage deposit.

Perhaps it was because we were going to be under the scrutiny of his family but when I pointed out to him that we should do everything we could to keep from being evicted this time, he agreed to find a job!

I thanked God. Perhaps things would be different, and there would be no need for a divorce. I hoped we could live like a family and be a couple who lived in love, patience, peace, mutual respect, and harmony. Perhaps this intuition that everything was going to change was actually because our marriage was going to improve. Perhaps no more beatings.

I felt I had somehow graduated from a very difficult university.

I sighed with relief and looked forward to moving this time.

• • •

After moving into the townhouse, things settled into a lovely routine for about three months. The freckled one agreed to work toward not only paying the bills but also to our other debts. Secretly, I hoped we would pay the overdue rents on our previous places.

He found a job that required travelling and staying away during the week. He came home on weekends and his weekly expenses were covered by the company. He was paid once a month, but that was fine. It was heavenly knowing money was coming in regularly.

For the first time since our marriage, I was allowed to open my own bank account for the family allowance. Prior to this, the family allowance was used for his own expenses but now I was allowed to use it for the boys. I was becoming a person again. It felt strange to sign a check.

Once, as I signed a check at the bank, I had a premonition I wouldn't be using my married name anymore soon. I stared down at the name.

I panicked. Now that things were looking up, I didn't want this to end. I was married. There was no reason to feel the marriage would fail now. I prayed and prayed that everything would be fine, but of course, I was reminded that this was His life and not mine.

I prayed I would do whatever His will required. But I knew whatever this next phase was, it would hurt. I pushed it to the back of my mind.

I regularly took the children to the playground to play with their little cousins. Eventually, I became bolder and shared some stories with my sisters-in-law. Gently, I asked them what they remembered of his temper.

Their stories were about times he would react aggressively, but they felt that after receiving Jesus into his life, he vastly improved. They hadn't been accosted by him for a few years.

One of my sisters-in-law sensed there was more to my question.

"Why? What's he done?" I loved these two sisters. I felt close to them and knew I could trust them.

"Well, he would lose his temper. At times." I didn't offer anymore. I didn't want to worsen a situation if it was improving. I just wanted to understand him more. Now I thought did.

One day the freckled one came home, announced he quit his job, and said that God gave him a board game idea that was going to make him millions of dollars. He wanted me to design the board and cards that went with it.

I was stunned but was careful to sift through this new information. We had been there five months, never missed rent even though money was tight. But we were doing much, much better.

"Well," I said carefully as my mind raced. "It sounds like a marvelous idea. I could do the design. But," I knew I were treading on thin ice, "why don't you keep the job while I do the design work? I will help you develop and shop it around. That way we keep our heads above water."

I didn't think I'd see it again. It happened so quickly that I was barely able to register the changing look in his eyes before something happened.

Suddenly, I felt my face whip the other way and almost fell out of my chair.

I regained my balance and sat slumped in the chair, holding my face. I was about to cry but instead did a dry cough. He had hit me so quickly I didn't see it coming. My heart was pounding, and I needed to catch my breath. I looked over to see where the children were.

Joel was upstairs, but I saw Ethan playing on the carpet. He was looking at us, shocked. Then his face scrunched up, and he started to cry. I got out of the chair to comfort him. As I swept him up, the freckled one followed me and swung me around. He held my blouse crunched up in one hand, and formed a fist with the other hand as if to punch me. His nostrils flared, and his mouth was set as he debated about hurting me.

"Please, not with Ethan in my arms," I cried.

The cries brought Joel down the stairs. He stood looking at his father holding me in a familiar stance. He cried, "Mommy".

"Don't cry, Joel. It's okay."

The freckled one changed his mind and delivered a hard slap on my face instead of a punch. That side now really burned. I knew a welt was going to show. How would I hide this from my sisters-in-law the next day?

He pointed his finger at me and jabbed my forehead. "You are going to shut your f---ing mouth, b----. If God is telling me to do this board game then that's what I'm going to do!"

"But I can't believe God is telling you that! We're finally paying rent and covering our costs. Why would God let our poor landlord down!? Think about it!"

With that he poked me in the forehead again, cutting my skin with his nail. Then he grabbed me and walked me backwards.

"Ethan!" I cried, as he was still in my arms. "Don't do this while I hold Ethan!"

He finally slammed my back into the wall behind me.

"Let Ethan see what happens to his mother when she disobeys." He body slammed me one more time against the wall and let go. Crying, I slowly slid down the wall. Ethan was crying at the same time, but the freckled one bent down and took him into his arms and tried to soothe him with gentle noises. He walked into the kitchen with Ethan looking over his shoulder at me, his mother, on the ground against the wall with blood on her forehead and big welts on her face.

"Please God, don't let this hurt my babies. Don't let this hurt my babies."

I remembered the scripture again. About enduring. But then I remembered the book. *How to Get a Divorce in Canada.*

I was greatly confused.

• • •

My sisters-in-law wondered why I didn't take the boys to the playground the next day or the day after. I finally took the boys out a few days later.

One of them looked at me.

"Are you okay?" She was a beautiful woman, with big hazel eyes full of gentleness.

I looked away and nodded. The boys were understandably quiet that day. Still not over the return of our own personal hell.

"If my brother does anything, you know you can talk about it. I won't say anything."

Even she was afraid of him. But I decided I would rather wait and see if it got better again just in case. I didn't want them hurt with the knowledge that their brother was a monster.

She gave me a big hug. Knowing someone understood helped. I had also come to learn she was also under the thumb of her own husband.

We understood each other's suffering.

For now, it was our secret. She didn't want to know any details. I didn't need to know hers. Why? It all added up to the same hellish story.

A few days later, I was vacuuming the carpet when Ethan punched the hem of my skirt with his little fists.

I looked down on the top of his beautiful blonde head. He looked so sweet. I stopped the vacuum cleaner and put it on its base. I ruffled his hair.

"What are you doing, Ethan?" I asked, smiling down at him.

"I'm punching Mommy like Daddy does."

As the air left my lungs, I fell to my knees and faced him.

"Ethan, Daddy doesn't punch Mommy." I held him tightly.

"Yes, he does. He punches like this." With that, he hit my cheek with his little fist.

I sat back and covered my face. Joel hurried over and put his young arms around me. He squeezed tightly as I cried. I reached out and held Ethan close as well.

Only one thing registered—that that monster was teaching my children to become monsters.

I was not going to let that happen. No matter what.

• • •

On this early summer evening, I had waited in the living room. The boys were bathed and dressed in their pajamas. Though I had rehearsed my thoughts and words, I was nervous.

It was time to draw the line in the sand.

The freckled one returned home after a meeting pitching the board game concept to the same friend who had lost his $100,000 in the last business venture. He seemed upbeat. Hopeful.

I prayed he would listen to me as he had done for a while before this last violent episode. Perhaps it was an aberration. A hiccup. Now that he was developing this board game, perhaps he was in a better frame of mind. Surely, when I pointed out what Ethan said, he would be appalled as I was.

After he took off his light jacket, he walked in from the hallway while I went to the kitchen to get his dinner. As he dropped his briefcase and papers, he went to the boys and lifted them up for a big kiss. Then while he washed his hands at the kitchen sink, I carefully began to speak.

"Something happened today which was very upsetting. Something I think you will be concerned over as well."

He looked over at me. He took the towel I was holding.

"What happened?"

"I was vacuuming this morning when Ethan came up to me and did something he's seen you do to me."

He went over to the table while I got his dinner plate out of the microwave oven. I placed the plate in front of him and sat down in the next chair.

"So?" he said.

I straightened up. "He punched my skirt with his fists, saying he was punching Mommy like Daddy does."

He picked up his fork but stopped and looked at me. "Okay. So, did it hurt?"

I took a deep breath. "Of course not, it's just that ..."

"That *what*?" He threw the fork down onto his plate. Some of the food splattered onto the tablecloth. He slapped his hands on the table. "So, now what is it, huh? Something else you want

The Kingdom of God and Playboys

a pound of flesh for?" He swiped the plate and utensils off the table with his arm.

I got up out of the chair.

I wasn't going to let this one go. He was not going to bully me this time.

I stood still and waited for him to come to me. He raised his finger and jabbed my forehead as usual. I didn't let him push me back, though, and fought to stand my ground.

"You're not going to bully me this time," I said softly. My voice quivered.

He grabbed my blouse at my throat and shook me. "Is that so? Is this bullying you? Tell me, is this bullying you?"

"You're not going to make monsters out of my sons!" I yelled. Then I pushed him as hard as I could. When he let go of my blouse, I turned and ran to the stairs. I needed time to think about what to say next. What to do next. How was I going to get out of this? And I wanted this to be out of view of my children.

At the bottom of the stairs, I turned to see him lunging toward me, his shoulders hunched, his long arms hanging, his hands forming fists. He raised one in a threatening manner.

"I'll show you what a monster is," he sneered coming toward me.

"I'm not going to let you do this to them," I yelled pointing at the children as I turned and ran up the stairs.

He ran after me. At the top of the stairs, I turned around to face him and then, suddenly, time stood still. Sound disappeared. All I could hear was my breathing and the pounding beat of my heart.

I pondered on how to deal with this crazy man. I argued that he was a monster who I felt should not be allowed to live and destroy the lives of my children. I also believed that if I didn't do something first, he was going to kill me this time. So I had to kill him. I felt my hands raising toward him. But I stopped and remembered that God had said, "thou shalt not kill." But what if one were protecting themselves and the lives of their children?

But then I thought what if he wasn't going to kill me after all, or the children as he always threatened. Then that meant killing him would have been for nothing. I debated, did I have the strength to push him hard enough so that he would indeed fall back down the stairs and break his neck? But he might survive, and he would surely kill me and the children.

Then I realized if I successfully killed him, I could be imprisoned. I wouldn't be around to protect my children from the world. They'd be without both their father and mother.

A cold sweat broke out on my forehead as I felt the muscles in my arms screaming to push him. *Hard! Hard*, they said!

In a split second, I went light years into a hell where others who had killed existed. I saw why they killed. Some for good reason. Others for much less valid reasons. I communed with them. I saw some who were black, lost souls. Some gray. But they were all in a class of their own. I was in a type of purgatory. I communed long enough so that when I came back, I felt their oily suffering film imprisoned in my body. That's what I was sweating out. I could smell it. I knew then I would never judge another who may have killed out of fear or for protection. They would have gone to this place where no one would want to go. And I was taken there to see because I seriously considered killing him. Almost as if by imagining it, I had actually done it.

Slowly, I watched his black eyes drill into mine as if he read what I was planning to do. Now it was a race. A race to kill each other.

I closed my eyes. I chose to do nothing. I surrendered.

The stairwell rumbled under and around me. I felt him tackle me. I felt him lift me off my feet. A scream came from my throat but it didn't seem real. It wasn't me anymore. As he threw me on the bed, I saw the open bedroom window. Perhaps if I screamed out that window, someone might hear me and come running into the house to stop this hell.

My eyesight turned to black as he threw a pillow over my face. As I fought for air, I felt him lean into me with all his weight and strength.

Strangely, I didn't care I couldn't breathe. I felt no panic. I felt nothing. I watched what was happening without any emotion. I saw and knew he was suffocating what was my body.

I watched until it died.

BOOK FOUR:

The Unsettled Years

"My dear friend, do not be bewildered by the fiery
ordeal that is upon you,
as though it were something extraordinary."

(1 Peter 4:12, NEB)

SEVENTEEN

Just Call me Lazarus

*"...he brought them out of darkness, dark as death,
and broke their chains."*

(Psalms 107:14, NEB)

The adrenaline rushed so fast at the moment of death, that the muscle memory remained on high alert. Even while the pillow was still pressed on the face, the chest muscles remembered to go up and down, in and out, ever so slightly. Knees dug into the chest kept them from expanding very far, but the memory was as stubborn as the person whose body it was. As soon as the knees were removed and the pressure on the pillow relaxed, tiny amounts of oxygen inadvertently entered into the upper reaches of the lungs though that was not what the muscles meant to do. They just wanted to party on, doing what they did best.

I travelled somewhere during that eternity where I was told it wasn't time to stay. I had to go back again.

The last time I returned after hanging off the bolt in the steering column feeling elated and happy, this time it was different.

My soul was tired.

The body was not ready. It was hard, but I slithered back into this non-functioning vessel and eventually felt the pillow slip off the face. Slowly I became aware of a cacophony of sound.

The body's programming had to be rebooted fully. Through the eyes, it did not recognize. The ears heard but did not understand.

Slowly, I understood enough to be aware of the larger object moving toward me. Then it floated me through shadow and light, down the stairs and into an arm chair. Finally, I understood this larger object was the freckled one. He was talking to me, begging me to respond, to say anything at all.

That loving, quiet Voice was much more discernable than before.

Tea.

I found my ponderous tongue, felt the teeth, and moved the jaw. All I could form was the sound 'T.' Relieved, he praised God that I could talk again. As he made me a pot of tea, the Voice spoke again.

Now is the time. The perfect time.

When he returned, placing the cup and saucer next to me on a little table, he asked what else I would like. Anything at all, he cried.

Tell him you want to see your mother.

"My mother. I want to see my mother."

He said we did not have gas for the car or money to get any.

Tell him to borrow it. He's good at that. It's nothing new to him.

"Borrow it."

"From whom?" he asked.

Tell him to ask his mother. She knows how he treats you. She could lend the money.

"Your mother."

The next day we were in his parents' car on the way to the bus station.

I was running away with the children.

EIGHTEEN

Match-Maker Pap and Here Come da Judge

*"Rise up, captive Jerusalem, shake off the dust:
loose your neck from the collar that binds it,
O captive daughter of Zion"*

(Isaiah 52:2, NEB)

"I'm sorry I have to do this."

I looked up at the Chief of Police. He was standing with his camera, waiting for me to indicate it was okay for him to take photos for his report.

"After we've finished here, you'll have to go to a doctor and get checked out. You have a lot of cuts and bruises, most of which are probably not evident, I'm guessin'."

I felt nothing. I didn't cry when I related everything to him that I had told Pap and Mam. I felt numb and strangely detached.

"And I would advise you to charge him."

I shook my head.

"Well, you're not thinkin' of goin' back, are ya?" He tried so hard to remain officious but looked surprised at the thought.

"I'm not charging." I was dead inside.

• • •

A week later I lay on the box mattress. My hand trailed toward the boys' little bodies on the mattress on the floor as if I didn't want them to disappear. It was too hot for all of us to sleep together on a single bed.

I fell asleep realizing I had better figure out the future for the boys' sake. Should I finish my degree or immediately start a career? Without realizing it, I started to take over my life again.

Did I not learn a single thing through the recent custom-made boot camp?

When we reach for Him, He surrounds us. When we pull away from Him—whether we do it knowingly or not—He watches from a distance while we do it *our* way. *Again.*

• • •

I took over the Chandlery Store for the Marina and eventually moved into a renovated apartment above the store. The two were connected by a back stairway. Many times, the boys played either on the stairs or behind the store's counter. It was a perfect set-up, though I jumped at any chance to take on other jobs that fit in with the schedule of the store. Pap gave me a little Omni car to get around. As a result, I did a slew of commercials for a local TV station and started sample selling on weekends or evenings at grocery stores.

I was going to make a future for the boys if it killed me. I was in a crazed state.

"Stop fretting about the future and money," Pap said as we were standing outside in the parking lot. "You have me."

I was all spruced up for an audition in Toronto. It was almost a two-hour drive one way. "I want to catch up on lost time," I said, grabbing his wrist and looking at the time. "I better go."

"Listen, you don't understand. Your Mam shouldn't be watching the boys every time you duck out for your hobbies."

I stopped for a moment. "Hobbies?"

He shrugged. "You should only worry about the children. That's all you have to do."

"That's not enough, Pap." Someone drove into the parking lot and passed us, spewing gravel dust around us. "I have to be both mother and father for the boys now."

Pap looked back at the car that had driven by. He was frowning.

"Was that the teacher that caused so much trouble with the girls?"

He waved his mitt at me. "No, he's long gone. After you left, I marched right down to his boat and kicked him off the property. I told him I didn't want his kind here."

"Wow, Pap."

"Yeah, he threatened to sue me. I told him to go ahead. He never did, of course." He took his cap off and repositioned it on his balding head. "I think you should stop everything. Run the store if you like, it's convenient. But you," he pointed his thick forefinger at me, "you should just focus on raising the boys."

It was a mantra for him.

"Pap, depending on a man for security makes me want to throw up."

"I've got the perfect man for you."

"I don't want a man, Pap. I've had it up to here with men!" I opened the door to the Omni. "I have to go, Pap."

He ignored me. "No, this guy is perfect. I would give my eyeteeth to have him as my son-in-law. I'll tell him to come tomorrow. The boys need a good role model." He closed the door gently and leaned into the window. "So, what is it today? Stupid commercial? Low-budget film?"

I squinted up at him. "A movie. Probably won't get it."

"Then why do you do it? Your Mam is tired of babysitting."

I looked up toward the stairs at the side of the building that led up to their apartment.

"Okay, Pap. I'll just do this one today, and then I'll see if I can get babysitting somewhere for next time." I started the car and put my seatbelt on.

"Tomorrow he'll come by."

Well, if Pap thought he was perfect, he must be perfect. And I was still an obedient and doting daughter. I still hadn't learned to keep Pap's face from hiding God's face.

• • •

The next morning, I stood in front of the Chandlery watering the petunias and geraniums I planted. A beautiful, red Buick Riviera convertible with white leather upholstery drove into the parking lot. It passed me and went down the hill toward the docks. I stood and watched Pap come out of the large boat shed and do a loud greeting. Pap motioned for me to come down.

I dropped the hose, turned it off at the tap in the wall, and sauntered over. I was embarrassed and heard that three-ring circus music playing in the back of my mind.

I recognized him. The Chief of Police.

"Sonny, you met my beautiful daughter."

The Chief grinned. "Yes, I have. How do you do again." His glasses were partially smoky and I could just barely make out his eyes.

"Sonny, I keep telling you I would love to have you as my son-in-law. How about taking my daughter out?"

I looked for a circus cannon to crawl in and be shot away from this crazy place.

"I would love that. How about the movies?"

Pap grinned and said, "You got a deal. Friday night?"

The Chief nodded. "Sounds good. There's a Clint Eastwood movie out. He's my idol. Honkytonk Man. Drive-in okay?"

"Hey, make my day!"

"Very funny," grinned the Chief.

"She'll be ready," said Pap, "and no funny stuff."

With that, I went to the movies with the Chief. Before I knew it, the Chief played Daddy to my boys.

Then I found out he was married.

"Oh, he's leaving his wife," Pap said.

"Ooookay."

So, I found myself driving out to the Chief's house to see if I could see his family through the windows.

What the heck did I fall into? I was back in dysfunction land.

• • •

Just as Pap predicted, the marriage broke up.

"We're expanding your apartment," Pap said to me. "There isn't room enough if the Chief is moving in. The poor guy is living in a musty motel room. And you can't live on your own with that crazy maniac of an ex-husband threatening to kill you all the time. It would make me sleep better at night."

"He's not an *ex*-husband yet, Pap."

"As good as."

• • •

1983

I sat in the large dusty courtroom fretting and feeling sick. My very first time at court. I was appalled to see there were so many strangers in the room. I leaned toward my lawyer.

"Why are all these people here?" I whispered. Even though my voice was soft, I could still hear it echo off the opposite wall. Everyone else was whispering loudly, too.

"They're all here for the same thing as you."

"You mean they'll all know our business?" I looked around at all the faces in the courtroom. "How embarrassing. I don't want them to know what happened to me!"

There was a commotion in the courtroom. "Shhhh, the judge is coming. Stand up."

I looked over as a very old, miserable-looking man in a judge's cloak came in with papers under his arm. Everyone stood. He sat down. Everyone sat.

"Do I have to say anything?" I asked.

My lawyer shook his head. "No, he'll have read your statement and the police report by now, and he has the photos. Only I will speak to him. You won't have a problem getting a divorce based on physical and mental abuse."

My heart kept skipping beats. I wasn't comfortable with so many people around but I thought that at least I would soon be vindicated. The abuse, pain, and suffering I had gone through would be recognized by a judge of the land. The freckled one would see that what he had done was wrong. Finally, my suffering would be brought to light, and then, perhaps, I would regain my dignity. I needed all the help I could get in finding it again. What was left of me was an empty shell.

When it was finally my turn, the freckled one's lawyer stood up.

"Your Honor," he said very clearly and gently. He motioned back to the freckled one who had tears running down his cheeks. "My client has been grief-stricken at not being allowed to see his two beautiful children. He is a gentle, loving man who wouldn't think of hurting them or his wife. We do not wish to argue the divorce petition, but we do insist that my client has visitation rights, even if supervised."

I looked at the judge in anticipation.

The judge looked at me. Then at the freckled one. He looked down at his papers and sighed.

Here it was, my vindication.

He raised his head, faced me again, and lifted his hand. He scowled and jabbed his finger in my direction to emphasize his words.

"I am so sick (*jab*) and tired (*jab*) of hearing these false reports by young, lying wives who claim to be beaten by gentle and obviously (*jab*) well-meaning men such as he. This court (*jab*) will not stand by and watch our legal system be abused by such filthy (*jab*) slander."

He slammed his gavel on his desk. But he might as well have hit me in the face with it.

"Divorce granted. Supervised visitation each weekend for a month and then unsupervised bi-weekly weekend visits. Custody granted to the mother (I could swear he sneered). Child support $25 a month."

I sat there feeling accosted. He just rendered me a lying, filthy young wife who is not to be believed by the entire world. He threw me aside like a used Kleenex full of snot.

I didn't care about any support. I knew the only reason I received two months of payments was that he had to prove he paid. As soon as they stopped checking, he quit.

In the meantime, Pap's sonny-to-be had continued on with his mid-life crisis and quit his position as Chief of Police. He was hired as a Professor of Security at the college and also cashed in savings and bought a GL 1800 Honda *Gold Wing* with stereo and air conditioning. And, of course, I was part of that crisis-induced change.

Later, Pap insisted I not drop the boys off or pick them up from their father.

"Let the Chief do it. The loser just goes out of his way to upset you every time. He'll behave himself with the Chief."

The following Sunday night, the Chief came back with a bleeding nose without the boys.

"Where are the boys?"

"He punched me."

I panicked. "Where are the boys?"

"He punched me."

"I know, but where are the boys?" I still believed the freckled one was quite capable of carrying out his threat to kill those beautiful little angels. If he had been so enraged that he would give the Chief a bloody nose, then surely, he was pushed over the edge.

"He wouldn't let me have them."

I was in the car before he even finished that statement.

I raced back praying to God he was still there. He wasn't. I drove everywhere looking for them. The irony was that I would've called the police, yet I had a fresh *ex*-Chief of Police at my apartment with a bleeding nose, caused by the very person I would've called him about.

Finally, after an hour, I raced home to see if he would call. I stomped back upstairs, and the Chief, who had a package of frozen peas on his nose, gave me a look that said that I was in trouble. But that was the least of my worries.

"Any calls?"

"Yes, that f---ing ex of yours. He hung up when he heard my voice. He's rung about ten times since then."

I looked over at the phone and silently prayed that it would ring soon.

It did. I pounced on it.

"Hello?"

"Don't ever do that again." The freckled one was angry. I could hear my boys crying.

"Do what?"

"Have a total stranger come to pick up my boys."

"Our boys," I said. "And the Chief is not a stranger to the boys."

"From now on you drop them off and pick them up. You do that again and I'll simply disappear with them." I continued to hear the boys' cries.

"Why are they crying," I cried. He had reawakened that frightened little mouse in me.

"Because they saw your boyfriend beat me up. Now they don't want to go back to you."

Up bubbled the frazzled, beaten, measly weakling. The rag of the woman he created with his threats and beatings. "Don't hurt them," I cried. "Please don't hurt them. Please let me have them. Don't take them away. Please let me come and get them. They need me …"

"They don't need a whore for a mother. They're better off with me. God doesn't want them to be with you. What kind of mother are you that you take another man into your bed when you belong to me?! You're nothing but a Jezebel. You know what they did to Jezebel? Remember? They threw her out the window and she was stomped into pieces. They could only find part of a hand. That's what's going to happen to you."

My boys could hear every single thing he said. *My God!*

I felt a hand try to take the phone away from me. I was an animal. I yanked it back and moved as far as I could away from the Chief. "Please, tell me where you are. Please, the boys' need to go to bed. Joel has school in the morning."

"What's school when you're in the kingdom of God. I don't care. Why should I care?"

"Please, let me have the boys," I cried. "If you don't I'll call the police."

"Police? Wasn't that supposed to have been a super policeman? Huh? The Chief? Ha! He couldn't beat up an old lady. Besides, what are they going to do? Shoot me?"

He, again, had full control over me. I quietened down. "No, they wouldn't."

"Right, they wouldn't. Now, if you'll behave, I will drive back. I will let you, and only you, take them. But they are upset. They don't want to go home with you. I've had to calm them down and tell them they must go back to you. I told them I'll see them again next weekend."

"But you don't have them next weekend. I've made plans for them. A birthday party."

"No, you're wrong. They don't want to go to a birthday party. I've arranged to take them to see their Nanna and Grandad. They'll be hurt if you prevent them from going to see them."

I felt it. That familiar suffocating control he always had over the boys and me.

"Also, I told the boys that your new man is evil. I looked into him. Everyone says he's evil. He's a bad man."

Zing. Another poison-tipped arrow.

Dutifully, I drove back and picked up my tired little babies. Ethan cried and clung to his father. Joel quietly got into the car. He looked drained, pale and frightened. That same look when we were all together as a family.

The boys refused to listen to the Chief at all from then on.

In return, the Chief treated my boys as if they were second-class citizens.

Then I landed a lead in a made-for-TV movie called, *Visit from Heaven*.

• • •

During shooting, I had to stay overnight at the Holiday Inn in a town an hour away. The Chief didn't believe I was actually shooting a movie, or that I had a lead in it, so he drove around and around the hotel looking for camera crews and activity. I don't know how he missed us. We were in a conference room, then in the swimming pool area. He may have missed us when we went back to the studio set up as a living room.

He thought I was having an affair.

I came home to find him angry and jealous. I had an early morning call, so I let his yelling and accusations roll off my back. He kept arguing while in bed, so I got up to sleep on the couch. I needed my sleep for an early morning call.

He threw a pot of cold water on my head.

I woke up with a start and pushed him away. It came out as a slap on his right knee while my eyes were screwed shut.

"You hit me!" he yelled and whacked me in the face.

I had to have extra make-up put over the welt under my left eye.

That was the end of the Chief.

• • •

1984

The freckled one, who was adept at crying on everyone's shoulders at the various churches and retreats he now frequented, was given money to buy whatever the boys wanted. He had money to stay in a motel for the weekend and to take them to McDonald's and other restaurants for their meals. He took them to Toys 'R Us as a traditional part of the weekend.

I, on the other hand, working three jobs at once, was proud to be able to pay all the bills and save up a little towards Christmas. But by the time their birthdays and Christmases came along, they had already been given every single toy they ever wanted. Consequently, this became a measure of how much I didn't love them and how much he did.

I lost control over my beautiful little children.

Then another form of ugliness reared its familiar head.

"Daddy said that Nonno and Nonna will cut us up into little pieces."

"Daddy said you don't love us and you'll kill us one day in our sleep."

"Daddy said you only want men to come and live with you. You won't want us."

"Daddy said you're wrong. My teeth won't fall out it if I never brush my teeth."

Daddy said, daddy said, daddy said.

• • •

Late at night, I would go out and walk along the docks to be alone with God. I prayed and talked with Him, praying over the children, praying over my parents, my little sister. I thanked God for everything good and bad. I'd look up at the stars and imagine the Milky Way and how little we were in comparison. How insignificant my problems were compared to everything else in this universe.

All the more amazing that God should care for someone like me, down to the tiniest detail of my life. Jezebel me.

I was tired of not being able to offer more for my children. I was tired of being a broken family. I started to feel Pap was right. The boys did need a different role model for a father.

I remembered something He taught me sometime earlier. That if we were all sitting in His living room, He would pass along a bowl of candies and tell everyone to help themselves. As a Host, it would please Him if we enjoyed ourselves and if we took what we wanted. Some people are timid and say "No thank you," and they pass the bowl on to the next person.

Then there are those who look into the bowl and take only one. They would like more, but they believe that having more would be a sign of greed.

But God says there is an endless supply of these candies and it pleases Him to no end to see us enjoy his kindness.

With this in mind, I looked at the stars above me and prayed: "God, if what You say is true, that your children can ask for so much, would You mind very much if I pray for a husband that is a solid and respectable man who could be a good father and a better male role model for my children? One who loves to work and does well. And God, I don't want to be poor anymore. Please let him be a millionaire but, more importantly, let me love him with all my heart. If that's what You can do for me, and if You don't mind, oh please, may I have that?"

I truly believed it was just a matter of time.

Be careful what you wish for. You will get it.

• • •

1985

It was freezing rain on a long weekend. Pap had a fire going in the small wood stove next to the counter in the Chandlery. I had a big pot of coffee on, its aroma caressing the cushions of warm air generated by the stove.

I had *James Galway's* beautiful flute playing "Nocturne." The beautiful flowing music echoed throughout the little store along with the crackling pop sounds of the wood stove. Hale and sleet pelted the large plate glass windows along the front wall creating flowing images of light, sparkles, and distortions of the view outside. Few cars parked right in front of the store. Most boat owners' cars were parked down by the docks, and because of the weather, most stayed tied to their docks where, undoubtedly, they were having a nice hot rum toddy in their cozy little cabins listening to their own choice of music as the rain pelted their cabin tops.

I stood by the counter listening to James Galway while arranging the chocolate bars and small toiletries under the counter.

I moved to the other end of the counter and reached under the glass where I had the larger instruments: compasses, depth finders, and barometers. I dusted them and repositioned them, swaying to the music. The boys were sitting on the stairs behind me, content with their toys.

Pap in his coveralls and Portuguese cap was splicing a rope. I was proud of Pap. He worked like a dog on that marina and he was succeeding.

Suddenly, the doors banged open, and five inebriated men exploded into the shop. Grins, guffaws, and bright eyes made Pap look up and grin broadly. They were men's men, just like Pap. They wore matching T-shirts with a boat's name on the upper right shoulder. They stopped and looked at Pap with his big grin and spliced rope on his lap.

"Hey, you do that kind of stuff?" the portly jovial one said pointing at Pap's lap.

"Yes, man, I could do this with my eyes closed."

The portly gent laughed. "Well, that's real old school!"

There was a skinny guy I didn't trust, a nice, happy-go-lucky one, and another who was quiet but pleasantly happy. A red-faced one with big eyes went and sat beside Pap.

"You're splicing that rope with a fid, right?" He sat with his legs spread, his ample girth leaning between his legs. He had big hands and white hair. He leaned in to watch Pap closely.

I looked over to another who walked the aisles and was moving along the life jackets. He had an arrogance about him I didn't trust. I watched him as he picked up things off the shelf, looked at their prices, and then put them back. "Your prices are far too high!" he complained.

I took offense. It was my store to run, and I did the pricing. "Well," I said, smiling broadly, "if you don't like them, you don't have to buy them."

For some reason, that made all the men applaud and cheer.

"Watch out, Carl. She's figured you out."

Carl looked over at me and laughed loudly.

"Oh, I have him figured out, all right," I said to the portly one. "He comes in here to check the prices, complain about them, and then try to bargain them down. I'll just send him back next door, where the prices are even higher, and he knows he can't bully them down. Uh-uh. My prices are what they are here, whether you like them or not. He can't bully me."

Carl brightened up, eyes sparkling, and he guffawed. He was shocked and pleased at the same time. Grinning, he came over to check the instruments under the glass.

"Coffee anyone?" I asked, holding up the bottle of rum.

"What kind of an establishment is this?" asked the portly, jovial one.

I pointed to Pap. "It's his. Well, his and my uncles. It's a family business. But Pap does all the work. This marina is what it is because of him. He created it singlehandedly."

Pap grinned. "That's my daughter. She's always trying to show me off."

I leaned against the counter, still keeping an eye on Carl, while I watched Pap joke with the others who gathered around the warm stove, the flames flickering and jumping behind the tempered glass.

"Do you sell Autopilots?"

I turned to look at Carl. "I can order them for you if this one here…" and bent down to get a box from under the counter, "isn't quite right."

He came over and picked up the box. "This doesn't have a remote control."

"That's okay, have a look at this catalog." I gave him the catalog and turned to check on the boys at the stairs behind me. I went over and ruffled Joel's hair, then Ethan's.

"They yours?" asked Carl, holding the open catalog.

I looked back at the boys. My darlings. "Yes, they are," I said proudly. "They're mine."

"They're well behaved. I can tell you're a good mother."

I looked at him. "I would give them the moon if I could."

Carl smiled. Then he looked down at a page in the catalog. He chose an Autopilot and I took his information and a credit card imprint. He looked at the credit card imprinter. "That's one of mine," he said.

I looked at the machine.

"You made this?" I held it up.

"Yup."

"That's great. Small world."

"Yes," he said. "They're practically around the world now."

"Well, congratulations," I said.

Soon the guys left. Pap cleaned up his equipment and went back upstairs to have supper. Anxious to get supper started for the boys, I was just about to close the shop when Carl showed up and knocked on the glass.

I was a little impatient with him because he had all day to finish his shopping, but he wasn't looking for something off the shelf.

It was me.

"I was wondering if you wouldn't mind going out for dinner with me next weekend." He said politely, though with that arrogant look

I eyed him. Almost every man who came tried to pick me up, sometimes even while their wives browsed through the shelves. I did not trust any man who asked me out.

"Are you married?" I asked, not very politely.

"No, I'm not. And I'm not dating anyone either."

I paused and said a little prayer. There was enough on my plate, and the last thing I needed was for the freckled one to hold my children for ransom again.

Go with him for dinner.

In a few weeks, after I put him through the children test, I was open to getting to know him. We spent hours on his C&C

38 boat over the next few months and took a week-long vaca-tion trip. I kept him a secret from the freckled one.

Five months later, we eloped to Hawaii.

NINETEEN

Trouble in Paradise

1985

A chorus of birds celebrated the beautiful early morning. We stood tanned and barefoot in the middle of a rich, thick banana grove in Ka'anapali on the Hawaiian island of Lahaina. Every once in a while, I felt a fat dew drop plop onto my curls. Holding hands, we watched the beautiful, colorful little birds dart around us. They were just as curious about us. I was so excited I thought I would faint as we waited for the Justice of the Peace to arrive with his wife who would act as a witness.

In Hawaii, I experienced many firsts: a cockroach, an allergic reaction to Macadamia nuts, fresh pineapple, Mahi-Mahi, whales frolicking and mating, resort life, fresh coconut, orchids, volcanic cliffs, and the smell of Jasmine. This was Paradise.

Carl and I bought brightly-colored wedding clothes. He chose a pair of white shorts and a bright pink shirt with Hawaiian birds in a white motif pattern. I chose a white wrap-around dress for our vows and a pink one for later.

Around our necks we wore thick pink and white carnation leis. He wore the white ones and I the pink. The heavenly smell will forever remind me of this beautiful wedding day.

I was in love. I was madly in love with a man for the first time in my life. I loved this man with my heart, my soul, and my body. And I thanked God for him every single day. I was walking on air. I felt beautiful, glowing, and finally *at home*.

With no twinges of angst or anxiety, I believed this was it. God had blessed this relationship, and it would last forever.

Carl wasn't born again. He wasn't quite sure what to believe, but the "unevenly-yoked" aspect of our relationship seemed to be less important because I had been "evenly-yoked" with a husband who almost killed me.

I thought middle of the road would be safer. I wanted no more yelling, no more swearing and no more violence in my life.

The boys were under Mam's care while we were in Hawaii, and I knew they were fine. Not having lived with Carl yet meant that the freckled one stayed in his lion cave and didn't make any threats. He knew very little about Carl.

Finally, we heard our Justice of the Peace.

"Good morning. What a beautiful morning to get married!" I turned to see a kind Hawaiian native son, but not his wife.

"She slept so soundly. I only woke her up enough to sign the witness signature, and then I let her get back to sleep. I hope you don't mind."

We both laughed and settled into a spot that allowed the three of us to stand together.

As the magical words of the marriage ceremony fell sweetly off the Justice of the Peace's lips, I reached out and felt God's presence all around me.

Am I doing the right thing? I asked.

Is this what you want?

Yes, very much, I responded.

With a big smile, the Justice of the Peace spoke those special words we were to repeat. I turned to Carl:

"… to have and to hold, from this day forward, for better, for worse, for richer, for poorer, in sickness and in health, to love and to cherish, till death do us part."

With tears in my eyes, I searched his green eyes, his face, and his mouth. I drank him in as if he were the finest wine in the world.

I smiled brighter as Carl spoke those special words. For a moment, I thought I saw the sparkle lessen in his eyes. Fear? Nervousness?

"… in sickness and in health, to love and to cherish, till *love* do us part."

Till love do us part. Not death.

He had made his vow conditional.

• • •

Immediately after the ceremony, we hopped on a small plane and flew to the island of Maui where we'd spend another few days We had an amazing wedding supper inside the opulent restaurant seated beside a sparkling stream that flowed past the tables. Water gurgled and lapped while we ate. It all added to the sense of being in this Paradise on earth.

That night, as skittish as a virgin on her wedding night, I had a lovely bubble bath as he watched the news

He said he wasn't in the mood.

He wasn't the next night either.

Finally, I asked him what the problem was. He sat back and thought about it.

"I guess the only way I can describe it is that you make love like a nun."

I laughed. "Well, that's funny because I did try to become a nun."

He didn't laugh.

"Well, can you teach me how to be the way you want me to be?" I asked hopefully.

He sighed. "I guess."

And he tried. I thought I had learned, but one night he surprised me with the harshest, ugliest sound in my ear I had ever heard.

With a massive grin, he had turned on a battery-operated dildo right in my face. I did not react the way he thought I would. I jumped back and yelled, "What the heck is *that*?!"

He looked at the vibrating thing in his hand, "It's a sex toy."

If he had warned me or talked to me ahead of time, I may have had the time to think about what to say. But he hadn't, and I didn't.

He never introduced or suggested anything else after that and slowly withdrew from our physical relationship.

BOOK FIVE:

The Rocky Years

"But if a man is a cause to stumbling to one of these
little ones who have faith in me,
it would be better for him to have a millstone hung
round his neck and be drowned
in the depths of the sea."

(Matthew 18:5-7, NEB)

TWENTY

Who's in Charge? The Playboy or the Prophet?

1986

I continued to work and pay for my own children's expenses. I wanted to be the one who cared for every need they had. We lived in a lovely home in an upper scale neighborhood. Nannies and gardeners were constantly moving through our street, and I had a housecleaner though I tended to clean the house before she came.

Our gardeners took better care of the rose gardens and box hedges than I ever could. Our swimming pool was opened and closed by a company, but I insisted on maintaining the pool. It was a pleasure to stand next to clear sparkling waters while gently scooping out floating leaves.

I thanked God every day for so much beauty and the fact that we no longer struggled for money. I had absolutely nothing to complain about.

Except for two things.

The freckled one: under his influence, the boys had difficulty enjoying being with Carl and I when at home. And Carl lived as if the romance was gone completely. Pressure from the freckled one did not help.

Quite often, when he felt the boys were enjoying themselves with us too much, he would take his turn and disappear with them for weeks at a time.

I called the police. I called the school board. No one could or would help me. There was no internet, no cell phones, no answering machines, no Facebook, so there were far fewer support outlets to turn to.

Each time I prayed and had to believe they were fine. But in the back of my mind, I allowed fears to take hold. How will they survive this emotionally? Would he kill them as he always threatened? Or would he disappear with them forever?

One saving grace was Dr. Bob, our friendly psychiatrist Carl took me to see.

The first time I went to him, it was solely to ask about the freckled one and how to deal with the brainwashing of the boys. But Dr. Bob had other ideas.

"First, we deal with you," he said, pointing with one of his nicotine-stained fingers still holding a burning cigarette. "We can't do anything to help the boys without first helping their mother."

I panicked. I needed to protect all the lurid and shameful secrets I held deep inside of me.

Please, I thought. *Don't go there.*

"I suspect you are very adept at hiding deep pain. Deep depression. You've crafted a wall around you that is skillfully put together A person looking at you would never guess what you've gone through in your life."

I started to sweat and looked around the room. Could I simply get up and walk away? But if I were to walk away, I would walk away from someone who could help my boys. I started to shake. I watched his eyes watch me. He saw right through me.

"There is nothing to be afraid of. But if you really are serious about dealing with your ex-husband—who, by the way, is a schizophrenic, bi-polar, narcissistic, and antisocial man—then I need to find out why you chose him as the father of your children to begin with. Only someone suffering from a tremendous amount of emotional and psychic pain, would do such a thing."

I felt panic rise in my throat. I wanted to swallow it down, but then tears took over.

"Please, we don't have to go there, do we?"

He threw his right leg over the arm of his chair. He scratched his groin and then flicked the ashes from his cigarette missing the overflowing ashtray. He inhaled noisily and sniffed. He looked off to the side as he took another drag.

"I think for you it's almost a matter of life and death. You see, I figure the pain is so strong and deep from your past that you have tried to erase it and take the easy way out."

I sat up straight, but my heart pounded with fear. "It's not an easy way out. It takes a lot of pain and courage. It takes a lot of Faith!"

He pulled his leg off the arm of the chair and placed his foot firmly beside the other foot. "That comment," he said as he leaned in toward me, "comes from a veteran." He sat back and stomped his cigarette out. It continued to burn. I watched the dwindling plume of smoke going in reverse as I heard him say, "Let us begin, shall we?"

• • •

Carl and I went once a week for counseling to deal with the freckled one, the boys, and our marriage and once a week I went by myself. Dr. Bob helped me see I was not to blame. It was always another who imposed on my body, mind, and emotions in my tender years. My belief in God he did not comment on except to say positive thinking was never a bad idea. And it was only the past and present pain he was interested in.

He came up with some very good ideas for dealing with the freckled one. Basically, he counseled me to ignore what he was telling the children about Carl. Carl and I were upset by the freckled one's ugly stories. But the whole idea was to keep the children from being scarred for life. It took self-discipline to not defend oneself by pointing out the wrongs in the other parent.

One day, we told Dr. Bob we had put the house up for sale. As a result of a bidding war, we sold it for $1.2 million, double our purchase price. We had no mortgage. Carl was thrilled. He told Dr. Bob he had interviewed inventors because he was looking for three good products to develop and market. He thought he was on his way to making multi-millions. Plus he said he wanted to buy a bigger boat: a 64-foot C&C we had seen at a boat show so he needed more money.

When Carl left to pay at the front counter, Dr. Bob took my arm, and pulled me back into the room, and closed the door.

"If I were you, I would take half of that $1.2 million and run away."

I blinked. Was he joking? "You're joking, right?"

He lowered his voice. "No, I'm not. He's not a nice man. I've known him a good number of years before you. I've seen him go through his first marriage and numerous relationships. He is a selfish man. He became a nice man when he met you, and today he may still appear to be nice. But one day he will get tired of being nice." He looked at me pointedly. "And he will get tired of you. I guarantee it."

I almost believed him, but I didn't want to. Yet, I couldn't help but think back on the vows we made in Hawaii. *Till love us do part.*

"Believe me. He is nothing but a *Playboy*. And you are his *Playmate*."

"His *Playmate*?" I asked, all the marked-up centerfolds from the past flashing before my eyes.

"Yes, his *Playmate*. His *Trophy*. He thought he would have a movie star on his arm. You know why he started to sail?"

I shook my head.

"Because his *Playboy* brother bought a 48-footer and has a new girlfriend every summer. What did Carl start with? A 20-footer first to learn how to sail? No. He immediately bought a 38-footer, and he didn't even know how to sail. And now what do you have?"

"A 48-footer."

"And what's he want now?"

"A 64-footer."

He sniffed. "That's right. And after that he'll want an even bigger boat. And he'll want an even more exciting *Playmate*."

My heart was racing.

"Take my advice. Wait till that's in the bank, then file for divorce."

"No, I can't do that, Bob."

"Why not?" He was serious.

"Because I love him. With all my heart. And we're married. That's forever."

He gave me a pointed look.

"I don't care about the money."

"What is love? It's nothing but an emotion. That guy out there has no inkling what love is. Or commitment." He stood up straighter before turning the knob on the door. "Well, it's your life. But believe me, your love will have absolutely no positive effect on him or your marriage. You will only end up broken-hearted." Then he opened the door.

When we left the building, we headed for our black BMW. Normally I would look straight ahead as I walked, always deep in thought after a session with Dr. Bob, but this time something told me to look up. A pretty woman walked toward us. I looked back at Carl. He was smiling at her with his eyes wide and sparkling. The same way he had looked at me at the Chandlery when he first came in, and I gave him a saucy reply. Then I looked at the woman.

She was reciprocating.

If I hadn't have been there walking with him, I knew he would have stopped to talk.

And eventually, he would have bedded her.

My husband, the *Playboy*.

TWENTY-ONE

A Tear in the Curtain of Love

1987

"Please, don't Pap."

"Oh, don't you worry. I know what I'm doing."

"No, I really think you shouldn't. I have a bad feeling about this."

"Carl is a successful businessman, and I have faith in his ability to make millions. I just want a piece of the action."

We were sitting in the kitchen before the house sold. Pap, my uncles, a couple of cousins, and my little sister invested in Carl's new company. He chose several new inventions: a remote thermometer which was ahead of its time, a multi-sprinkler for the garden, and a computerized medicine dispenser. He also thought he'd try a gadget that kept socks together in the wash.

We moved out of the house a little closer to where the freckled one lived and a small company Carl co-owned with two partners whom he then bought out. He let that one run under a manager and started another limited company to overlook the research, development and manufacturing of the various new products he bought from their inventors.

Within a couple of years, Carl built up the business into an empire with offices in Southern Ontario and the state of New York. During the next few years, he blew through all the money: ours, Pap's, my uncles', the banks' and everyone else's. One day he came home with mortgage papers for me to sign.

"I'm not signing those papers," I said, fearful of the inevitable.

"If you don't sign these, I will divorce you." He looked at me in a cold, dry way.

He stopped having shareholders' meetings and closed the various offices he had opened. All he had left was a massive mortgage on the house and the one small business he had neglected. Now, however, it seemed a bit of a lifeline.

One night, while I was praying, it struck me that even though it looked like we were going to lose everything, I still had been given everything I prayed for that night at the marina. *I hadn't been specific enough*, I grimly joked to myself. I felt ashamed. Ashamed that I had stood there on the docks praying to God for riches. Riches that were fleeting. A husband who no longer loved me. I realized I had a lot to learn when choosing how and what to pray for. I had been so selfish. I choked with shame and remorse that I had been so self-centered.

In the meantime, Carl was challenged to enlarge the little company he had left. It brought out his aggressive and creative entrepreneur. He was finally somewhat distracted in his work life.

• • •

Something new developed. I had begun praying differently, asking for growth and humility. I meditated and tried to improve myself, fill myself with love and strength, truth and joy. This new development happened at the same time I began to have more trouble with my hip and back, as walking long distances was sometimes unbearable. One day, while driving through the parking lot of a mega mall, I felt a nudge to go to the main doors first. A car pulled out of a spot right in front of the doors as I rolled up.

The next time I faced a potentially impossible distance to walk, I followed the nudge and drove straight to the main doors, and again a car pulled out as I drove up. There was no handicapped parking in those days and I was so grateful having my own personal and heavenly help to find closer parking.

As time went on, I began to hear more specific directions.

Go straight, turn left and go to the end. You'll see someone pull out just as you get there.

I did, and, again, they did.

A more personal *relationship* was strengthening slowly but surely. It confused me at first. Why would God worry about where I parked? But it kept happening.

• • •

Carl was easily bored with life. He planned trips every three months or so. We went all over Europe, the United States and the Caribbean. He decided one trip by the toss of a coin—Heads for a train trip to the West Coast across Canada and Tails to the East Coast.

Carl flipped the coin. Tails. We were on our way to New Brunswick by Via Rail.

The freckled one discovered we were once again going on a trip and that Joel and Ethan were to be staying with Pap and Mam. About a month before the trip, it was the freckled one's weekend with them and after they climbed into his dusty car, he closed the doors on them and stepped toward me. I took a step back. My heart still skipped beats when I was near him and I always had the feeling I had to run for my life. That or be so nauseous and I would vomit.

He held up his forefinger and pointed at me. I felt the venom.

"You're one rotten Jezebel of a mother. You don't deserve them. One of these days, you'll find that they simply won't come back. They hate you. I have to force them to come back. Just be careful." He gave me an evil eye and took a step back. I watched as he turned and opened the driver's side door and stepped in.

I pretended nothing untoward happened when I saw the concerned look on Joel's face as he watched us through the window.

I bent over, smiled and gave a big happy wave. I blew him kisses. My eyes searched the back seat as the car pulled away to wave goodbye to Ethan. Ethan didn't look up. He had already found a He-Man toy that was apparently in the back seat.

As the freckled one drove away, I had a sense of foreboding.

That Sunday evening, there was no one at the meeting spot. I waited over an hour, scouring the highway up and down from the bridge, hoping against hope they were only held up. I raced home and called him but there was no answer. I waited half the night. No word.

Carl came down in the early hours and saw the wreck that I was as I sat on the edge of the family room couch, my eyes swollen from crying, Kleenex twisted in my hands while I kept the phone close to me.

"Oh for f—ck's sake. He's just playing you. Come to bed."

I burst into tears. How could he possibly not understand what I was going through?

After two weeks and no word from the freckled one or the boys I tearfully announced, "If I don't find the boys, I'm not going on this trip."

Carl dropped his fork on his plate. The sun was setting behind him through the patio doors and light started shimmering throughout the kitchen as the waning sun bounced off the rippling waters of the pool out back.

"You are going." He leaned over his plate and interlaced his fingers as he cradled the plate with his outstretched arms. I loved those arms. Those hands. I loved this man. But he did not have a big heart.

I covered my face and shook my head. I heard him shove his chair back and lope away, muttering. "I almost wish those kids never came back. This is not the life I thought I was going to have with you."

I looked up, stunned and heart-broken. "How can you say such an ugly thing!" I yelled.

He stomped back. "One of these days you're going to have to choose. Either it's them or it's me."

I suddenly stopped crying. An ultimatum? Was that an *ultimatum*? I didn't dare respond.

That night:

I stood at a hot wood-burning cooking stove. I was so big and round my bosom almost touched the hot edge of the stove. My apron covered my round belly. I wore layers of clothing. A heavy woolen dress with a subtle tan and green stripe in the weave. Underneath was a bunched-up nightdress. Under that, I had heavy woolen bottoms. I wore gray-brown woolen stockings with a hole in the back of my calf. My worn leather boots were high and could barely be tied tighter over my round calves. My feet hurt.

A little boy sat eating in an old wooden chair behind me. He was in a dark, dirty green heavy wool top and bottom.

There was one single oil lamp hanging from the rafters over the rectangular wooden table.

I let go of the ladle, overwhelmed with fear. I needed to save another child. A boy slightly older than the toddler in the highchair. I hurried into the black, narrow hallway and turned right toward the front door. I hiked the skirt and apron up a little as I clomped down two rickety wooden steps to the front door. I opened the door and pulled it shut as I took two steps down into the street.

There were storefronts across the road to the left. All were dark.

The cold, crisp air was moist as sleet fell on my hot cheeks, barely cooling them. I hurried to the right toward the main corner. Then I turned right again to run up the hill, but I couldn't. I was too heavy. My feet caked with mud, and my dress' dragging hem got caught under my shoes. Several times I fell forward. My hands broke my fall but got cut and hurt by the frozen mud. I began to lose my breath. I couldn't breathe.

At the top of this hill, I sat on a rock ledge to catch my breath. I was wheezing, and my heart was pumping hard. In front was the hill going down, where I came from. To the slight right, I saw an old wooden house with a light on in the front room. Slightly to the left was a white church with one steeple. To the immediate left, I saw a small tree, it's wet, black branches dripping with melting ice. To the immediate right was another tree and beyond that a red brick wall.

I started to panic. I was only halfway up the big hill on my way to the new school. I thought it was on fire, and I couldn't get to my son.

I couldn't get to my son. I couldn't get to my son. Oh Lord, I was dying of a heart attack. I couldn't breathe, and I couldn't get to my son.

"Wake up! Wake up!"

I opened my eyes. It took a while before I realized I was safe in the bedroom with Carl.

"You're having a heck of a dream. Are you okay?"

I cried and he let me cling to him like a baby. My heart ached. I was so afraid to leave the children behind while on this trip to the East Coast.

• • •

Dr. Bob snorted, wheezed, and looked off to the side of the room. Then he exhaled rings of smoke.

"Shit, she knew what she was getting into," Carl went on. "I want to go on these trips. I'm not going to let some jackass dictate how I'm going to live my life. He already is, for God's sake."

I looked straight ahead. What could I do? These were my boys.

"I realize it's very difficult for a mother to keep things in perspective. But the more you cling to them, the more he does things to spite you. You may find that he will let his grip loosen the more you loosen up," said Dr. Bob.

I looked over at Carl. He looked from Dr. Bob to me and shrugged. "I think you should listen to Bob. That's what we pay him big bucks for."

• • •

We stepped off the train in St. John and struggled with our suitcases up the hill to a hotel for the night. In the morning, we picked up a rental car and made our way down the coastline.

It was getting dark by the time we reached a place called *Torryburn*. We thought we would go just a bit farther and start looking for a place to stay for the night.

The ocean fog came in and almost choked the surroundings. We knew from the map that we were driving along the shore, but we saw nothing beyond the edge of the road. Our headlights highlighted the thick fog ahead. We slowly made our way, only passing one or two cars. A sign came up.

"*Rothesay.* That can't be too much further."

Carl was driving. "Let's stop there. This fog is so thick we can't see anything anyway."

We continued slowly and eventually drove along another body of water. At an intersection, we turned right and followed some old streets through the hills that were strangely familiar.

We drove by a street that reached high along a hill. I looked up. My heart skipped a beat.

"I've been here before." I turned to look at Carl.

He slowed down. "No, you haven't."

"But I know all this. I know what's around the corner. These houses. From my dream.""

"I guess we'll check it out in the morning."

We checked in at an inn and the next morning we walked the streets. I pointed out things I knew had changed. Up the hill was a rock ledge, now a cement wall, and there was a statue nearby. The trees were there, but much larger. The one on my left in my dream was gone.

"And look," I pointed at the white church. "There's the church. Except it has two towers now." I turned and looked at the red brick building next to the statue. It was the Town Hall.

Carl was used to my *insights*. We spent the rest of our time tracing the steps of the woman in my dream. Her house was gone, now part of a parking lot for a tall warehouse-looking building. We spoke to the young couple who lived in the house next to my dream house, and they let us in. It was the exact same footprint. The same builder had built both houses.

We returned home, touched by the magic of the East Coast. However, the haunting feeling of the woman in my dream never left. In fact, she would call us back and eventually call me there on my own.

TWENTY-TWO

Both Playboy and the Prophet Win

1993

Dr. Bob had been right. After the trip, the boys were anxious to come home. I loosened my grip and stopped worrying about the effect the freckled one had on the boys. I just made it as happy a home as I could. I agreed to change our arrangements to half custody so that we each had the boys three and a half days a week. They were home schooled and they appeared to fair better once the stress between their father and I lessened. We settled into an almost comfortable routine.

Years later, Carl was sitting at his desk reading a newspaper when he called me over. "Look at this," he said, pointing to an article. I bent over and looked. The headline was "Go East Young Man" and was about a couple who left Toronto to start an entirely different and charmed life in New Brunswick. He looked up at me. "We're going back. I want to take another look at the real estate prices there."

"Okay," I said. I couldn't get New Brunswick out my mind as well.

This time, we drove. We decided to go through the U.S. and the drive was comfortable and the days sunny. The landscape was absolutely breathtaking. We were very close to Saint John when freezing rain came down and froze everything into a sheet of ice. The brilliant sun and the bumper-to-bumper traffic took a long time, but it gave us the opportunity to talk.

Carl wanted to buy a second home. He had liked what he read in the newspaper of the couple who had bought a house in Rothesay and started a Bed & Breakfast.

"Not that I want to have a B&B. I want to be on that ocean. After seeing Rothesay and experiencing your dream, I feel as if we're supposed to be there."

He echoed what I thought precisely.

By the time we limped into Rothesay, we didn't hesitate to get into action the next morning.

We walked into a real estate office and asked about seeing some houses. We met a delightful man who took us for a grand walk throughout the town. We saw four houses. Then we realized the warehouse building where the dream house had been, was also for sale.

We waited a day before seeing the warehouse. It had been a factory where they made blocks and tackle for the tall ships, as well as other wooden products such as sweeps and oars.

Our realtor suggested we join him and his wife at a pub that night. We parked along Main Street and walked into a large red building perched on the shoreline. Music wafted out of the open doors. I followed Carl into the pub and immediately our realtor saw us and came toward over.

"Glad you could make it. Here, let me introduce you to my wife and a few friends."

He led us to a large table of people. He introduced us to his lovely wife, a gentle and sweet woman. Then he introduced us to the rest of the table. One by one, the people shook our hands or waved with a smile and a nod. At the head of the table sat a bearded man and his wife.

"Hi," said the bearded one. He seemed jovial and friendly. He was one of the owners of the pub. His wife simply looked at my outstretched hand and looked away.

Ice queen, I thought.

As the evening wore on, and we ordered food and wine, I watched the gentleman and his wife closely. She seemed to sneer at everything her husband said, but he seemed completely oblivious to it as he talked and gestured the entire night.

He likes to talk, I thought. But he was a pleasure to listen to.

When Carl and I returned to the motel, I said, "Boy, that marriage won't last another three months." I was so relieved that we were somewhat happily married. "Oh, Carl, we're so lucky to have each other. I'd hate for us to ever lose each other. I just can't imagine living without you." I reached over and hugged him and snuggled my head into his neck.

He let me hug him for as long as I wanted.

The next day, our realtor took us to see the large warehouse. We fell in love with it.

By the time we returned home from this short but magical trip, we were in the middle of putting an offer on the building by fax.

As we pondered the counter offer, we knew we were happy with it, but we wanted to think about it some more. We wondered if this was the right thing to do. We would have to put a mortgage on it. Could we handle it?

Carl was sitting in his office armchair; I sat at his feet.

"What does your gut tell you?" Carl asked me.

I checked deep inside. It was almost as if I heard it clearly spoken.

The mortgage and costs will always be covered by rental income.

I nodded. "The costs will be covered by rental income. I have a feeling that as soon as we buy it, we'll get a call about renting it."

Carl looked at me for a moment. "Okay, let's sign that counter offer."

Within days of acquiring the building, we got a call from a large movie studio in Los Angeles. They wanted to rent the top two floors as a production office for a big film they were producing. There were already two rental spaces downstairs with tenants. The costs for the coming year were more than covered.

I believed we were right on track with what I thought God wanted for us. When I called to make sure everything was settled at the warehouse, a girlfriend of mine answered the phone. This confused me. Perhaps I dialed her home number by accident.

"Oh, I'm sorry. This is funny. I didn't mean to call you. I was calling our building in Rothesay," I said, laughing.

"You did call Rothesay. So, this is your building? Wow. What a small world. I'm the Production Coordinator for the production!"

I took this as confirmation that it was all a perfect move and meant to be. Little did I know exactly how.

• • •

1994

Carl did a wonderful job injecting life into the small business. In four years, it had outgrown its small factory. He started to rent other spaces within the area until it became quite clear that it made better sense to amalgamate the various locations into one large building. So he put the smaller factory up for sale and the same realtor began to help him find a larger building to buy.

Then *it* happened.

Because he was such a lovely and beautiful person, and we seemed to be so very much in love lately, I forgot it might happen at all.

Carl started to feel a bit under the weather. I loved him and comforted him. I made him my Nonna's amazing chicken soup and other meals he loved to eat. I hugged him. I did everything I knew he loved. It went on for weeks.

Then he became distant and quiet.

I left on Friday nights to work on a little cabin at my parent's fishing retreat. It had about nine little cabins. Everyone in the family got the chance to choose a cabin and fix it up, so that they had a place to go to. It sounded magnificent.

We chose a little one close to the main cabin. I created stained glass lights for it, scrounged up old furniture I painted white with hot pink and turquoise detailing.

One night I was sleeping on a futon mattress in a sleeping bag when something woke me at 4:00 a.m. I worked on the cabin the next day, and that night again I woke up at 4:00 a.m.

I came home on Sunday afternoon, and he was quiet.

I asked if he would consider coming with me to help the following weekend, but he said he wasn't interested in getting dirty and covered in mice *shit*.

The next weekend, each night I woke at 4:00 a.m. I knew it had something to do with Carl.

And a woman? My insides frozen but I knew what my tentacles were telling me. I just knew.

That Monday at dinner, I thought I'd bring an end to the silence because I now realized that God was trying to tell me something. I was blind to His direction for so long, I was caught up in the warehouse in Rothesay, the cabin, a documentary I was producing, writing screenplays, and going to auditions, and worrying about the freckled one and the boys. In other words, I had forgotten the most important thing in life.

His guidance. Now I had to face the results of my neglect and I could almost swear it was another woman. I tried to push that into the back of my head. Tried to believe I didn't get it right.

"Carl, does it bother you that I've been going to the cabin?"

He adjusted his glasses and looked at me. "No."

"Did I do something wrong?" Perhaps it was buyers' remorse with the warehouse in Rothesay, but that turned out well. "Something is bothering you, but you won't talk about it."

Carl continued eating. I realized I had to be a little more direct.

"I have been loving. I have been trying to do everything possible to make you happy."

He looked up. "Oh no. You've been very loving and very patient."

I sat back. "Well, then. If it's not me, what is it?" *Please let it not be another woman.*

He suddenly pushed his chair back and stepped out the open patio doors. It was a gentle early summer evening, and the sun hadn't yet set. I followed him to the edge of the wide terrace steps that went down to the pool and sat down beside him when he parked himself on the edge of one of them.

I put my arm around him and bent down to look into his face. He was staring down at his feet. "What is it?" I asked softly, lovingly. "Please tell me."

There was a very long pause before my world ended.

"I'm leaving you."

With that, he stood up, went through the kitchen, into the mudroom, and out into the garage. Then I heard him start the BMW and drive out of the garage.

I shot up and ran to the side gate, yanked it open, and ran out into the driveway.

Just in time to see his car disappear.

The *Playboy* won out.

And ultimately, so did the freckled one.

TWENTY-THREE

A Woman Scorned

I bent over the real estate sign and regretted not bringing along a little jackknife. I used the edge of my car key instead. With perseverance, I was able to cut through the plastic ties that kept the nameplate hanging on the real estate sign.

I took the nameplate to the back of my van and threw it in with the remainder of the nameplates—perhaps twenty.

I had driven all night throughout the area. My mission was to take down all the name plates I found that belonged to the real estate *Playmate* who stole my husband, the *Playboy*.

I had already gone to speak to her and threatened to crucify her if she continued to see him. Of course, she disregarded me, and if anything, Carl scolded me for inconveniencing *her*.

At first, he insisted there was no woman involved. When I told him that I knew who it was, I begged him to stay, but he didn't want to be disloyal to her.

Disloyal to *her*.

Dr. Bob did an 'I told you so.' He also told me that I should let him go. He wasn't worth it. That it was, after all, just a journey. He was in one car now moving in another direction. I was left alone in a car and could choose whatever direction I want to go.

Bullshit.

How could I let a man go who still carried my heart in his hands? That one heart you can only give away once in your life? I couldn't breathe. I couldn't think.

Carl blamed me. She had nothing to do with it. I wouldn't give up my boys. He hated them and didn't want to see them again. He said I was of poor class, I came into the marriage with nothing, though he conveniently forgot he lost over a $1million of my family's money. He regretted ever knowing me and just wanted to get rid of me.

Everything he didn't like, he blamed on me.

Again, Dr. Bob said *I told you so.*

Ironically, his family and friends took me in to nurse me. I could not function. I had just acquired a job as an on-air Special Events Radio Announcer for a local FM station. It took every inch of fiber and strength deep inside me to be able to speak live on air and not break down into a blubbering, incoherent mess.

I never said a word in anger to him. I didn't want to hurt him one iota. But I did her. So, I hurt her where it would really hurt.

By taking down all her real estate signs.

I also went to her business, licked my finger, and wrote on the front window that she had stolen my husband while doing business. I wrote it backward so everyone in the office would be able to read it once the sun hit that window Monday morning.

Carl loved homegrown tomatoes which were coming in quickly in my little garden. They were massive and juicy, so I took a basket with me to work. After work, I planned to go to my brother-in-law's house where I knew Carl and the woman were staying.

He hadn't given me the dignity of fighting for him. My heart was still beating, but he didn't care. I was afraid it would shrivel to dust, and there'd be nothing I could do to reclaim it. It would take a heck of a lot more than an extramarital affair to hurt me. I told him such.

"I'm not the first this has happened to, Carl. Look where I've come from? What I'm hurt about is you *leaving* me. Why can't you stay in the house? Let this affair run its course."

"I told you. I can't. She won't have it."

"*She* won't have it? Carl, you're killing me."

I knew the only way to save myself years of grief, years of empty sockets looking out at a world that reflected only lost future years, was to see them together. I loved that man. I knew where every freckle was. I knew what to do when he had a migraine, and I was the only one who could take the pain away. What will he do when he's down, and I'm not there to reach out and wrap him with my heart and soul? The soul that has seen so many difficult times. The soul that shyly looked out its window and reached out to touch this man, to trust this man with my secrets and my pain. The only man I ever trusted with my inner child, the inner 16-year-old innocent who learned not to trust men at all. There is only one card in life that reads: *I trust you with my pain. You have the power to save it, to eat it, to destroy it, but I trust you.*

I know you won't throw it away.

I believed you wouldn't throw it away.

I hoped you wouldn't throw it away.

You threw it away.

And now you won't tell me where you left it. Which wastepaper basket is it in? Is it crumpled up like a used hamburger wrapper? Did you know the red was not ketchup? It was blood? And that bit of meat is what was left of my dignity? That little bit I gave to you to protect?

And now I have *nothing*?

I had to see them together for myself.

I climbed through my brother-in-law's kitchen window and waited for them to come home. I sat in the kitchen facing that little basket full of giant tomatoes with a love letter tucked in for him. Perhaps to catch him in a moment of regret.

I wanted to see them walk in together. In fact, except for that day when I threatened to crucify her, I didn't know or remember what she looked like. I couldn't envision them as a pair.

After an hour of waiting, I thought it was better if I sat in the living room. That way I could see them hold hands as they walked up to the front door. And this way they would see me, at the same time, sitting there in the living room. They could face me together.

I got up and walked into the hallway.

I forgot about the security alarm.

It suddenly whooped and hollered. It was deafening.

I didn't rush. I knew that it would take the police a while to get there. I once knew the code but in my grief, my brain didn't think straight.

So, I calmly opened the front door and walked out. No worries about locking it behind me now. I walked to the radio stations' jeep, got in, and drove slowly down the street.

I turned left to the end of the subdivision to see fireworks going off on the neighboring university campus. They whooped, banged, and hollered. In fact, I could tell where the security alarm whooped and hollered behind me but the sound waves were almost identical.

I had no choice but to drive through the campus. I rolled down the windows, grinned, waved, and honked at the people on the bleachers as they whistled and called to me in return.

They thought I was there to promote the radio station.

By the time I made it to my father-in-law's a few miles away, I could hear the police sirens heading for my brother-in-law's home.

TWENTY-FOUR

Graduating to Speaking with Angels

"…they are like angels in heaven…"

(Matthew 22:3, NEB)

I thought I would go crazy with the pain of losing him, but then that familiar *voice* came through the angst and directed me to get into the car and drive to the neighboring town.

Why there? I didn't have any reason to drive there. Having learned to follow that voice, however, I knew I had no choice. I got into the car and drove to that particular town.

Once there, I was directed to drive onto a side street and found myself at the back of one of the most beautiful Roman Catholic churches I had ever seen. How did I miss that? Those spires can be seen from miles away.

I stopped the car, turned the headlights off, and looked all around.

Nothing. Just darkness. I waited for some direction.

Drive into that parking lot. Look for a red door.

I looked over to the left and saw a parking lot off to the side. It was badly maintained. I started the car and drove over the broken pavement to where a little red door was at the back of the church.

Go through that little red door.

"But it'll be closed, I'm sure," I responded.

Go through that red door.

I got out of the car, walked over to the door, and tried it. It was unlocked. I poked my head in. It was around 9:00 p.m. and I wasn't sure if what I was doing would be considered trespassing.

No matter. Isn't it my house? Am I not allowed to bring one of my own into my house?

"Yes," I said aloud. "Thank you, Jesus. Thank you, God."

I walked in through a utilitarian-type entrance into a barely lit side aisle. I stopped and looked around the beautiful interior. It was dark. There were very few lights on, but I could see it was magnificent. Though St. Basil church had its own beauty, this one was incredible. It reflected a strong, large supportive community. There was an air of dignity about it.

Walk to the center of the church and then go to the back to sit in the last pew.

By this time, I was on the edge of tears. Being so close to God was frightening and humbling. Such direct and ongoing *direction* was emotionally overwhelming. I could barely see, but as I worked my way, zig-zagging through the pews, I reached the back of the church. There was not a soul around. I sat there for a while and let myself soak in the quiet beauty of my surroundings.

Come to me. Down the aisle.

I got up from the creaky pew and moved down the center aisle, keeping my eyes on the altar in front me.

Prostrate yourself as you would if you had become a nun.

Once before, I remembered prostrating in front of God. It was at an evangelical church when I was with the freckled one.

I got up and walked slowly down the middle of the center aisle. I got down on my hands and knees first. Slowly, I sank down onto the floor and put my face on the carpet. Then I spread my arms to the side. I stayed like that until I was told to get up.

Up.

Slowly, I walked back to the last pew, bent with humility. I grasped the pew before sliding onto it. I knelt on the kneeling cushion and clasped my hands.

I was crying so hard I desperately needed a fresh Kleenex or a cloth. I looked around for a bathroom but didn't see one.

As I looked to the side of the altar, an explosion echoed somewhere in the bowels of the church. A man walked briskly into the center aisle from between the columns carrying a roll of paper towel. He passed me without looking and turned right behind me. I heard him open a door. I looked back to see where he went. He opened a closet hidden behind a statue. Then he shut it and left, going the other way.

"Thank you, Jesus."

I got up, went to the closet behind the statue, and opened it. I tore several sheets off the roll that he had left on a shelf, went back to the pew, and blew my nose.

This made me cry even more. Such a small detail. He would think of that.

I'm never gone.

I felt a massive warmth around my body. As if I had been wrapped in strong, warm arms.

Go home and rest.

Drained, I left. But not before turning back to look at the altar, the ceiling, the statues, and the lights.

Once I climbed into my bed, I slept like a baby.

I knew I wasn't alone in this ordeal, but it was going to be a painful struggle. Not only did I have to be weaned from Carl, but I was also losing our home, which my boys and I loved. I was going to lose constant contact with Carl's family whom I adored. Our friends would undoubtedly feel torn.

But I did leave that church knowing one thing burning in my heart; within a year, I would be living amongst the gentle folk in New Brunswick.

• • •

After some heavy-duty meditating and prayer, I went out to jog around the neighborhood. I was stronger. I knew I wasn't alone in this journey of change. I wasn't afraid of the future now.

There was a specific streetlight that always shut off as I passed underneath, but I never thought much about it. Perhaps my blonde hair reflected back the light to the sensor. Perhaps the color of my clothing did the same. But this time I was wearing black and a woolen cap.

In the past, I would watch a car drive underneath that light. Or happen to see a couple of young people walk by during the night.

It only happened to me.

Then a realization set in. This particular light, all these years, was God's way of telling me I wasn't alone.

Then one day, I saw them.

• • •

After the first snowfall, I couldn't jog down the road, so I shoveled a path around our winterized pool and started doing laps.

At one point, when I passed the far-right corner near the changing house, I thought I saw three forms. As I continued jogging down to the other end, I looked back, but there was nothing. The next time I passed, they were there again. This time, I continued to look down at my feet as I jogged by.

The next time I passed them, I realized they were not in physical form.

And then I recognized them. They were the ones I saw when I was about twelve years old back on the 'street' when my face was covered in Noxzema. The night of the big fight between Pap and my drunken uncle.

I reached out with my mind and started a conversation with the one that seemed to be the leader. I told him/her that I remembered them. I said that I remembered they told me men would be a constant source of suffering for me.

I felt the main person reach out to me. In return, I asked what his/her name was.

Sam.

"Hi Sam," I said out loud. It struck me that the name was neither male or female. "Is that why you have a name that is both male and female? You are an angel?"

Yes.

It was then that he reminded me I had felt his presence while a student at university. My heart quickened. I hadn't made the connection.

"I remember! You were standing by me as I slept. I was sleeping in someone's residence on campus. You woke me after I had floated out the window and flew over the flat fields and power lines near the campus."

So, I had had another out of body experience at university. But I thought it was a dream and never thought of it again. Sam heard my thoughts.

You needed to feel free.

"Wow," I said. Then I stopped jogging and went back into the house.

Was he following me? Do I say *excuse me?*

I am with you always. If you need me, you will feel me. If you are caught up in the world, I stand by. Know I am here.

• • •

University.

I finished my summer contract with the radio station.

"University?" I asked Sam.

Yes.

"Wow. Okay. I'd love to go back to the university," I answered. I thought about it and realized the only option was the closest campus forty minutes away. It fit into the boys' and my schedules.

I gathered together my papers, applied and was accepted.

Excitedly, I studied Medieval History, Environmental Law, Chinese Philosophy, Women in History Studies, and Modern Art History. The internet was now available in a primitive form, but it was only accessible through a few library computers.

I took the boys with me whenever I could. Consequently, they were exposed to the campus and the library. As I did my papers, they wandered the campus, and got to know it well.

My courses were precisely chosen by Sam.

Medieval History I assumed was about Europe during the Dark Ages. I thrived on history, so I was confused when the professor came in that first day and wrote on the board, *Religio*.

I wondered what that had to do with history.

Then she wrote *Rules and Regulations*.

She turned around and said, "*Religio* is Latin for rules and regulations and is the root of the word religion."

Whatever else she said, this statement made a lightbulb go off in my head. I finally saw the difference between faith and religion. If someone were to ask me, are you religious, I would say no. But most people thought that meant I did not have a faith. So, I would say yes, but then people asked what church I belonged to. I did not believe in any particular church.

I believed in God.

I believed in Jesus.

And I believed I walked with an entity named Sam. My whole life was influenced by these relationships and now my days were even more so. My body was the walking church I attended every moment of my day.

"Rules and regulations are manmade," she said. "And medieval history is basically the history of the Catholic Church, also known as the Dark Ages, which had many rules and regulations. It was a time of very little enlightenment."

Manmade rules = very little enlightenment.

Chinese philosophy was also a Sam surprise. Through the study of the Tao, I saw the resemblance between that and other forms of worship of a higher power.

To me, the Tao Path was the path I walked. Not having the wherewithal to properly describe the Way or the Path means we can only describe the finger that points to it.

How many fingers are pointing to a Higher Power? How many different religions and philosophies are there that believe in something better than ourselves?

I began to think there were potentially just as many *fingers* to describe the Power as there are *people* on this planet.

Studying Women in History delved into the issues that were part of our gender in a patriarchal society. The course gave me tools and language to understand my own experience as a woman, especially one within a society that almost ignored the everyday plights of being in a female body. Although the spotlight seemed to have waned over Hugh Hefner and his *Playboy* Dynasty, the wave of sexuality was still strong, perhaps stronger. By this time, fashion racks in Walmart and Zellers displayed provocative outfits which prostitutes used to wear but they were now the fashion for six year olds.

Children's Beauty Pageants were about to be given a good hard kick with the murder of five-year-old beauty pageant star, JonBenet Ramsey[14]. The sexual revolution had evolved to involve even female children. Whereas in my day, teenagers and women were taught to feel ugly if they did not fit into a sexy mold, now toddlers and very young girls were at risk to grow up disliking their bodies. They were put through the objectification of their bodies by their own parents. These young girls were forced to dress in revealing and promiscuous outfits and to perform talent skits and dances which were very sexual in nature. They were naturally magnets for sexual predators.

Needless to say, the course allowed me to feel I wasn't alone and many of the students were of like mind as myself. There were key historical women of history who were simply not written into the textbooks and it was a pleasure to learn that there were strong female mathematicians, historians, scientists and politicians.

---

[14]   JonBenet Patricia Ramsey, a popular child beauty queen of 1995, was murdered in her family home in Boulder, Colorado on December 25, 1996.

Environmental Law gave more insight into how we are destroying God's planet. One lesson that stood out involved the petri dish with a tiny presence of bacteria and enough nutrients for it to thrive. The professor said our planet earth was the petri dish, bacteria was mankind, and the nutrients were all the earth offered to sustain us.

The bacteria did exactly what it was designed to do. It consumed all the nutrients until there was nothing left. Then the entire bacteria culture died.

I learned many things that shaped the next stage of my life. And because the boys went with me to the campus, it also shaped my boys.

My special, wonderful boys.

TWENTY-FIVE

Damsel in Distress in Paradise

"He took away our illnesses and lifted our diseases from us."

(Matthew 8:17, NEB)

1995

When I told Pap about what I was thinking to do after the school semester, he thought I was nuts.

"How are you going to find work in a third-world country like that?"

"Pap, it's a province of Canada."

"It's a welfare state!"

"What about the boys?" Mam asked. We were sitting in the main cabin of their old fishing resort. Pap was busy straightening out the walls with tension wire and ratchets. Through the window, the sun reflected off the choppy waters of the bay. The lights danced merrily on the old rafters above us and on the old fireplace made of round beach stones.

"I told the boys I want them to come with me to New Brunswick," I said taking another sip of coffee. "It would be good for them."

"What if the boys don't want to go with you?"

I had thought about that at length. "Then their father will stop focusing on destroying my relationship with them. With me further away, he no longer would have control, and I wouldn't be a scapegoat anymore. There'd be no one else to blame for everything. The boys know that Carl left because of their father, so I think they'll be questioning *him* more now."

"Let's hope," Mam said, reaching for the coffee pot.

"Besides," I said excitedly, "It also means that, if they choose to stay with their father, when they visit me, they'll be with me for at least a couple of weeks or whole summers at a time. And once they see how beautiful it is in New Brunswick, they'll want to stay. It will be a far less hectic schedule than the three and a half days on and off for each of us with joint custody every week. There will be a lot less manipulating and brainwashing going on. The boys can only take so much."

"And if they do stay? How will you possibly afford everything? They can eat a house in one sitting."

"I'll find something. I have a gut feeling work won't be a problem. I'll be back as often as I can, whether I fly or drive."

Pap sat to save his back and shifted in his chair impatiently. "Oh, come now, let's be realistic."

He still didn't understand that I followed a path. One that I was not walking alone.

I left their cottage with two cats in tow and a van packed to the hilt with fragile objects and houseplants. The rest of my furniture was already shipped and stored in Saint John.

Two days later, I arrived at the warehouse and it felt great to be there.

I put on my foul weather jacket and deck boats and stomped down the stairs to go into town and look for a phone booth. I walked through the parking lot where my dream lady once lived, onto the sidewalk, and turned right, as she did. Then at the corner, I turned right again to go up the hill. I thought of her tripping over her heavy skirt, rushing to get up the incline. I looked up at the top of the hill at the statue and wall where she sat catching her breath, perhaps even to die. That dream was still a fascinating mystery to me. And it eventually brought me here to live.

I found a public phone and waited as it rang at my parents' place while I looked down the hill and onto the harbor. I promised to call to let them know I arrived. I couldn't wait to tell Pap about the boats at anchorage. The trawlers at the wharves and the pile of scallop shells along the wharf was so deep and high they reached over the water's surface.

I felt so fortunate to be alive and to stand there at the phone looking over a harbor in a town where people were gentle, and the history was rich.

After they were satisfied I was still in one piece, I drove to the pub Carl and I visited. Half an hour later, I stood at the busy bar and asked if I could apply for a job. The girl called over a red-headed lady who told me they weren't hiring.

The next day was Sunday, so I dressed up and put on my heels. The entire town was empty of traffic and pedestrians. I walked up and down those hills looking for a Roman Catholic Church. I found every other church except that. My feet were killing me in those heels, and I realized one did not walk up and down hills with heels on. Dressing up and wearing high heels as they did in Toronto was not something one did here.

I gave up looking, went down a block, and turned left onto a street I hadn't yet walked. As I turned, I looked to the right and noticed a little brown man step out of a Bed & Breakfast. He was just about to light a cigarette.

I looked away and headed for home. Soon I heard him walking behind me, and I hurried, not wanting to talk to anyone.

"Excuse me, but how many people live in this town they call Rothesay."

I turned around. "I don't know, but I do know there are only 900 taxpayers," I said.

He laughed. "You must be a very good businesswoman," he said. We talked about taxes, businesses, and real estate. A half-hour later, he hired me as his business manager and chauffeur.

Through him, as I drove him to meetings or picked up his family from the airport, I learned a tremendous amount about the culture of Pakistan and about how some Muslims lived. I also learned there were moderate Muslims who drank alcohol and did not pray five times a day.

During one of his business meetings, he asked me to quickly deliver a document to someone he knew in Saint John. I rushed over, found the office, and knocked on the door. A voice told me to come in. I introduced myself to the gentleman sitting at the desk, gave him the document, and then, suddenly, he walked around his desk and locked the door behind me. He came back to sit on the edge of the desk in front of me. He looked me up and down.

"Aren't you the most beautiful woman I've seen in a while," at which point he grabbed me and started nuzzling me in the neck. I pushed him back, unlocked the door, and rushed out, flushed and upset.

When I told my boss what happened, he laughed. "Oh, that's because you are blonde and beautiful. In our home country, women don't do business like you North Americans do. Men figure it is easier to seduce you."

"But that was sexual harassment," I said.

"You may call it that, but you ask for it here, don't you agree?" He grinned and nodded his head side-to-side.

He proceeded to tell me what "good" women did and did not do. "So, you should not be surprised when a real man comes here in a culture that is sex crazy. How can you blame a man?"

"But he touched me!" I argued.

"Did you not put make-up on? Did you not curl your beautiful blonde hair instead of hiding it under a veil? Are you not a walking billboard?"

This rattled me.

When one of the people he interviewed as a potential business partner offered me a job, I took it right away and said goodbye to my boss and his family.

Within two months of coming to New Brunswick, I was now into my second job as Marketing Manager and Head of Website Development for a computer animation studio. They were in production with a German company creating computer animation for a series that would become an underground cult classic.

In the meantime, I flew home every second week to spend the weekend with my boys. I rented snazzy cars each time just to give my teenage boys a thrill. I sent them to Young Drivers' Ed, and they both got their licenses.

Someone mentioned they needed a car driven from California to New Brunswick, so I spoke to my manager and arranged to fly down for several appointments with production companies in Los Angeles. Then I would drive the car back.

I flew to Santa Barbara, rented a car, and drove to Los Angeles for the meetings. After my meeting with DIC Comics, where they showed me their latest acquisition in Sailor Moon, I stepped into the elevator to find a young man standing in the corner. We spoke as we went down twenty floors or so. Suddenly, he stepped over and pressed me against the wall of the elevator.

When the door of the elevator opened, we were in the parking garage. I tried to loosen his grip. I had to talk sweetly to calm him down. All the while I looked for a security guard but I could see no one. Not another soul. He followed me to my car. He wouldn't let me go until I promised to give him my phone number in New Brunswick, and he gave me his.

Somehow, I got into that car and drove away. He called for months, but being so far away, I knew he couldn't do anything to me. Eventually, he gave up. Long distance was very expensive in those days.

I figured it would take ten days to drive the car back. Around the eighth day, I was in Burlington, having driven from Los Angeles to Fort Bragg to pick up the car, then back down to Los Angeles, and on to Las Vegas, Nevada. I stopped to win enough money at a slot machine to do my wash in a laundromat in the Lux Casino. From there I went through Utah and saw the great Mormon temple. I saw the amazing cliffs of Colorado, then Nebraska, Iowa and Illinois, just barely touching the outskirts of Chicago. Then I went through Indiana, Ohio where I was tempted to find Paul's family, Pennsylvania and finally into New York state before crossing the border at Fort Erie. I wanted to say a quick hello to the boys before I went on through Ontario, Quebec, and to New Brunswick.

Driving a car across the US alone was uneventful until I stopped in Ontario for the night. A man approached me in the restaurant. When he found out I was from Europe, he asked if I would try on a body condom he had bought in Amsterdam. This was during the AIDS epidemic hysteria. Apparently, creative solutions for safe sex were on the market now. The sexual revolution had evolved once again while Hugh Hefner was five years into his second marriage to a former *Playmate*. He had two children with her and had already left the running of *Playboy Enterprises* to his daughter from his first marriage, Christie Hefner. Hugh Hefner changed after surviving a stroke in 1985. Circulation of the magazine had plummeted and AIDS put a temporary brake on the sexual revolution.

In a recent interview, Hugh Hefner sat in his trademark silk pajamas drinking diet and caffeine-free Pepsi. "We are a schizophrenic nation…We were founded by Puritans, who escaped repression only to establish their own…The relationship between the sexes is in many ways suffering from even more confused messages than ever before. You have the religious right and some left-wing feminists both taking conservative postures on sexuality and the images of sex. There is within the women's movement an antagonism towards sexuality and towards the opposite sex…"[15]

I had wondered how he would've faired if he had lived in my shoes.

It was still a sex-crazed world.

• • •

1996

Just as I had hoped, Ethan came over a number of times to stay. He would go to work with me and he got to know the computer

---

[15]   Los Angeles Times Interview, July 31, 1994.

animators, learning about the different programs they used. He thrived within that environment. And I was right, the freckled one didn't call every night, as he did before when we had half of the week each. I saw Ethan relax and make himself at home both in Saint John and Rothesay.

Joel was getting ready for university now. He worked at a summer job and was accepted at the same university he fell in love with during the time I worked in the library on my papers. I was so very proud of him.

Then it happened.

I was at my desk when the phone rang. I picked it up and answered it.

Then I heard Carl's voice. My heart jolted, and I thought, *I KNEW IT!*

"How are you?" he asked.

I told him I was doing fine. Then I said, "Oh Carl, you are never out of my thoughts. I think of you all the time."

"Well," he said, "I think of you all the time as well."

WOWEEE! "Oh Carl, oh my gosh. I knew you'd come back. Please, come and live with me. I still have the warehouse. I don't care if you've lost everything. We'll have each other, and you would love it here." I listed all the reasons why he would love being in New Brunswick. "But if you don't want to stay here, that's okay. At least we'll be together again!"

"That's not what I meant," he said.

I stopped. I thought I heard wrong.

"What do you mean?"

"I've lost everything. I've filed for bankruptcy. And you've got something I want."

"What's that?"

"I'm suing you for the warehouse."

I sat back in shock. "Why are you doing this to me?"

"I don't care if it hurts you. I'm just letting you know."

I slowly hung up on him. The sound of the phone clicking onto its cradle was like the echo of a massive bronze door closing.

My heart closed on Carl. Though the love would burn for another twenty years, I gave up hope of ever having that marriage back.

Throughout the entire ordeal of his extramarital affair, the abuse, the humiliation, and the constant ugliness he threw my way, I never said a nasty word to him. I never raised my voice. I never made any threats to him.

Only her.

This time, I sat down with pen and paper and wrote a very long letter outlining my love for him. Then I told him what my uncles and cousins had wanted to do to him. I also truthfully told him I held them back from going after him. And that now, if he tried to sue me, I had no other option but to protect the future of my children and tell my uncles and cousin to go have a field day with him.

He knew what they were capable of. He used to call them a mafia family. But I also knew that he was not a courageous man. His fear of them was much larger than their need to hurt him.

He never bothered me again.

• • •

One day, shortly after the call, I was driving through St. John and suddenly became aware that something was slowly taking over my mind.

I couldn't remember where I was going. As if my mind were disintegrating, I also forgot where I was coming from. Shaking and fighting to keep my mind focused, I quickly pulled into a parking lot and stumbled to a phone booth. By the time I got to the phone booth, I couldn't remember what I had to do. I fought to keep thoughts in my head. Somehow, I remembered I needed change. I had to remember where it was. Then I had to keep reminding myself what it was that I was trying to do. Then I forgot why I needed the change that was in my hand.

After fighting to keep a train of thought, the only number I could remember was my sister's in Ontario. I called her and quickly told her I was forgetting how to use my head. My brain. My hands. I forgot where I was. I didn't know what province I was in. I couldn't remember where I lived.

She talked me through the episode, the first of many.

A doctor later told me I had *MS* and *Crohns* and that the episode was an anomaly. I arranged for someone to housesit for me while I rushed back to Ontario to be near family. At the same time, I made sure the boys would be fine if something happened to me.

I seemed to have times where I was lucid, so I found a job that did not have set hours. When I was ill, I did not have to go in. If I became ill during the day, I could quickly slip out to the hospital. I found a doctor nearby, and he wanted me to call the moment I had an episode so they could take tests while the episode was underway.

• • •

1996

One day, my doctor called me in.

"Have you ever had an accident or were you ever in a position where you couldn't breathe for a period of time?"

He was younger than me, new to the field of medicine, and unusually diligent in his approach. I was grateful for his care.

"What do you mean exactly? I had a car accident when I was a teenager."

He looked at my file on his desk, "Yes, I remember you mentioning the accident. That was the cause of your hip and back problems, and, of course, part of your stomach problems." He shook his head and sat back. "But these episodes cannot be generated by an accident unless you'd been underwater for a period of time, or if you were suffocated by something."

The blood drained from my face. "Could a pillow held over my face long enough for me to die cause it?" I said this very softly. I did not want him to misconstrue it as sarcasm or jest.

His eyes widened and overwhelmed his glasses. Deep circles formed under his eyes.

"Yes, that would definitely be what I've been looking for. Is that what happened?"

I nodded and looked down at my hands. I frowned. I didn't like having to talk about the freckled one.

He sighed, sat up, and shuffled his papers around. "Well, yes, that would definitely be the reason for what you are experiencing. Tell me what happened."

I hesitated. Then I realized he needed to know precisely. I told him. I also mentioned what the doctor I saw afterward surmised about my health. "He said I was lucky to be alive."

"Most definitely. Basically, your brain was starved of nitrogen. It can leave lingering problems that do not show up until much later. In easy speak, it's a syndrome of disintegration. Your cognitive abilities have been affected. There is a minimal amount of damage. What happens is your brain isn't sending electrical signals properly. When you have an episode, your brain basically is shutting down, so you literally feel like you are disintegrating into thin air."

I still walked with the legacy of the freckled one.

BOOK SIX

The Later Years

"I wrote, I may say, to see how you stood the test,
Whether you fully accepted my authority."

(2 Corinthians 2:9, NEB)

TWENTY-SIX

Almost Twenty Years with the
Bearded One and Living Like Job

1997

It was unusually warm in New Brunswick. Musicians crawled the streets, the annual Folk Harbor Festival taking over almost every private home as a billet for visiting artisans. Musical geniuses. People from all over North America were visiting to watch and listen. I had guests over for dinner and they were overwhelmed by the ocean breeze, the aroma of lobster, baked potato, and Greek salad. Wine flowed. I needed no stereo to set the mood. The singing and instrument playing from both waterfront and high up on the hill filtered down to my second story balcony.

I invited the bearded one, whom Carl and I had met at the pub during our first trip to New Brunswick years before. I bumped into him and his little daughter when I went to see a fishing boat at the harbor rigged out to scour the ocean for shark.

His little daughter came up to me, though she had never met me, and announced that it was her father's 50th birthday. He informed me that he and his wife had split up a few years prior. On impulse, I invited them for dinner.

He was late. I saw a small red truck pull up in the drive below us, gravel and dust spewing and wafting up to sprinkle us with sneezing powder.

"Who's that?" a guest asked appalled.

I looked over the railing. A truck I didn't recognize, but the golden locks of hair and beard gave him away.

"Oh, another guest. I invited him and his little daughter. They're late."

I pushed my patio chair out ready to play the hostess. I stood at the top of the wooden stairs and watched as this man, unusually dressed in fall or winter clothes as an effort to dress up, scrambled out. He took off his coat, buttoned at his neck, and held a bunch of spring flowers in one hand and a bottle of wine aloft in the other. He shook his locks and grinned up at me. I sensed everyone behind me craning their necks to see.

Then, as a superhero would fly towards the woman he craved and wanted, he sped up the steps, his coat billowing behind him. He put the bottle on the railing, grabbed me by the ribcage with his free arm, and dipped me back over his bony knee. He kept me there, his crazy blue eyes looking straight into my mind and a sparkling grin close to my face that went straight to my heart. Then suddenly the flowers were squeezed between my face and his. I smelled the flowers. I smelled Geraniums and Banana trees and fresh pineapple on a Hawaiian shore. He had opened my heart.

That was the beginning of another marriage which lasted 19 years but ended predictably badly. As predicted by the freckled one almost each time I called the boys and he happened to answer the phone. But the bearded one was a brilliant man, with endless charismatic charms reminding me of my uncles. And like my uncles, behind doors he was troubled and drank and there was much, much yelling and arguing. As if he lived to argue each and every day. Even in his shower, he cursed and swore at some imaginary foe.

I was no one special. Another to blame for all and sundry. And of course, it was familiar to me. Whereas another would not accept it, I seemed to revel in it though it caused me much grief and depression.

What almost destroyed me, from the very day we finally married two years later, however, was that he stopped reaching out for me. I began to feel perhaps there was something boring about me while being intimate. I was such a sensual creature and in truth, his withdrawal was difficult for me to accept. It was almost a physical shock to find myself once again in a dysfunctional marriage. But, of course, again, I was committed and, again, loyal. I reasoned at least there was no beating.

By now, being a very slow learner even with God's help, I recognized I was caught in an endless cycle and depression hit once again. I was well aware that in life we do the same thing over and over until we finally learn the lesson. But this lesson I decided to wait out. I was never going to end this marriage.

That was a challenge to God without me knowing it.

A few years into the marriage, my back gave way during a trip through Disneyworld and I ended up finishing the trip in a wheelchair. Shortly after that, along with the stress of driven work, daily arguments and drunken accusations, the chronic pain in my back and hip had become so intense and uninterrupted that I physically collapsed.

I was in bed for three years and eventually graduated to a wheelchair and was told I would never walk again.

As *Job*, I was made helpless.

• • •

Those seven years of sickness were a blessing from God. Money still came in, as I had more rental properties and still listings and commissions owing through real estate. I once again bonded with Sam and did a waltz between walking beside him and communing with God and then conversely getting caught up with the distractions of this physical world. My doctor, who was a close friend of ours, amazingly did house calls on a regular basis for me.

By some miracle, Ethan had decided to move in with us just prior to my collapse and I saw the irony. It was Ethan who took care of me during the times he was home from work and evenings he sat with the bearded one downstairs, the two of them equally bright and comical, their drunken revelry and guffaws floating up the stairs to my ears, amusing and entertaining me.

It was not lost on me that the bearded one was the happiest he had ever been in our marriage during the seven years I was ill. Not once did he yell at me. It was a very peaceful time for both of us.

One day, after having graduated to the wheelchair and slowly taking over the care of the house on wheels, I decided I was not going to be stuck in the wheelchair. I knew in my heart that all I had to do was push my boundaries.

I decided to paint the kitchen cupboards in order to have to reach by pushing up on the countertops. I forced my wheelchair in and out of the house to garden, pushing my wheelchair backwards with my feet up and down the slope of my yard, my cat on my shoulders hitching a ride.

I decided also that I was going to be back in the work force and while still in that wheelchair, started a gift shop on the bottom floor of another building I had bought prior to getting ill. After a year, I progressed to a cane. Then slowly I was able to do short walks without one.

With my return to health, my marriage suffered once again. And the more I was living openly with my Faith, the more it bothered the bearded one. He believed himself to be superior to those who were 'morons' and believed in a God.

Our weakest link was the bearded one having access to all the scotch he wanted throughout the day in his pub and at night wine and scotch at home. This helped keep his manic disposition buoyed until the inevitable crash late into the evening. Sometimes it ended with grumbling and loud fretting. but as time went on, more and more occasional explosive rage.

• • •

2009

"Let it go."

I looked over from the hot steamy kitchen to my sister-in-law at the far end of the groaning dining room table. She had an unusual gift of carrying on a conversation. She was a bright, literate woman, well-read, with a photographic memory, who knew a little bit of every subject under the sun. It wasn't so much what she was saying that caught my attention. It was more the fact that she had stopped talking entirely. She was looking as elegant as ever with her manicured hands raised in mid-air. As if she had been in the middle of explaining the secret of this amazing universe and then suddenly an unexpected flaming meteorite slashed across the edges of infinity without her consent.

Her entire being was riveted and focused on her brother, my husband, the bearded one.

I stepped closer, ignoring my wet hands dripping soapy water all over the floor. When the bearded one did something, it took all your focus away from whatever you were doing.

And the bearded one was never boring to live with.

He sat next to one of our guests brought by my sister-in-law. They were visiting from Ontario along with their beautiful, gentle golden lab. My stepdaughter and another couple completed the cramped table.

I looked over as the guest turned to his right facing my husband. The guest's girlfriend sat wide-eyed opposite them. She looked frightened.

Then I heard our little poodle growling.

I looked under the table. The guest had a hold on his dog's collar. A gentle giant compared to my smaller dogs and my sister-in-law's cocker spaniel. My little poodle bared his teeth at the gentle giant.

"Just leave the dogs alone, they'll figure it out for themselves." I looked at the bearded one. He had that look about him. The one that said he would gladly take on a challenge with a moron.

"I asked you very nicely if you would please take your dog away from mine," said the guest.

I stepped forward. "Sure, I'll take him away. He's not being very nice to a guest. Come here." I patted my knee, and our other pompoo slowly crawled out from underneath the table to me. I patted his head. I looked at our poodle. I whistled. He wouldn't look at me. I was just about to reach under the table when the bearded one suddenly put up his hand to stop me. He didn't take his eyes off our guest. He leaned forward over his bony knees and let his long hands hang between his legs. He did a funny shake of his head and then his shoulders. He grinned, looking at our guest sideways.

"Whose house is this anyway?" He then sat back and stared down his nose at the guest. The guest refused to budge.

"It's your house, and we are your guests. You said it was all right to bring our dog, who by the way, is the gentlest dog you could ever know. Your dog is frightening my dog. Please take your dog away."

"I'll do it gladly," I began.

Again with the hand up in the air towards me.

"Your wife is kind enough to do so. Let her do it."

The bearded one had met his match.

"Please let me ..." I started again.

Again, with the hand of his, except this time the bearded one pushed his chair back at the same time causing it to fall against his daughter's thigh. He stood up and blew up his chest like a balloon with ribs.

The guest stood up and blew up his own chest. He was a head shorter, but he was game for a fight.

"Danny, please sit down," started his girlfriend.

This time *she* got the hand sign from *him*.

Suddenly, as if timed perfectly, the two roaring giants went at each other.

Everyone still seated rose up in their places yelling and screaming. The guest's girlfriend was trapped on the other side, as were the couple beside her, but she tried to tackle the table and crawl over it. Glasses fell; wine spilled. My stepdaughter froze and looked straight up at her towering father. I saw their shadows rise over her face. For her, it was a horror movie.

I flew forward past my stepdaughter, grabbed a handful of husband hair and t-shirt, and yanked back as hard as I could, screaming at him to stop. It was as if he didn't hear me. He strained forward, but his t-shirt was locked in my curled fingers. I watched the t-shirt rip over his back. He was slowly getting closer and towering over our guest. Two jungle animals, fangs exposed, fur rippling over their muscles of steel.

I then kicked at the back of the bearded one's knees hoping to buckle them, but his legs were hard as tree trunks. I kicked and kicked. Finally, my sister-in-law pushed passed them and ran to the phone.

"I'm calling the police!" she screamed.

When he heard this, the bearded one suddenly turned, threw a few more threats and expletives at our guest over his shoulder, and pushed past me through the kitchen. I heard him stomp up the hall, slam the door to his man room, leave the room, and slam the door again. He left the house slamming the door. I heard the car door slam, and then he burned rubber leaving our driveway.

I looked out the window in the dining room to see if there were any cars coming our way. I secretly prayed that no one hit him and vice versa.

Apparently, he sped over to his best friend's house, but when he learned that the police could be after the bearded one, he refused to let him in.

Then the bearded one sped to Saint John and crashed at Ethan's place. Ethan took him out for sushi so he would calm down. While there, the bearded one threw back a couple of bottles of Sake and happily accosted the two pretty Japanese waitresses. When he started flicking lumps of sticky rice off the chopsticks onto the ceiling, the manager came over and kicked them out.

Ethan, who was bigger than the bearded one, practically carried him back to his apartment and let him collapse on the couch for the night.

Even as I write this, knowing full well that this reflects a dysfunctional aspect within me, though at the time it was appalling,

I still love that brilliance and passion. It was like watching my father kick my uncle out the front door.

You see. I can't point any fingers. I always am where I am because of my blind-spots.

Constant 'connecting' with God eventually sorted that out. And I didn't have to lift a finger.

TWENTY-SEVEN

A Great Earthquake

"...when suddenly there was such a violent earthquake
that the foundations of the jail were shaken:
all the doors were opened,
and all the prisoners found their fetters unfastened."

(*Act 16:26, NEB*)

2014

Pap called from their winter home in Alabama. They were heading home early because my little sister was diagnosed with colon cancer and needed an immediate operation.

Pap drove straight through from Alabama without any sleep. They were beside my little sister the moment she rolled into the operating room.

The operation went well. Once she was sent home, she was told not to pick anything up heavier than five pounds. Unfortunately, she and her husband had already given notice they were moving out of their apartment and into a new one. She was not allowed to pack either. The whole process of moving was a little beyond my brother-in-law, who was a sweetheart but couldn't do it on his own.

Pap and Mam returned to their new house east of Toronto. Mam wasn't feeling well, so went to the doctor for a check-up. She also had a malignant tumor in her ear canal and a cluster of tumors down the main artery of her neck. Pap called to give me this latest update.

"Well, how is Mam reacting to the news?" I could hear her crying in the background.

"Oh, you know your mother, she exaggerates everything."

I heard Mam scream at him that she could die on the operating table.

Pap turned from the phone, and I heard him say, "Oh come now, everyone has to die some time!"

Mam screamed even louder.

Yup. I had to go to Ontario to take care of both my sister and Mam.

I bid the bearded one so long and asked him to take the time to think about our marriage.

Then I got into my little white Honda Civic and drove back to Ontario pondering on how my marriage could be saved. I had no inkling of how my life would change as a result of my trip. God had plans for me and when God has plans, things start to get stirred up.

• • •

I arrived in Ontario and ended up staying five weeks. During that time, there was nothing but upheaval. A young man in fatigues proceeded to do a shooting rampage, killing three RCMPs and wounding two others, not five kilometers from where I stayed for the night after the first day of driving. I listened with a broken heart to the news the next day on my last leg to my parents. This was Canada after all. It just wasn't what Canadians *did*. The whole country was in shock.

My parents and I left in separate cars early the morning of Mam's pre-op consultation. As we exited the highway onto a major road, a car came out of the blue and T-boned me into my side, pushing my car completely out of the intersection.

Later, after the consultation at the hospital, I got into my smashed up car with contact and insurance information in hand from the other distraught driver, and simply headed north to my sister's place. On the way there, I suddenly fell ill. At first it felt like a heart attack, and then I felt an episode of *disintegration* coming on for the first time in years. I pulled off at the gas stop to wait for it to pass, thinking back on the freckled one. As I was sitting in the sun slowly recuperating, my cell rang, and it was Joel in tears.

"Mom, they think Dad won't live another month or so. He's dying."

The symptom of *disintegration* that hit me was his father's legacy to me, and his father was now on his death bed.

After all this time and all this distance, we were still connected.

I continued to my little sister's in a contemplative mood. My life with the freckled one came back in great detail during that long drive. But I still knew in my heart marrying the freckled one was what God wanted. For three reasons: God, Joel and Ethan.

Immediately after my long drive there, my little sister, recuperating from her operation, wanted to do some shopping. She looked great considering she had just had a close brush with death. We went back outside to the car, and, thinking she had gotten in the back seat already, I proceeded to run over her feet.

I stopped right on top of them.

As her screams echoed throughout the street, I had to drive back off them.

I took her to the emergency room, and we sat the whole evening watching news of the young man in fatigues who killed the three RCMP.

They X-rayed my sister's feet. While we waited, I wheeled her into another waiting room where I banged her feet against the counter. An hour later, the doctor appeared in the doorway with the results of the X-rays. He was smirking.

"Well," he started, then stopped to look to the side. Controlling another smirk. He looked at me. "Are you the one who drove over her feet?"

I nodded.

"How'd you do that?"

I shrugged. I couldn't talk.

He looked down at the file, then lifted it up to hide his face crumbling in suppressed laughter. Then he lowered it and cleared his throat. "We looked at your X-rays, and I am happy to say that you've had a miracle. Not a single bone is broken."

"Wha-?" My sister had that dumb look people get when things don't add up. "But her *whole car* ended up on my feet."

The doctor leaned back against the counter and crossed his hands over the file. "What kind of car?"

"A little white Honda Civic," I said.

"Well, you were lucky. It could've been a Hummer."

"A what?"

He turned to my sister. "Your sister can go back to New Brunswick knowing she didn't hurt you after all."

"Thank you so much," I said stiltedly.

He left rather quickly.

I pushed her out into the emergency waiting room. When I paused, she got out of the wheelchair and walked to the exit.

The next day, she wanted to shop again and I lost my wallet. It seemed there was no end of mishaps on this journey.

• • •

I spent the rest of the weekend packing my sister's things, moved, and unpacked them. Once they were settled into their new apartment, I drove back to my parents' house.

Finally, the big day of Mam's operation arrived. They had to give Mam three times the medication to get her dozy. Even then, she was wide awake when they wheeled her into the Operating Room. She didn't want to go to sleep. She swore she wasn't going to wake up from the operation. Her doctor was patient and arranged for soft, oriental music to play in the background. Finally, Mam fell under the spell.

Half a day later, she pulled through like a trooper. We were led to the ICU to see her.

They warned us about what they would do. They removed the ear canal and replaced the artery down the side of her neck with one from her arm. They also took a skin graft from her back to plug the ear. They weren't sure if they were going to be able to reposition the ear, but they would do all they could save it. Mam's doctor knew how she loved to wear earrings and had promised to do his very best.

We walked in quietly because she was sleeping. From the side, she looked fine. Then as we walked in front of her, we got the full effect.

It was the Bride of Frankenstein!

Half her head was shaved, and she was stapled around her head and down her neck. There were more staples down the length of her arm. As we stood there staring at her, she woke up. She broke out into a glowing smile, her eyes wide and glistening.

"I saw the face of God! I saw him!" She laughed. "I saw God!"

I stood there, amazed. I believed her.

Pap laughed and snorted. "Oh silly. That's the medicine talking," he said with a snort.

She looked over at him with those wide, beautiful aquamarine eyes. "You think? But I could swear I saw Him. It was beautiful!" Then her eyes dimmed, the smile lessened, and I saw she believed Pap.

She had seen the face of God.

• • •

Mam immediately asked for her pink negligee. Then she had me do her hair. She put on lipstick and told every nurse and every doctor she felt fine and asked when she could go home.

"Oh, you have to stay for at least five days," said the nurse.

"Oh no. I don't think so," said Mam.

"Mam, you just went through a major operation," I said.

"I feel fine!"

"Mam, you're on painkillers, and you need twenty-four-hour care. You have nurses coming and going."

"I don't need nurses. I have you."

On the second day, because she was so adamant, they let her go home. She had broken a *record* according to the nurses and doctors.

It was then I who gave her twenty-four-hour care with painkillers every two hours around the clock for four days. Not three shifts of nurses. But me. And it almost killed me, but I loved waking her up with her medication, see her smile up at me, and say in her own way, "*My Florencine of Nightingale.*"

At night, for the short time I was in bed, *He* was there. God was comforting me, teaching me new insights. One lesson focused on how people exaggerated things. Through either laziness or believing they lack the time, they don't tell things as they really are. He told me people have lost the ability to use words properly. Words had power. And this power was being abused badly.

I was in the habit of staying away from needless negative statements. I believed the words that come out of our mouths have power. We have power. And we continuously abuse this particular power.

The lesson now was *diligence* in speech. He taught me that I must use words precisely. Not to be tempted to change facts or water them down. Truth had dignity.

Okay, I said. I thought about it because I thought I already had but really didn't.

You must remember.

I said, "*Yes*, I will do that. I promise."

Sam started to teach me about sensuality. Being starved for a loving touch of any kind for almost 18 years, He showed me that gently touching my own arm, letting a finger trail along the skin, was satisfying and sensual. He was teaching me something I never knew.

I was happy to have my *conversations* with Sam and God back again. I realized that my life with the bearded one, though I still prayed, did not offer the peace that nurtured an ongoing close relationship with God. I also understood what God had been doing to me throughout the whole five weeks I was in Ontario. With all the upheavals, just like the boot camp I went through on the sailing trip so many years before, I was being shaken and worn down physically and mentally. My system was upset and rattled by all the mishaps and accidents that kept happening. I became putty in His hands once again.

After Mam recuperated for a couple of weeks, I kissed Mam and Pap goodbye, and I drove back to New Brunswick. The entire trip was full of music and little *whispers* telling me how much God loved me. Many times, I could barely hold back tears of joy. I didn't deserve so much love. I was flying high.

Little did I know what was in store for me when I got home.

• • •

Two days later, as I rounded the bend toward the last cove on my way to my little house, I saw it sitting in the distance. Sam said loud and clear, *This is your home.*

It was so sudden, out of the blue, and in earnest, I laughed out loud and said, "Yes, I know. I love my home."

When I drove into the driveway, Sam told me to go through the back door.

I walked through the courtyard that was now full of weeds. I wasn't really surprised, as I always did the outside work. The bearded one didn't see it. Still, I was a little disappointed to see it so badly maintained.

I wasn't surprised to find the back door unlocked, so I turned the knob and stepped into the house, only to surprise the bearded one, who was sitting in the armchair in the back corner facing the other way. He had put himself in a strategic spot to see me enter through the front door. I had ruined the effect.

He was sitting with one ankle resting on the other knee, his hands and fingers intertwined in his usual judgmental way.

He had been drinking.

He was surprised I came from the back door and swiveled the chair around. "Well, look what the cat dragged home. Sneaking in through the back way, are we?"

I took off my shoes and sat on the arm of the chair in front of him. I settled down and searched his face. I saw now why I had to go through the back. I sensed he had written a script for tonight, and I'd already changed it by not coming through the front. For the first time, I felt bad for him. I started sensing how I personally caused him this angst, whatever form it was. I purposely hadn't called him while I was gone. It put him into an aggressive mode instead of what I had hoped for—open arms, a massive hug, and an eagerness to work together to make *us* work.

Don't say anything. Listen.

"You have nothing to say?" he asked, lifting his hands and dropping them. "Cat got your tongue?"

I remained quiet.

He bent forward, "Are you in love with someone else?"

I took a deep breath. "Yes, I am." His face dropped a little. This was not what he had written. "I'm in love with Pap, Mam, and my family. I'm in love with God."

"So, what are your plans, then?"

"After being there, I see I have to move back. Eventually, take care of Pap and Mam."

"And when will that happen?" He resumed his quiet haughtiness.

"In a year. Or two."

Suddenly he threw an envelope at me. I didn't manage to catch it in time, so it dropped to the carpet. I picked it up and looked at the front. It was from a psychologist I saw before leaving for Ontario. I needed to speak to someone about our marriage. It had been opened. He had read it.

"So, you went to see a shrink."

"Yes, I did. You didn't want to see one, so I went alone to figure out how to save this marriage."

He suddenly got up, and as he did, he threw his wedding ring at me. He walked into the kitchen. I turned to look at him.

"I want you out of this house, now." He stood by the kitchen island.

I got up, walked to him, and put my keys and bag on the island. "Well, I'm not going. This is my home."

This is your home.

"No, this is my house, and I want you out."

"I'm not leaving," I said, standing straighter.

"If you go up those stairs I'll throw you back down."

I pointed to the ceiling. "I'm going to sleep up there. That's my bed. It was mine before I met you."

At this point, the bearded one blew up his chest and lunged towards me. At his full height, the top of my head reached his chin. He towered over me.

"You get the f--- out of my f---ing house. I don't want to see your f---ing face anymore." With each "f" word, he pushed me further back with his chest. I struggled to keep my balance.

He's trying to break you. He wants you to strike out at him, so he can hit you back. He needs a reason to say why he's kicking you out.

It seemed that being quiet and not getting upset made it worse.

He bent down and bellowed such expletives into my face that I wanted to throw up. I couldn't take it anymore and thought *before I say or do anything I shouldn't, I had better leave.* So, I picked up my car keys and left the house.

As I walked towards my car, Sam stopped me.

I told you, this is your home.

I turned right around and went back into the house instantly refreshed and strengthened. The bearded one was already upstairs on his cell.

"Yup. She's out. She's gone. I have the house. Nope, she won't come back." He started crunching down the stairs.

He was talking to his daughter, but she was used to our arguments. I yelled up as loud as I could. "No, I'm not gone, and I'm not going away either. Hi, I'm back."

"I'll call you right back, kid," he said quickly, but I could tell my stepdaughter had already hung up on him, probably in shock and ashamed that she'd been caught being an accomplice to his plan.

We were completely off script now. I took my bags upstairs and got ready for bed. He gave up trying to kick me out and also got ready for bed. He was flabbergasted at my catching him in the act.

I settled down on the floor next to my side of the bed which was where I usually slept the way my back was. There was no way I was sleeping next to that man.

"So, you want this marriage to end?" I said from the pillow on the carpet.

He paused. And in a lighter tone said, "I'll think about it."

I peeked over the blankets and looked at him. He had an arm behind his head and he was staring up at the ceiling.

Don't even think about opening that door, girl, Sam said. *And don't sleep here after tonight. We must give him a clear message.*

The following night, I slept in the barn. The next day, in the kitchen, it started again.

"I want you out!"

Diligence. Facts. Carefully-weighed words.

"If this marriage is to end, then we do it right," I said. "We go for counseling, and if that doesn't work, then we keep it amicable, and we sell everything together. We stay in the house until it's all settled."

"I'm not going to live in a house with you. You know you are an idiot. The whole world knows exactly what you're like. Everyone hates you. They love me, so they tolerate you. Everyone knows what you're really like."

I put up my hand to stop him. "Tell me definite things. Not generalities. What don't they like about me?"

Remember. Words.

"Well, you're," he looked around quickly, "you're stubborn, you're hard to work with. Everyone says so. Everyone hates you."

"Why do people find it hard to work with me? I do a lot for people. People ask me to do something, and I do it to the best of my ability. People always work with me."

He was getting steaming angry again. I was preparing a lunch to take with me to the rental apartments to work there. He wasn't going it seemed.

Later, I called Ethan from my cell on the way to the apartments.

"Listen, Ethan, I just want to let you know. Nothing's happened, but he tried to throw me out of the house last night. I'm sleeping in the barn, but I might consider sleeping on the boat. It's a little cold yet, but it's getting too uncomfortable with him."

"What's he done now, Mom?" He was concerned, but I didn't want him upset. I just wanted someone to know that something was up in case something happened. The bearded one twisted too many stories. Someone had to know what was going on.

"Well, when I got home, he threatened to throw me down the stairs. This is just in case, okay? I'm fine."

"You and I both know what he's capable of, Mom. Call the police."

"No, I don't want them involved. Please, I'm okay."

Unbeknownst to me, he called the police anyway. He explained the situation. They told him I should talk to the RCMP in my area. So, he spoke to the RCMP himself.

The next few days I tried to stay out of his way, but twice he caught me in the kitchen. Each time, he couldn't get me to leave. Finally, while I was getting ready to sleep on the boat, he tried to start another argument. He became more heated and frustrated with my lack of response. He lunged at me with an expletive, pushed me hard, and I fell back against the fridge. Everything toppled off the top. I looked at the things scattered on the floor, and something said, *Run!*

So, I ran. I broke my little toe on the corner of the center island as I scrambled out of the house to my car. As I was closing the car door, I was startled to see him right behind me. He pulled back the door and slammed it against my leg but held back a little at the last moment. I was able to fend it off enough with my hand. Then I started the engine and scrambled out of the driveway. He clung to the car as I backed out, swearing at me.

I was shaken. I called Ethan to tell him what happened but said I was okay.

"I just didn't know what to do with him anymore. I can't control him. He's so big, and I'm no match for him. He threw me against that fridge like I was nothing."

"Mom, I already called the RCMP. They told me to tell you to stay away from him."

"Well, that would be an easy thing to want to do now."

"They want you to call them. Now, especially. He assaulted you, Mom. You have to call. If you don't, then I will."

"Please don't bother them. I'll sort this out."

I immediately drove over to the marina where my little boat was still in the cradle. I saw that my cell phone was almost dead but I had left my charger at the house. So, I turned it off and settled down for a very fitful night.

In the morning, I turned on my cell. My mailbox was full with messages from the RCMP.

I called them back. They insisted I come into the station. I tried to tell them everything was fine, but I had no choice but to go.

So, absolutely shaken and rattled, I drove to the station.

While I waited, Sam reminded me.

Diligence in facts. Truth. Nothing but the truth. No personal attacks or despairing remarks. What you say is important.

I sat stunned for a moment realizing Sam had been preparing me for this since Ontario.

Finally, they came into the room and asked me what had happened.

I settled down and told them everything. I didn't exaggerate. I did not hold anything back. I told it like it was.

Then they tried everything possible to tell me I should charge him.

I refused.

"Well, if you won't charge him, then it's in our laps now. We have no choice but to charge him ourselves because we have a zero tolerance for any kind of abuse."

"Even if I beg you not to?" I asked, surprised.

They didn't even answer. "We recommend you find a safe place to hide for tonight."

My heart sank. If they charged him, then it was the end of our marriage.

Failure.

Again.

TWENTY-EIGHT

The Fall of the Lion

They came to the house while I quivered in someone else's home, fretting over the coming pain and humiliation for a man who had embarked on a mission to do the same to me. They put handcuffs on the great lion, the bearded one, with his manic passion for life and his own superiority, and a twisted mind tortured by some distant sin and pickled by alcohol.

This man caught my heart in a way that demanded I admire and look on as he shot through the sky like a rocket with everyone facing the blazing light in awe. I tried to fill that void in him.

Now, 19 years later, he sat at an RCMP station negating everything I said. He was charged with assault and for being a public danger because of his drinking and driving. He was not to have any contact with me and not to touch alcohol for one year.

This is your home, Sam reminded me. I was amazed how the entire proceeding had been set up by God. It was a rescue mission. As if the heavens knew I would be sucked into the great comet's tail once again and left half dead on a sick bed, this time not able to think or do for myself. Become under complete control by the lion.

I stood in the doorway of the man room and surveilled the papers, boxes, and the dust. *Oh, the poor man,* I thought.

The mighty do fall, said Sam.

• • •

As time wore on and the comedy unfolded, I went from extreme distress to feeling at peace. I slept better than I had in almost 18 years. There was peace in the house, and within a short period of time, it reflected on me. I smashed the wall open between the man room and the dining room to create an elegant, dignified office. I put down new white carpeting. I fixed an ancient leak and a gaping, crumbling hole in the wall behind the stove.

He told everyone who would listen—friend and stranger—I had created a set up to get rid of him. He could not bear to face what he had done and how it was taken completely out of his hands in such a surreal and precise way.

I struggled with the sense of failure that comes when a marriage dies. But in my case, this third failure intensified the shame and humiliation.

The freckled one's voice whispered, *Jezebel*.

If I hadn't gone to a counselor prior to our break-up, I would've believed I was a destructive and impossible person to live with. But she told me it was simply my tendency to choose the wrong husband because of my upbringing and conditioning.

I kept choosing the handsome, passionate, aggressive, heavy drinking uncles of my youth. I knew nothing else. I loved them. I was proud of them. I held them up as movie star gods. Now, in the mausoleum of my heart, I buried the love of three passionate men with their own deep and overwhelming streak of superiority.

There wasn't a humble bone in any of their bodies.

TWENTY-NINE

From Jezebel to Angel

2015

Joel, now Assistant Professor at the university I went to in my teens, proposed to his girlfriend of ten years with a candy ring. He timed it for during a trip of mine to Ontario and also invited her parents. He presented her with the massive cherry-flavored ring.

Her parents and I were elated.

Eight months later I came back to help with the wedding preparations. They set up a massive tent with a dance floor on the beautiful 100 acres horse ranch where they rented a house.

Hours before the ceremony, I was dressed for the occasion and waited to help greet family and friends when my tall, handsome son hurried into the hallway.

"Mom, Dad's here," Joel told me breathlessly.

The dying freckled one had arrived. The prophet. *Jezebel. Jezebel.*

He was barely alive. He had already lost a leg and was about to lose another to diabetes. He was permanently in a wheelchair.

I prayed to God for strength and to guide my reaction as I met him after all these years. This was the nemesis of all nemeses. He still hated me. I was the fallen woman. I was Jezebel. What was I to do? Deep down I was frightened of this man who was now a weak cripple. At the same time, I knew how silly that was. How could he hurt me now?

His eyes, his words, his thoughts in my head. He still had a poisonous bite.

I looked out and saw a large dark van. An oversized wheelchair was set on the driveway, ready for the man. I stepped closer to the window. So close I fogged up the window as I did the porthole on that ship coming into New York harbor and seeing the Statue of Liberty lit up in the dark, new world. I sensed as I did at the age of four, that this meeting would change my life somehow.

There was movement on the other side of the van. Joel took the wheelchair and brought it to that side. Both disappeared from my view. I heard my blood pumping in my eardrums and impatiently wiped at the window to see better.

Slowly a big man wheeled out into the open. He had a white beard down to his middle. He wore a massive baggy suit. The freckled one. The mighty prophet of God. The teacher of this Jezebel and master with the whip and curtain rod. The father of my two beautiful and amazing sons, Joel and Ethan, whom he tried to brainwash, make brain dead, forced murky-colored glasses on their innocent beautiful young eyes and given filters labelled "whore" to stick on when with me.

I looked down at my dress and shoes. I checked the hemline to see how high it was. I touched my hair to see if I had sprayed it too heavily, and I wondered if my makeup was too thick. Surely, he would break out in expletives at me, in front of those around us, while my eldest stood by. Surely, he would want to spit at me, point his quivering finger at me and pronounce that God wanted to wreak fire and brimstone on my soul, the whore. My eyes watered with a hot fever. I wanted to run away like an animal in front of a wall of widespread flames of wrath and vengeance.

I was my boys' mother, the mother of *his* children.

Go and greet him.

"Oh, Lord," I said to the misty window.

You must go and greet him.

Almost at the point of hyperventilating, I walked to the door and stepped out into the sunshine. Slowly I moved toward him and the wheelchair. With each step, I remembered something of our painful yet glorified past. I remembered him at 100 Huntley Street. I remembered him ordering the cars to move out of our way in the name of Jesus. I remembered traipsing on the runway with my blonde curls bouncing with every glamourous step, and then being married next door at God's command. Another step and it was the first time he swore at me. The next step was him stepping over my body while I lay weeping on the floor eight months pregnant and battered by him. I took another step and he smashed me against the wall while holding baby Joel. Another and we were being evicted. Another and my crying baby Ethan is pushed against my breast after having little sleep for months. Then another and I pushed myself to lug furniture so hard that I miscarried another soul I wanted to save from this monster. I stopped. I knew what the next step was. He hadn't noticed me yet. Joel was fretting over his father's coat and tucked it in the back of the wheelchair. I took another step, and I was at the top of the carpeted stairs debating whether I should push him to his death before he killed me and decided to accept my fate instead. One more step, and I came back from a place where they said I wasn't finished with my life yet. It was when I came back and was able to hear that mysterious, heavenly, loving voice of a power that was beyond understanding.

I took another bold and tentative step and smiled at the man who was old ahead of his time, born two thousand years too late, his beard looking like it had been painted on by a master painter of the sixteenth century. His freckles were the same. His nose was the same. His hazel eyes were the same. Less hair on his head but still the red-blonde of his youth with a touch of gray. He smiled and exposed a toothless mouth, a mouth neglected and teeth rotted away by the very sweet and starchy food that took his leg away and almost killed him the year before.

I reached out my hand.

He reached out with his.

"Who is this beautiful angel walking toward me. Thank you, Jesus. Praise the Lord."

This is what I wanted you to hear. This is what you are.

As he held my hand, a massive weight lifted off my shoulders, and I could feel myself floating away. Joel saw my holy vindication, and I wondered if he saw the massive, gray, murky cloud rise from my head.

The prophet put his other hand over mine as I bent down and gently spoke.

"It's me, Tina. I am the mother of your sons. What a wonderful celebration this is for us. Our eldest is getting married."

His hands went limp as he looked on myopically. I felt his mental feelers reaching into my mind, and I into his, and he jolted back in revulsion.

His hazel eyes changed to pure black, and he withdrew his hands.

I stood up, smiling, straightening out my sore back, pretending not to have noticed. I watched this man, who molded a major part of my life, being awkwardly wheeled away, his weight making every little bounce and shaking of the chair amplified. I watched his bulk bouncing helplessly, his feelers still pointing and looking my way in confusion until he and his feelers disappeared into the house.

● ● ●

The next year the Lion of Moses—the father who gave me two talented and special young men, the man whom people adored, hated or feared, the messenger who whipped God's wrath onto my soul and helped change me from a vain, Catholic glamorous model and actor to a humble, broken creature prepared for the pouring of God's Holy Spirit—this misdirected prophet finally died at the age of 70 hours after screaming from his hospital bed demanding that his longsuffering lady-friend finally hand over his chocolate bars.

Thus, another prophet, wielded by God's hand as a mighty tool but still flawed in his humanity, passed away from this realm.

THIRTY

God Always gets the Last Word

2018

A few years later, I stood under massive, powerful arc lights as I quivered pressed against the Wailing Wall outside the old city of Jerusalem. I looked down at a little slip of paper in my hands, and then down at my black Pumas. I had an intense urge to take them off for I felt I was standing on holy ground. I was about to make a call through the holy phone booth.

I looked up and over and spied a dusty, solitary tendril of green plant-life clinging to a crevice in the ancient stone crammed with other women's prayers. I saw that little frail stem as a symbol of me, clinging desperately to the face of God.

I searched and then found a crevice with a little space. I folded my little slip of paper as tiny as it would go and tucked it in.

Mine was not a prayer of need for once. They say God gives you the prayer to pray, and my pencil only wrote gratitude and praise from a humbled heart and soul, my spirit's eyes wide open, feeling the tangible presence of God wrapping around me.

Though I asked for absolutely nothing, I realized later that one of the most sublime miracles of my life happened. While there, I felt an intense rush of warmth go through my body along with a familiar tingling sensation that went from the top of my head down through the middle of my feet. Shortly afterward while sitting in the safety of my friend's sister and Rabbi brother-in-law's home in Jerusalem, I began to feel a lightness of being. Our conversation led me to share something of my journey which I would never have dared share before.

Then suddenly I received a text. It was news back in New Brunswick of a young friend I knew who was struggling with the pain of sexual abuse and drug addiction. She had hung herself. I was stunned. I thought of that frail little bird of a young girl who was so difficult to reach.

As I pondered on this, an email came through telling me that a man who had a grudge against me was telling people in my community of friends and acquaintances a sordid sex-based lie about me.

I helped a community theater group save money by switching to a more hands-on website. Consequently, this man lost their ongoing contract.

As a woman having lived a life of subtle and not-so-subtle forms of gender abuse, I recognized this man's need to debase me as another form of it. His lie was extremely dirty and crude. I felt bullied and I was tempted to feel that familiar pain and sense of helplessness.

The timing of both text and email stopped me in my tracks. Then I heard Sam gently say.

You have to write your story.

"Oh my God, Sam, I can't. It would kill me to think of all those things I've hidden away."

You can do it now. And you are older. Older women guide younger women. The wisdom of experience. More women need to heal and be set free to live their lives fully.

"I don't know about wisdom but I guess I can show how I survived. How God's Hand reached down so many times. But why me, Sam? I'm so far from perfect."

No one is. Just do it.

Like a prisoner facing the electric chair, I sat down at my computer and wrote my sordid story. In a rant, I dug up things I had forgotten long ago. Things I did not want to face ever again. But they poured out. I cried a lot and, one day, I was so sick, I couldn't leave the bathroom. It almost killed me.

Then my computer *crashed*. Everything was lost.

Everything.

I didn't back up a single thing.

I was appalled. It took so much out of me to write it. But then I understood.

When God is in charge and does something, it's very startling.

You have written it all down and now I have erased it.

Oh. Of course. God was giving me a fresh start.

This was important: I needed to move on. Over fifty years of my life was wasted and it was time I finally got over what others had done *to* me. I needed to forgive. To move on.

I had stuff to do.

I just hoped I would live to be a healthy one hundred years old to make up for lost time, because now that I was no longer imprisoned by the shackles of the past, I felt I could do anything I set my mind to. And suddenly I wanted to do everything!

Like Ebenezer Scrooge in Dicken's Christmas Carol, it was a very giddy feeling.

I felt as free as a prepubescent teenage boy.

Well, almost. The older I've become, the more shy I am in my bathing suit. Prepubescent teenage boys take over swimming pools and do cannon balls as if they were the center of the universe seemingly without a care in the world.

They love life.

And, I knew, so should I.

And, therefore, so should you.

This is not meant to be disrespectful to anyone who is not of the same mind—but for me, believing in something bigger and better than myself saved my life.

I realized that getting stuck on mistakes was wrong because these do not ruin the rest of your life. And how can we learn if we never make mistakes? Mistakes should be celebrated and given dignity by learning from them.

I believe we choose our lives beforehand. That amazingly bright light I *saw* in that 17-year-old girl so many years ago was extremely intelligent.

That's why when bad things happened to me, I couldn't entirely point fingers elsewhere and feel sorry for myself. I intuitively felt I had *chosen* these things in order to refine something *in* me.

I do know one thing. I was His from the moment I felt His Hand on my shoulder at the age of six in that front pew in St. Basil Church. When I ached to climb up onto the statue of Jesus cradled in his mother's arms to give Him a kiss and make him feel better.

And, *Playboy*? Hugh Hefner died on September 27, 2017 at the age of 91. As a lifestylist, he left behind a massive legacy that affected most of the world. He changed our culture and fashion landscape in profound and destructive ways and not just for the female sex. He helped distort the way men looked at women and stole from them the ability to become part of a mutually-respectful and committed couple. This unit is the first building block of a family. Today, society is completely in upheaval due, in part, to the loss of strong family units which help form strong communities.

Most of the men in my journey who emanated Hefner have gone into dust like him. These men who caused so much upheaval and waste in my life are now *harmless*. I think about them and they appear to be little specks in the distance. The overwhelming emotional storms and pain they caused have subsided. There is peace. Calm.

I have now moved back to Ontario to within five minutes' drive of Pap and Mam, mainly to help ensure they live in their own home until they are well over a hundred. The interesting thing is? They look exactly as they did in that vision that saved my life on that sad moonlit night so many years ago.

We went shopping a little while ago and I caught Pap threatening to kiss a sales lady putting on a tie for him. I'm sure he thought it would be a compliment and meant well.

He shakily pushed on his cane with all his might to straighten out his badly-curved spine, and shot that beautiful, charming charismatic smile I love and admire so much. Beautiful Mam, looking like Grace Kelly would have looked if she had lived into her eighties, sat regally nearby looking on. She shook her blonde head, understood, and simply looked away.

I know in my heart that God loves them both and is proud of their unique fighting spirit.

And I have been so blessed in sharing this journey with them.

Damsels in Distress: Depression

Depression is a form of mental illness which can be persistent, destructive, and sometimes lead to fatal consequences. It was one of the main struggles in my life. Looking back, I clearly see what lessened depression's effects in my distress. For all *damsels in distress,* I have listed them below:

D = Dreams of new things you can do or be if time and money were no object.

A = Arts consist of theatre, music and art. Go and act, play, listen and create!

M = Meditating is rebooting. Flush out negative and fill with light, love and rebirth.

S = Structure is putting one foot ahead of the other. Make a list and stick to it.

E = Environment can be changed. Lose the *negative* and find more *positive.*

L = Love. You are not alone. Somebody loves you. And *you* must love you.

S = Sports. Activities. Inhale great amounts of air. Sweat out the grit.

I *dreamt* about everything. I even looked at catalogs and imagined buying everything I wanted. I dreamt of adventures with my sons. Like Disneyworld. Dreams do come true!

What saved me in my teens was *music, art and theatre.* And one should always have a *designated room* to be surrounded by their work and their favorite music.

Meditation was a major tool. I imagined inhaling light and clearing out the blackness and pain. This process is extremely effective.

I began a life-long process of making *precise lists* every day. In my darkest period, the day was broken down into 15 minute segments which included brushing my teeth, brushing my hair.

I *moved away and created a new environment* which did not have reminders of my ex-husband, his mistress, and my first husband's manipulation and threats.

I *knew I was loved by a higher power.* And I finally *learned to love the little girl in me.* The one who was still crying, still hurting. I hold her in my arms to comfort her and never let go.

I loved *skating, gymnastics, basketball, cycling and swimming.* When I *danced,* though I was under-weight, I took vitamins, protein powders and cut out sugar, gluten, and red meat.

So, go and create a different life. Tailor it to fit the more positive version of you and yours. It not only could heal you, but your family as well. May you be filled with light and love!

About the Author

Tina Assanti is blessed with two absolutely amazing sons. She is a published author and writes under an assumed name. She is a former model and actor, on-air radio announcer, videographer and supporter of Women's Issues. She produced and directed the documentary, *Breaking the Cycle of Violence: Second Stage Housing* and is a former Board member of Toronto Women in Film and Television (WIFT). She taught Self-Improvement and Modeling courses for women, Motivational seminars for Business Students, and Acting and Modeling for children from 4 to 17. She studied journalism, film production, screenwriting and Fine Arts and History at York and Guelph Universities.

Today, Tina is a Certified Deeper Path Coach and Motivational Speaker who believes we are all God's Amazing Creatures. With her high-spirited love and exuberant warmth, she helps women and teens by-pass their pain and head straight to the very heart of their exquisiteness.

For more information contact Tina at: information@tinaassantibooks.com or dollivertwist2014@gmail.com.

Books Forthcoming
by the Author

Corrie and the Red Rose Accordion
Italian Bodies of Change